ADVANCES IN HOSPITALITY AND LEISURE

ADVANCES IN HOSPITALITY AND LEISURE

Series Editor: Joseph S. Chen

ADVANCES IN HOSPITALITY AND LEISURE

EDITED BY

JOSEPH S. CHEN

Indiana University, Bloomington, USA

2004

ELSEVIER
JAI

Amsterdam – Boston – Heidelberg – London – New York – Oxford
Paris – San Diego – San Francisco – Singapore – Sydney – Tokyo

ELSEVIER B.V.
Radarweg 29
P.O. Box 211
1000 AE Amsterdam
The Netherlands

ELSEVIER Inc.
525 B Street, Suite 1900
San Diego
CA 92101-4495
USA

ELSEVIER Ltd
The Boulevard, Langford
Lane, Kidlington
Oxford OX5 1GB
UK

ELSEVIER Ltd
84 Theobalds Road
London
WC1X 8RR
UK

First edition 2004

British Library Cataloguing in Publication Data
A catalogue record is available from the British Library.

ISBN: 0-7623-1158-4
ISSN: 1745-3542 (Series)

⊗The paper used in this publication meets the requirements of ANSI/NISO Z39.48-1992 (Permanence of Paper). Printed in The Netherlands.

CONTENTS

LIST OF CONTRIBUTORS

Marcjanna M. Augustyn	Department of Leisure, Tourism and Hospitality, University of Wolverhampton, UK
Jeffrey A. Beck	The School of Hospitality Business, Michigan State University, USA
Hsin-Hui Chen	School of Management, University of Surrey, UK
Joseph S. Chen	Department of Recreation and Park Administration, Indiana University, Bloomington, USA
Rachel J. C. Chen	Department of Consumer Services Management, University of Tennessee, USA
Shao-Cheng Cheng	Department of International Trade, Chinese Culture University, Taipei, Taiwan, R.O.C.
Ronald F. Cichy	The School of Hospitality Business, Michigan State University, USA
Yuksel Ekinci	School of Management, University of Surrey, UK
Tadayuki Hara	School of Hotel Administration & Regional Science Program, Cornell University, USA
Tzung-Cheng Huan	Graduate Institute of Leisure Industry Management, National Chia-Yi University, USA
Chu-Min Huang	Ambassador Hotel, Taiwan, R.O.C.
Li-Jen Jessica Hwang	School of Management, University of Surrey, UK

Colin Johnson	Department of Hospitality Management, San José State University, USA
Michael L. Kasavana	The School of Hospitality Business, Michigan State University, USA
Bonnie J. Knutson	The School of Hospitality Business, Michigan State University, USA
Willy Legrand	Department of Hospitality Management, The International University of Applied Sciences Bad Honnef Bonn, Germany
Francis A. McGuire	Department of Parks Recreation and Tourism Management, Clemson University, USA
Sandra Naipaul	Montclair State University, USA
William C. Norman	Department of Parks, Recreation and Tourism Management, Clemson University, USA
Joseph T. O'Leary	Recreation, Park and Tourism Sciences, Texas A & M University, USA
Harmen Oppewal	Department of Marketing, Monash University, Australia
H. G. Parsa	The Ohio State University, USA
Nina K. Prebensen	Department of Hospitality and Tourism, Finnmark College, Norway
Peter Ricci	Rosen School of Hospitality Management, University of Central Florida, USA
Arthur Seakhoa-King	Department of Tourism and Leisure, University of Luton, UK
Marianna Sigala	The Business Administration Department, University of the Aegean, Greece
Arjun J. Singh	The School of Hospitality Business, Michigan State University, USA

Philip Sloan   Department of Hospitality Management, The International University of Applied Sciences Bad Honnef Bonn, Germany

Dana V. Tesone   Rosen School of Hospitality Management, University of Central Florida, USA

Maurizio Vanetti   Fribourg University, Switzerland

Jetske van Westering   School of Management, University of Surrey, UK

Kuo-Ching Wang   Graduate Institute of Recreation, Tourism, and Hospitality Management, National Chiayi University, Chiayi, Taiwan, R.O.C.

John A. Williams   Department of Hotel, Restaurant, Institution Management & Dietetics, Kansas State University, USA

Tae-Hwan Yoon   School of Management, University of Surrey, UK

AIMS AND SUBMISSION GUIDELINES

Advances in Hospitality and Leisure (AHL), a peer-review publication, aims to promote seminal and innovative research outputs pertaining to hospitality, leisure, tourism, and lifestyle. Specifically, the series will encourage researchers to investigate new research issues and problems that are critical but have been largely ignored while providing a forum that will disseminate singular thoughts advancing empirical undertakings both theoretically and methodologically.

The inaugural issue includes the articles on critical literature review that discuss the shortcomings of past research and provide the guidance for future research agendas in relation to hospitality, leisure, and tourism issues. In addition, empirical papers with a new investigative theme are included. In total the issue contains 10 full papers and 6 research notes.

For submission to future issues, please review the following guidelines.

Originality of Manuscript: The manuscript should represent an original work that has never been published elsewhere nor is being considering for publication elsewhere.

Style and Length of Manuscript: 12 pt Times Roman font; double spacing; APA; 7,000 words (Full Paper) or 4,000 words (Research Note).

Layout of Manuscript: First page: title of paper and author information; second page: title of paper, 100-120 word abstract, and keywords; third page and beyond: main text, appendix, references, figures, and tables.

Text of Manuscript: For literature review articles, please include introduction, critical literature review, problems in past research, and suggestions for future research. For empirical research papers, please include introduction, methods, findings and discussions, and conclusion.

AHL requires electronic submission. Please use an email attachment with Microsoft Word format to the editor Dr. Joseph Chen (joechen@indiana.edu) or send a diskette to Tourism Management Program, HPER Building #133, Indiana University, Bloomington, Indiana 47405, USA.

EDITORIAL BOARD

FULL PAPERS

IS THE SERVQUAL SCALE AN ADEQUATE MEASURE OF QUALITY IN LEISURE, TOURISM AND HOSPITALITY?

Marcjanna M. Augustyn and Arthur Seakhoa-King

ABSTRACT

Efforts aimed at evaluating quality in leisure, tourism and hospitality have concentrated predominantly on measuring perceived service quality using the SERVQUAL scale, either in its original form or with modifications. While these studies are of great theoretical and practical value, the focus on measuring consumer satisfaction may limit the potential scope of the quality-measurement process. This is particularly true in assessing the quality of complex services such as those found in the leisure, tourism and hospitality sectors, which may require the application of a range of measures that will collectively contribute to the identification of quality levels. This article critically evaluates the potentialities and limitations of the SERVQUAL scale in measuring quality in leisure, tourism and hospitality. It concludes that the SERVQUAL scale is a necessary but insufficient measure of quality within these sectors and specifies implications for future research.

Advances in Hospitality and Leisure
Advances in Hospitality and Leisure, Volume 1, 3–24
Copyright © 2004 by Elsevier Ltd.
All rights of reproduction in any form reserved
ISSN: 1745-3542/doi:10.1016/S1745-3542(04)01001-X

INTRODUCTION

The importance of continual quality improvement in leisure, tourism and hospitality is widely accepted by both academics and practitioners. Evidence exists that implementation of effective quality improvement programmes significantly contributes to achieving high performance levels by organisations (Bitner, 1990; Boulding et al., 1993; Buzzell & Gale, 1987; Evans & Lindsay, 2002; Rust & Zahorik, 1993). However, designing effective quality improvement programmes requires the systematic measurement of the existing levels of quality before any decisions on the direction of further improvements are made.

The measurement of quality is, however, complicated as it involves an evaluation of both the quality of a product[1] that is offered to customers and the quality of all processes that contribute to the creation of these products. The difficulty in measuring quality increases in the case of highly complex products. Leisure, tourism and hospitality products represent this category as they normally combine a range of individual but complementary services, goods and software that contribute to a specific leisure, tourism or hospitality experience.

The question of how to measure quality is central to both the total quality management (TQM) school of thought and the more recent service-marketing school of thought. Both schools agree that organisations need to set customer-focused standards against which the quality of processes and outcomes can regularly be measured and that a range of tools should be utilised in the process of quality measurement. However, they differ in their view of who the customer is, what constitutes the customer-focused standards and how to evaluate conformance to these standards. In particular, while TQM-oriented scholars developed a wide range of measures of both internal and external quality they have never attempted to develop an instrument for direct measurement of quality from the consumer perspective. Instead, they utilise a range of measures amongst which consumer satisfaction and consumer perceived value are most frequently used. In contrast, the development of a direct measure of consumer perceptions of service quality has been central to service marketing scholars. The work within this area was initiated by Parasuraman et al. (1985) who claimed that the knowledge inherited form the quality management literature was insufficient to fully understand service quality. Consequently, they embarked on a programme of in-depth qualitative and quantitative studies that resulted in the development of a multiple-item scale for measuring consumer perceptions of service quality, known as the SERVQUAL scale (Parasuraman et al., 1988). Since then, most studies relating to measuring service quality concentrated on evaluating the levels of perceived service quality at the expense of developing other measures of service quality.

Efforts aimed at measuring quality in leisure, tourism and hospitality mirrored these general trends that have been dominating the service marketing school since the mid-1980s, and concentrated predominantly upon evaluating perceived service quality. The SERVQUAL scale has been applied either in its original form (as developed by Parasuraman et al., 1988), or has been modified to reflect some of the unique features of the leisure, tourism and hospitality sectors or to address some of the inherent weaknesses of the original SERVQUAL scale. Examples of applications of this scale within the context of leisure, tourism and hospitality include measuring the service quality of U.S. recreational services (Crompton & MacKay, 1989; Hamilton et al., 1991; Taylor et al., 1993), travel and tourism industry (Fick & Ritchie, 1991), historic houses (Frochot & Hughes, 2000), resorts (Tribe & Snaith, 1998), hotels (Akan, 1995; Ekinci et al., 1998; Gabbie & O'Neill, 1997; Knutson et al., 1991; Saleh & Ryan, 1991), restaurants (Stevens et al., 1995), and fast food outlets (Johns & Tyas, 1996). Several writers have also considered the appropriateness of the conceptual and methodological assumptions that underpinned the development of the original SERVQUAL scale and their implications for the measurement of perceived service quality in leisure, tourism and hospitality (e.g. Ekinci & Riley, 1998; Frochot & Hughes, 2000; Ryan, 1999). These studies are of great theoretical and practical value and provide sound foundations for addressing the question of whether the SERVQUAL scale, despite its inherent weaknesses, is an adequate measure of quality in leisure, tourism and hospitality, given the complexity of the products offered within these sectors. They also constitute a platform for specifying a research agenda for the future.

THE INHERENT WEAKNESSES OF THE SERVQUAL SCALE

The development of the SERVQUAL scale was grounded in service marketing theory which at that time did not provide sound conceptual foundations for investigating service quality (Parasuraman et al., 1985). While service quality was defined as meeting or exceeding customers' expectations (Gronroos, 1983; Lovelock, 1981; Parasuraman et al., 1985), the interpretation of this definition assumed that perceived service quality results from the comparison of the expected service with the experienced service (Gronroos, 1983; Parasuraman et al., 1985). Consequently, the expectancy-disconfirmation theory underpinned the development of the SERVQUAL scale, which attracted a great deal of criticism from several writers (e.g. Babakus & Bolter, 1992; Buttle, 1996; Carman, 1990; Cronin & Taylor, 1992, 1994; Ekinci & Riley, 1998; Llosa et al., 1998). Such interpretation of the service quality definition also resulted in the direct use of the expectation construct as a comparison standard against which perceptions of actual performance were assessed (Parasuraman et al., 1988), which again attracted widespread discussion within academic circles. Another weakness of the SERVQUAL scale recognised in the literature relates to the dimensionality of the scale, as the application of this instrument within various service contexts yielded inconsistent results in terms of the number and the type of dimensions identified. Although other limitations of this scale have also been recognised, these three weaknesses are of particular importance in addressing the issue of whether the SERVQUAL scale is adequate for measuring quality in leisure, tourism and hospitality and therefore deserve more in-depth discussion.

The Disconfirmation Paradigm as the Basis for the Development of the Servqual Scale

The theory that informs conceptualisation of service quality in the service marketing literature and subsequently the development of the SERVQUAL scale is the expectancy-disconfirmation theory. This theory was originally developed to explain how consumers reach satisfaction decisions (Oliver, 1980) and it is unclear why Parasuraman et al. (1985) have drawn upon this theoretical framework in order to explain how customers evaluate service quality. Indeed, several writers challenged Parasuraman et al.'s (1985) approach (e.g. Babakus & Bolter, 1992; Buttle, 1996; Carman, 1990; Cronin & Taylor, 1992, 1994; Ekinci & Riley, 1998; Llosa et al., 1998). Such a direct application of the expectancy-disconfirmation theory within the service quality context has, however, major theoretical and practical implications.

From the theoretical perspective, the application of the expectancy-disconfirmation theory within the context of service quality has led to a debate as to what the SERVQUAL scale is actually measuring: is it measuring the levels of perceived service quality or is it measuring consumer satisfaction (e.g. Cronin & Taylor, 1992, 1994; Ryan, 1999). Parasuraman et al. (1988) maintain that the SERVQUAL scale measures service quality, which is defined as an attitude, a long run overall evaluation. In contrast, satisfaction relates to the evaluation of a specific transaction (Bolton & Drew, 1991; Oliver, 1981). However, according to Cronin and Taylor (1992, 1994) the principles and the structure of the SERVQUAL scale indicate that the instrument facilitates measuring the satisfaction with specific transactions rather than the overall service quality. While Parasuraman et al. (1985, 1988, 1994) argued that customer satisfaction and service quality are related constructs, critics maintained that such a conclusion is premature since the debate regarding the relationship between customer satisfaction and service quality has not been resolved despite a number of propositions made to explain this relationship (e.g. Bitner & Hubbert, 1994; Cronin & Taylor, 1992; Lee et al., 2000; Parasuraman et al., 1994; Taylor & Baker, 1994). Emerging results from recent empirical studies (e.g. Sureshchandar et al., 2002) are increasingly indicating that while consumer satisfaction and service quality share a unique relationship, they are distinct. Rust and Oliver (1994), based on Oliver (1993), identified two bases for differentiating these two constructs. Firstly, they argue that service quality is a more specific construct than overall satisfaction, since it is based on the product and service features, while dissatisfaction judgements can result from any dimension, quality related or not. Secondly, they argue that a company has to have a certain degree of control over the attributes of service quality whereas consumer satisfaction may be affected by aspects that are completely beyond the company's control. Oliver (1993) also noted that service quality perceptions do not necessarily require experience with the service whereas satisfaction evaluation does require the service to have been experienced. Within the leisure sector, Crompton and MacKay (1989) also noted that satisfaction, which is a psychological outcome, is different from service quality, which is an attribute of service.

In practice, the confusion over the service quality and consumer satisfaction constructs has led to the application of the SERVQUAL scale to measuring both consumer satisfaction (e.g. Wisniewski, 2001) and, more frequently, service quality (e.g. Akan, 1995; Ekinci et al., 1998; Fick & Ritchie, 1991; Gabbie & O'Neill, 1997; Juwaheer & Ross, 2003). Yet these two constructs, although related, are distinct and thus require different approaches and tools for measuring them.

Expectations as a Comparison Standard in Measuring Service Quality

The use of the expectation construct as a comparison standard against which actual performance is assessed presents a number of problems that have direct implications for measuring service quality in general (Cronin & Taylor, 1992; Teas, 1993) and quality in leisure, tourism and hospitality in particular.

Firstly, recent studies suggest that the expectation construct itself is still vague and further research is required to provide a full understanding of this construct and its determinants (Devlin et al., 2002; Ekinci & Riley, 1998; Johnston & Mathews, 1997; Kozak, 2000). For example, some researchers define expectations as predictions of future performance (Oliver, 1980), some as the desire or goals (Spreng & Olshavsky, 1993) and others as norms based on past experience (Cadotte et al., 1987).

Secondly, the expectation construct is dynamic as it is influenced by a number of factors including past experience, word-of-mouth communication, personal needs and a firm's external communication to customers (Parasuraman et al., 1985). Although some researchers (Boulding et al., 1993; Zeithaml et al., 1993) argue that the normative "should be" expectations are more stable than the predictive "will be" expectations, it is only when one standard is compared in relation to another. The problem of the dynamic nature of expectations can affect the measurement of quality particularly in tourism. Kozak (2000) notes that due to the length of time spent during the holidays, tourist expectations can be continuously updated by performance throughout the duration of the holiday and it may therefore be difficult to distinguish between expectations and performance.

Thirdly, expectations are subjective. Subjectivity entails that judgements of perceived service quality can differ from one individual to another and therefore can be contrasted with objective quality, which involves an emotionally detached or unbiased judgement of an aspect or feature of a thing or event (Holbrook & Corfman, 1985). To reduce the level of subjectivity, the developers of the SERVQUAL scale defined expectations in terms of a tolerance zone (Zeithaml et al., 1993). The proposed standards comprised three levels of expectations: the desired, adequate and predictive. The desired level referred to what customers hoped to receive, i.e. what customers believed "can be" and "should be" received (Zeithaml et al., 1993). The adequate level reflects the level of performance the consumer feels acceptable, i.e. the "minimum tolerable level" (Miller, 1977). Finally, the predicted level represents what the customer believes is most likely to occur. Parasuraman et al. (1994) modified their original scale to incorporate the concept of a zone of tolerance but these modifications did not substantially help in clarifying the expectation construct. Even the developers of the SERVQUAL scale themselves (Parasuraman et al., 1994) contended that many issues regarding the expectation construct remain unresolved.

Dimensionality of the SERVQUAL Scale

The SERVQUAL scale measures perceived service quality along five generic service quality dimensions, namely reliability, assurance, tangibility, empathy and responsiveness. Although Parasuraman et al. (1988) claim that the instrument is generic, the application of the SERVQUAL scale continues to yield inconsistent results in terms of the number and the type of quality dimensions. These dimensions can range from as few as one to as many as nine (Buttle, 1996). More importantly, it has been observed that the number and the type of dimensions vary depending on the service sector under investigation. The issue of the dimensionality of the SERVQUAL scale attracted particular attention within the context of leisure, tourism and hospitality and this is explored further below.

APPLICATION OF THE SERVQUAL SCALE IN LEISURE, TOURISM AND HOSPITALITY

Despite the inherent weaknesses of the SERVQUAL scale, this instrument has been widely used for measuring consumer perceptions of service quality in leisure, tourism and hospitality. While some researchers used the original scale developed by Parasuraman et al. (1988), others modified it with a view to capturing some of the unique features of the leisure, tourism and hospitality sectors and/or addressing some of the inherent weaknesses of the original instrument (Table 1). The rationale for using the original SERVQUAL scale or for introducing modifications differed across various studies but three general tendencies can be observed.

Firstly, researchers who applied the original scale for measuring quality in leisure, tourism and hospitality (e.g. Gabbie & O'Neill, 1997; Hamilton et al., 1991; Ingram & Daskalakis, 1999; Ryan & Cliff, 1997) argued that the service dimensions identified by Parasuraman et al. (1988) sufficiently represented the most significant aspects of services the perceived quality of which they intended to measure. In particular, Ryan and Cliff (1997) argued that the original SERVQUAL scale was a suitable instrument for measuring quality in travel agencies because the dimensions of the SERVQUAL scale highly corresponded with the factors that Albrecht (1992) and LeBlanc (1992) identified as those that customers used to evaluate service quality in travel agencies. Although both Albrecht (1992) and LeBlanc (1992) identified other factors that might seem different from the five dimensions proposed by Parasuraman et al. (1988), Ryan and Cliff (1997) argued that the SERVQUAL scale measured the most significant ones and incorporated the other factors determined by LeBlanc (1992) (i.e. price confidence, agent continuity and recovery) and Albrecht (1992) (i.e. corporate image and competitiveness).

Secondly, researchers who modified the SERVQUAL scale by introducing additional items claimed that the original scale did not sufficiently represent the unique features of services that constituted the object of their investigations (e.g. Akan, 1995; Ekinci et al., 1998; Frochot & Hughes, 2000; Juwaheer & Ross, 2003; Knutson et al., 1991; O'Neill et al., 1999; Saleh & Ryan, 1991; Stevens et al., 1995). For example, Saleh and Ryan (1991) explained that not all of the SERVQUAL scale items were immediately applicable to a hotel. Consequently, they modified this scale using some of Martin's (1986; cited in Saleh & Ryan, 1991) 40-item scale questions developed for the assessment of restaurant services as well as Saleh and de Cuardo's (1989, cited in Saleh & Ryan, 1991) 40-item scale for measuring Spanish hotel services. This has resulted in the development of a 33-item scale for measuring service quality in hotels.

The additional items that the researchers included in their scales were derived mainly from literature although more recently several researchers undertook some

Table 1. Examples of Application of the SERVQUAL Scale in Leisure, Tourism and Hospitality.

Researchers and Year of Study	Object of Evaluation	Comments
Crompton and MacKay (1989)	Recreational services	
Knutson et al. (1991)	Hotels and motels	Modified SERVQUAL scale called LODGSERV (26 items)
Fick and Ritchie (1991)	Airlines, hotels, restaurants, ski areas	
Hamilton et al. (1991)	Parks	
Saleh and Ryan (1991)	Hotels	Modified SERVQUAL scale (33 items)
Luk et al. (1993)	Organised tour services	Modified SERVQUAL scale (19 items)
Taylor et al. (1993)	Recreational services	
Bojanic and Rosen (1994)	Restaurants	
Getty and Thompson (1994)	Lodging industry	Modified SERVQUAL scale called LODGQUAL
Patton et al. (1994)	Hotels	Application of LODGSERV
Akan (1995)	Hotels	Modified SERVQUAL scale (30 items)
Lee and Hing (1995)	Restaurants	
Stevens et al. (1995)	Restaurants	Modified SERVQUAL scale called DINESERV (29 items)
Gabbie and O'Neill (1996, 1997)	Hotels	
Johns and Tyas (1996)	Foodservice outlets	Modified SERVQUAL scale – perceptions only
Gabbie and O'Neill (1997)	Hotels	
Lam et al. (1997)	Private and estate clubs	
Ryan and Cliff (1997)	Travel agencies	
Suh et al. (1997)	Hotels	
Ekinci et al. (1998)	Resort hotel	Modified SERVQUAL and LODGSERV scale; (18 items)
O'Neill et al. (1998)	Hotels	
Qu and Tsang (1998)	Hotels	Modified SERVQUAL scale (35 items)
Tribe and Snaith (1998)	Resorts	Modified SERVQUAL scale called HOLSAT
Ingram and Daskalakis (1999)	Hotels	
O'Neill et al. (1999)	Surfing event	Modified SERVQUAL scale (21 items)
Wong et al. (1999)	Hotels	Modified SERVQUAL scale (27 items)
Frochot and Hughes (2000)	Historic houses	Modified SERVQUAL scale called HISTOQUAL (24 items) perceptions only
Heung et al. (2000)	Airport-restaurant	Modified SERVQUAL and DINESERV scale (33 items)
O'Neill and Charters (2000)	Wine tourism	Modified SERVQUAL scale called WINOT (22 items)

Table 1. (*Continued*)

Researchers and Year of Study	Object of Evaluation	Comments
O'Neill et al. (2000)	Dive tour operator	Modified SERVQUAL scale called DIVEPERF – importance/performance
Fu and Parks (2001)	Restaurants	
O'Neill and Palmer (2001)	Accommodation facilities, water based adventure theme park	Modified SERVQUAL scale – importance/performance
Atilgan et al. (2003)	Tour operators	Modified SERVQUAL scale (26 items)
Getty and Getty (2003)	Lodging industry	Development of new scale based on Parasuraman et al. (1985) ten original dimensions
Juwaheer and Ross (2003)	Hotels	Modified SERVQUAL scale (39-items)
O'Neill and Palmer (2003)	Theme park	Modified SERVQUAL scale (22 items, 5-point scale)

Source: Based on literature review.

primary studies with a view to identifying supplementary attributes of services under investigation (e.g. Frochot & Hughes, 2000; Juwaheer & Ross, 2003). While these modifications led to the development of new and occasionally re-named scales (see Table 1), in conceptual terms the majority of these instruments followed the principles and the structure of the SERVQUAL scale, predominantly for practical reasons. Heung et al. (2000), for example, stress the relative simplicity and the relatively low cost of using the SERVQUAL scale as well as its potential for producing valuable information on an organisation's service quality. Similarly, Atilgan et al. (2003) used the SERVQUAL scale as the skeleton for the development of a modified instrument for measuring quality because "it is mostly used, valid and generally accepted measurement tool" (Atilgan et al., 2003, p. 413).

Thirdly, several researchers modified the original SERVQUAL scale more substantially with a view to addressing some of its inherent weaknesses (e.g. Ekinci et al., 1998; Frochot & Hughes, 2000; Johns & Tyas, 1996; O'Neill and Palmer, 2001; O'Neill et al., 2000). In doing so, they followed another approach to measuring service quality proposed by Cronin and Taylor (1992, 1994), who were the most critical of the SERVQUAL scale within the service-marketing field. Cronin and Taylor (1992, 1994) argued that if service quality is best conceptualised as an attitude, then the adequacy-importance model of attitude measurement is the most appropriate measure of service quality. They subsequently developed a SERVPERF scale, which assessed service quality in

Table 2. Examples of Service Quality Dimensions Identified in Leisure, Tourism and Hospitality Studies Against the Original Dimensions Found by Parasuraman et al. (1988).

Researchers/ Year of Study	Object of Evaluation	Approaches to Data Collection	Technique of Data Analysis	Outcome
Parasuraman, et al. (1985, 1988)	Credit Card, Banking, Brokerage, Repair Services, long distance telephone company	Focus groups; stage one: 97-item questionnaire (10 dimensions); Stage two: 34-item questionnaire (7 dimensions); Stage three: 22-item questionnaire SERVQUAL (5 dimensions); quota sampling; sample size: 200 at each stage; respondents recruited by a marketing firm in a shopping mall in the USA	Factor analysis	5 dimensions (Reliability, Assurance, Tangibility, Empathy, Responsiveness)
Saleh and Ryan (1991)	Hotels	Modified SERVQUAL scale; 33-item questionnaire from literature, five-point Likert scale; self-completed questionnaire in the presence of two researchers; stratified random sampling; sample frame: 4-star hotel guests, Western Canadian city; 170 usable questionnaires	Factor analysis	5 Dimensions (Conviviality, Tangibles, Reassurance, Avoid Sarcasm, Empathy)
Akan (1995)	Hotels	Modified SERVQUAL scale; 30-item questionnaire adapted from the original list of ten service quality dimensions of Parasuraman et al. (1985); four-point scale; sample frame: hotels in Istanbul, Turkey; sample Size 228	Factor analysis	7 Dimensions (Courtesy and competence, Communication and transaction, Tangibles, Knowing and understanding the customer, Accuracy of hotel reservations, Accuracy and speed of service, Solutions to problems)
Lam et al. (1997)	Private and estate clubs	Original SERVQUAL scale translated into Chinese with some changes to the wording; Questionnaires sent out by mail or distributed to members of clubs in Hong Kong; 96 usable questionnaires:	Factor analysis	Replicated the 5 SERVQUAL dimensions

Bigne et al. (1997)	Travel Agencies	Modified SERVQUAL scale; original 22 items used with changes to the wording	Factor analysis	Replicated the 5 SERVQUAL dimensions
Ryan and Cliff (1997)	Travel Agencies	Original SERVQUAL scale; questionnaire mailed to respondents; random sampling from the electoral register for Palmerston North, New Zealand; 210 usable questionnaires	Factor analysis / Cluster analysis	3 Dimensions (Reassurance, Reliability, Tangibles)
Ekinci et al. (1998)	Resort hotels	Modified SERVQUAL and LODGSERV scale; change of items' tense from present simple to past; PERFORMANCE only; 38-items questionnaire; sample frame: two seaside Turkish resorts; 113 usable questionnaires	Factor analysis	2 dimensions (Tangibles, Intangibles)
Qu and Tsang (1998)	Hotels	35-item questionnaire based on literature review including items from Parasuraman et al., 1988; Sample size 270	Factor analysis	6 dimensions (Price and value, Staff skills and performance, Extra amenities, Facilities and atmosphere, Availability and efficiency of service, Reliability)
Wong et al. (1999)	Hotels	Modified SERVQUAL scale; 27-item questionnaire (called HOLSERV) from literature; Sample frame: Five mid-luxury hotels (3–5 stars) in Australia; 155 usable questionnaires	Factor analysis	3 dimensions (Employees, Tangibles Reliability)
Frochot and Hughes (2000)	Historic houses	Modified SERVQUAL scale extended by items relating to historic houses; 24-item scale (called HISTOQUAL); 5-point rating scale; PERCEPTIONS only; interviewer filling the questionnaire; sample frame: visitor to three historic houses in England and Scotland; convenience sampling; 790 usable questionnaires	Factor analysis	5 dimensions (Responsiveness, Tangibles, Communications, Consumables, Empathy)

Table 2. (*Continued*)

Researchers/ Year of Study	Object of Evaluation	Approaches to Data Collection	Technique of Data Analysis	Outcome
Getty and Getty (2003)	Lodging industry	Development of new scale based on Parasuraman et al. (1985) ten original dimensions amended through literature review and in-depth interviews with service users to identify scale items representing each of the 10 dimensions; 63-item questionnaire mailed to frequent-traveller business owners from 12 large U.S. cities; Stratified random sampling; 222 usable questionnaires; 45-item scale after purification; second data set; 229 usable questionnaires; purification of scale to 26 items (LQI scale)	Factor analysis	5 dimensions (Tangibility, Reliability, Responsiveness, Confidence, Communication)
Juwaheer and Ross (2003)	Hotels	Modified SERVQUAL scale – 39-item, derived from exploratory interviews with ten hotel managers and 25 tourists of different nationalities. Mauritius; 401 usable questionnaires	Factor analysis	9 dimensions of which 4 were similar to Parasuraman et al. (1998)

Source: Based on literature review.

terms of the perception of performance only. Such an approach avoids many of the problems inherent in the SERVQUAL scale, including the existence of multiple comparison standards and the weaknesses of the expectation construct. However, the SERVPERF scale measures service quality along the same five dimensions of service quality proposed by Parasuraman et al. (1988) and such an approach does not address the problem of the dimensionality of the SERVQUAL scale.

The five generic dimensions of service quality represented in the SERVQUAL scale have indeed rarely been repeated in studies within leisure, tourism and hospitality, as presented in Table 2. While the results of these studies may indicate that quality dimensions are contextual, it should be noted that the research methodology literature recognises four major sources of measurement differences; the respondent, the measurer, situational factors and the instrument (Cooper & Schindler, 2001). Indeed, a more in-depth analysis of approaches to data collection adopted by researchers who attempted to measure perceived service quality in leisure, tourism and hospitality (see Table 2) indicates that these four sources of measurement differences may have significantly contributed to the fact that these studies yielded inconsistent results. Although Parasuraman et al. (1988) suggested that the SERVQUAL scale could be "adapted or supplemented to fit the characteristics or specific research needs of a particular organisation" (Parasuraman et al., 1988, p. 31), from the methodological point of view it cannot be expected that modified scales would produce the same results. In fact, every attempt to modify the SERVQUAL scale to reflect the needs of the leisure, tourism and hospitality industry produced a new instrument and only studies that use exactly the same instrument for measuring a particular construct may produce similar results. This, however, has not happened in leisure, tourism and hospitality, with the exception of LODGSERV and DINESERV that have been used on more than one occasion (see Table 1). Consequently, it should not be surprising that studies measuring service quality in hotels for example identified as few as two and as many as nine dimensions of service quality (see Table 2).

IS THE SERVQUAL SCALE AN ADEQUATE MEASURE OF QUALITY IN LEISURE TOURISM AND HOSPITALITY?

In order to address the question of whether the SERVQUAL scale is an adequate measure of quality in leisure, tourism and hospitality, two issues need to be considered. Firstly, whether the attributes and dimensions of service quality adequately represent the attributes of quality in leisure, tourism and hospitality.

Secondly, what the role of the SERVQUAL scale is in measuring quality in leisure, tourism and hospitality.

The SERVQUAL Scale and the Attributes of Quality in Leisure, Tourism and Hospitality

The fact that the original SERVQUAL scale was frequently supplemented with new items indicates that the SERVQUAL scale does not sufficiently represent the unique attributes of leisure, tourism and hospitality services. What also emerges from the review of previous related studies is the fact that there is no consensus as to what the attributes of service quality for individual leisure, tourism and hospitality services are. For example, depending on the type of secondary sources that were used for the identification of additional attributes of hotel service quality, the modified SERVQUAL scales contain from 27 (Wong et al., 1999) to 38 (Ekinci et al., 1998) attributes. More recently, several primary studies were undertaken with a view to establishing the features of service quality in the lodging industry but the results of these studies do not bring us any closer to understanding what the attributes of service quality in the lodging industry are. Indeed, in the first stage of their study, Getty and Getty (2003) identified 63 attributes of service quality in the lodging industry, which were subsequently reduced to 26 through a two-stage process of scale purification. In contrast, Juwaheer and Ross (2003) identified 39 attributes of hotel service quality. Such inconsistencies in results indicate that extensive primary exploratory studies are needed in order to establish how consumers interpret the notion of service quality in the lodging and other leisure, tourism and hospitality industries.

It is also worth noting that the dimensions of service quality identified by Parasuraman et al. (1985, 1988) were consistently used as the starting point for identifying the additional attributes of service quality in leisure, tourism and hospitality and for supplementing the scale. Such an approach has two shortcomings. Firstly, the dimensions of the SERVQUAL scale are predominantly related to the quality of highly intangible services and may not fully reflect the nature of services found within the leisure, tourism and hospitality sectors. While it is accepted that leisure, tourism and hospitality services share many characteristics with other services, they nonetheless possess unique features such as temporary and shared rights of use, involvement of the public, private and voluntary sectors as well as local communities (Swarbrooke, 1995). Furthermore, many leisure, tourism and hospitality services are characterised by a higher proportion of tangibles than intangibles within the service bundles, which according to Johns and Howard (1998) has implication for measuring their quality. It may therefore be the case that the scope of investigation under the "service quality" umbrella is insufficient to capture the meaning of quality in leisure, tourism and hospitality. This is particularly true in the case of assessing the overall quality of a specific leisure, tourism or hospitality experience which depends upon the quality of a range of individual but complementary services that frequently are delivered by more than one provider. It is also unknown how consumers evaluate such complex services or experiences. Indeed, Ryan (1999) notes, that ". . . attempts at applying services marketing theory in the field of tourism have been directed towards specific components of the industry and not the totality of the holiday experience. The question that arises is whether the holiday is experienced and assessed as a holistic experience or as a sequence of events" (Ryan, 1999, p. 15). Clearly, while the SERVQUAL scale has a potential for application in the assessment of individual services, its usefulness is less clear within the context of complex leisure, tourism and hospitality experiences.

Finally, it is unclear whether the attributes of services included in the SERVQUAL scale represent the attributes of an "ideal service" or a "quality service." At the stage of their exploratory study, Parasuraman et al. (1985) were searching for "descriptions of an ideal service [and] the meaning of service quality factors important in evaluating service quality" (Parasuraman et al., 1985, p. 44). A quality service and an ideal service are not, however, synonymous as quality refers to the "degree to which a set of inherent characteristics[2] fulfils requirements, [where] inherent, as opposed to assigned, means existing in something, especially as a permanent characteristic" (ISO, 2000, p. 7). Previous studies did not clarify this issue either as the researchers who focused on supplementing the original SERVQUAL scale with attributes of leisure, tourism or hospitality services did not indicate whether these new attributes represented an "ideal" or a "quality" service.

The Role of the SERVQUAL Scale in Measuring Quality in Leisure, Tourism and Hospitality

Parasuraman et al. (1985, 1988) developed the SERVQUAL scale with a view to measuring consumer perceptions of service quality along five service quality dimensions. They claim that "it appears that judgements of high and low service quality depend on how customers perceive the actual service performance in the context of what they expected" (Parasuraman et al., 1985, p. 46). However, they also stress that "when expected service (ES) is greater than the perceived service (PS), perceived quality is less than satisfactory and will tend towards totally unacceptable quality, with an increased discrepancy between ES and PS;

when ES equals PC, perceived quality is satisfactory; when ES is lower than PS, perceived quality is more than satisfactory and will tend toward ideal quality, with increased discrepancy between ES and PS" (Parasuraman et al., 1985, pp. 48–49). This statement implies that the scale may have been designed to measure the level of *satisfaction* with perceived service quality (from unacceptable to ideal) rather than the level of service quality itself (from low to high). It may also explain why Parasuraman et al. (1988) used the expectancy disconfirmation theory (originally developed to explain how consumers reach satisfaction decisions) as the basis for the development of the SERVQUAL scale. The debate concerning the appropriateness of the conceptual underpinnings of the SERVQUAL scale indicates that this instrument may indeed be more appropriate for measuring the levels of consumer satisfaction rather than the levels of service quality. Several writers agree with this view. For example, Ryan (1999) considers this tool as a good measure of customer satisfaction provided that the results are interpreted carefully. Similarly, Pizam and Ellis (1999) consider the SERVQUAL scale as a measure of consumer satisfaction. While the question of whether the SERVQUAL scale would measure overall consumer satisfaction with an "ideal service" or consumer satisfaction with certain attributes of a "quality service" remains open, the SERVQUAL scale is an important measure of consumer satisfaction.

However, while measures of consumer satisfaction are essential in the assessment of quality, a range of other measures and indicators need to be employed to gain a comprehensive and more objective picture of quality levels. For example, the European Foundation of Quality Management recommends the use of four groups of measures in evaluating the levels of quality both within service and manufacturing industries and regardless of the size of an organisation (EFQM, 2003). These groups of measures include customer results, people results, society results and performance measures. The first three groups comprise perception measures and performance indicators while the fourth one comprises performance outcomes and performance indicators. Within the group of customer results alone, the range of perception measures includes customer satisfaction, overall image, relevance of products, perceived value and loyalty while performance indicators comprise measures such as repeat business, number of complaints, value for money, performance against customer-based objectives, number of commendations and number of lost services. Similar ranges of measures and indicators are associated with the other three groups of results. Thus, measures of consumer satisfaction, that may include the SERVQUAL scale, only partly contribute to the evaluation of customer results and a whole range of other instruments is needed to adequately measure quality. Consequently, the results of studies that utilise the SERVQUAL scale (either in its original or modified form) do not say much about the levels of quality in leisure, tourism and hospitality sectors. They merely indicate levels of consumer satisfaction with certain attributes of services under investigation.

Implications for Future Research

The critical analysis of the potentialities and limitations of the SERVQUAL scale presented in this article indicates that while this instrument may be useful in assessing the levels of consumer satisfaction with certain attributes of services, it does not adequately measure the overall quality of complex leisure, tourism and hospitality services. Indeed, as explained in the previous section of this article, measuring consumer satisfaction contributes only partly to an understanding of how well an organisation performs in terms of the levels of quality delivered. Therefore, the SERVQUAL scale as a measure of consumer satisfaction is a necessary but insufficient measure of quality in leisure tourism and hospitality.

This proposition has significant implications for future research. It raises a question of how quality in leisure, tourism and hospitality could be measured. It is not only the question of what other measures of quality (apart from consumer satisfaction) are appropriate. It is predominantly the question of whether quality can be measured directly from the consumer perspective as proposed by the service marketing literature or whether, in line with the TQM theory, indirect quality perception measures (e.g. consumer satisfaction, overall image, perceived value, loyalty) should be developed instead. Addressing this question is central to specifying the future direction of research in the area of measuring quality in leisure, tourism and hospitality. Any attempt at answering this question should, however, begin with due consideration of conceptual issues associated with the notion of quality in leisure, tourism and hospitality. The quality construct is highly abstract and composed of a number of concepts which usually have different and confusing meanings to the parties involved in their evaluation. The literature on research methodology (e.g. Cooper & Schindler, 2001) emphasises that without a clear, operational definition of a construct under investigation (i.e. without specifying the characteristics of the construct and how they are to be observed), the measurement process will be flawed. One of the latent but significant contributions of the previous studies that attempted to measure quality in leisure, tourism and hospitality is the fact that there is no uniform operational definition of quality within these sectors. Indeed, most researchers developed their own operational definitions of quality of individual leisure, tourism and hospitality services for the purpose of a particular study, mainly in terms of the characteristics of the quality construct. This may indicate that either the common inherent characteristics of quality in leisure, tourism and hospitality have not as yet been identified or that the quality construct is highly contextual and different characteristics represent the quality of individual leisure, tourism and hospitality services. If it is found in the course of in-depth qualitative study that such common characteristics can be identified (either in relation to all leisure, tourism and hospitality services or in relation to distinct groups of services within these three sectors), and that all of these characteristics can be directly observed by consumers, then it might be possible to develop an instrument that would directly measure perceived quality in leisure, tourism and hospitality. If, however, it is found that the quality construct is contextual, in terms of either the characteristics of the construct or the ways in which they can be observed, then no further efforts aimed at developing a direct measure of perceived quality in leisure, tourism and hospitality should be undertaken. Instead, the research focus should be placed solely on developing sound indirect measures of quality in leisure, tourism and hospitality that would contribute to observing the inherent characteristics of quality leisure, tourism and hospitality services. This process could ultimately lead to the development of a quality index that incorporates all associated measures.

The process of developing sound measures of quality in leisure, tourism and hospitality proposed in this paper is a long-term one and requires a great deal of effort on the part of researchers. However, this process is unavoidable, if research and theory on quality measurement is to progress and benefit the leisure, tourism and hospitality practitioners.

NOTES

1. For the purpose of this article, product is defined as a "result of a process," which may be either a service, or a good (hardware or processed materials) or software (e.g. information) or their combination (ISO, 2000).

2. Characteristic are further defined as distinguishing features and can include physical, sensory, behavioural, temporal, ergonomic, and functional features (ISO, 2000).

REFERENCES

Akan, P. (1995). Dimensions of service quality: A study of Istanbul. *Managing Service Quality, 5*(6), 39–43.

Albrecht, K. (1992). *The only thing that matters.* New York: Harper Business.

Atilgan, E., Akinci, S., & Aksoy, S. (2003). Mapping service quality in the tourism industry. *Managing Service Quality, 13*(5), 412–422.

Babakus, E., & Bolter, G. W. (1992). An empirical assessment of the SERVQUAL scale. *Journal of Business Research, 24*(May), 253–268.

Bigne, E., Martinez, C., & Miquel, M. J. (1997). The influence of motivation, experience and satisfaction on the quality of travel agencies. In: P. Kunst & J. Lemmink (Eds), *Managing Service Quality.* London: Paul Chapman.

Bitner, M. J. (1990). Evaluating service encounters: The effects of physical surrounding and employees responses. *Journal of Marketing, 54*(2), 69–82.

Bitner, M. J., & Hubbert, A (1994). Encounter satisfaction versus overall satisfaction versus quality. In: R. Rust & R. L. Oliver (Eds), *Service Quality: New Directions in Theory and Practice* (pp. 77–95). London: Sage.

Bojanic, D. C., & Rosen, L. D. (1994). Measuring service quality in restaurants: An application of the SERVQUAL instrument. *Hospitality Research Journal, 18*(1), 3–14.

Bolton, R. N., & Drew, J. H. (1991). A multistage model of customers' assessment of service quality and value. *Journal of Consumer Research, 17*(4), 375–384.

Boulding, W., Kalra, A., Staelin, R., & Zeithaml, V. A. (1993). A dynamic process model of service quality: From expectations to behavioural intentions. *Journal of Marketing Research, 30*(1), 7–27.

Buttle, F. (1996). SERVQUAL: Review, critique, research agenda. *European Journal of Marketing, 30*(1), 8–32.

Buzzell, R. D., & Gale, B. T. (1987). *The PIMS principles.* New York: Free Press.

Cadotte, E. R., Woodruff, R. B., & Jenkins, R. L. (1987). Expectations and norms in models of customer satisfaction. *Journal of Marketing Research, 24*(August), 305–314.

Carman, J. M. (1990). Consumer perceptions of service quality: An assessment of the SERVQUAL. *Journal of Retailing, 66*(1), 33–35.

Cooper, D. R., & Schindler, P. S. (2001). *Business research methods* (7th ed.). New York: McGraw-Hill.

Crompton, J. L., & MacKay, K. J. (1989). Users perceptions of the relative importance of service quality dimensions in selected public recreation programs. *Leisure Sciences, 4,* 367–375.

Cronin, J. J., & Taylor, S. A. (1992). Measuring service quality: A re-examination and extension. *Journal of Marketing, 56*(3), 55–68.

Cronin, J. J., & Taylor, S. A. (1994). SERVPERF versus SERVQUAL: Reconciling performance-based and perceptions-minus-expectations measurement of service quality. *Journal of Marketing, 58*(1), 125–131.

Devlin, J. F., Gwynne, A. L., & Ennew, C. T. (2002). The antecedents of service expectations. *The Services Industry Journal, 22*(October), 117–136.

EFQM (2003). The *EFQM Excellence Model.* http://www.efqm.org/.

Ekinci, Y., Riley, M., & Fife-Schaw, C. (1998). What school of thought? The dimension of the resort hotel quality. *International Journal of Contemporary Hospitality Management, 10*(2), 63–67.

Ekinci, Y., & Riley, R. (1998). A critique of the issues and theoretical assumptions in service quality measurement in the lodging industry: Time to move the goal post? *Hospitality Management, 17,* 349–362.

Evans, J. R., & Lindsay, W. M. (2002). *The management and control of quality* (5th ed.). Cincinnati, OH: South-Western.

Fick, G. R., & Ritchie, J. R. B. (1991). Measuring service quality in the travel and tourism industry. *Journal of Travel Research, 30*(Fall), 2–9.

Frochot, I., & Hughes, H. (2000). HISTOQUAL: The development of a historic houses assessment scale. *Tourism Management, 21,* 157–167.

Fu, Y. Y., & Parks, S. C. (2001). The relationship between restaurant service quality and consumer loyalty among the elderly. *Journal of Hospitality and Tourism Research, 25*(3), 320–336.

Gabbie, O., & O'Neill, M. A. (1996). SERVQUAL and the Northern Ireland hotel sector: A comparative analysis – Part 1. *Managing Service Quality*, *6*(6), 25–32.

Gabbie, O., & O'Neill, M. A. (1997). SERVQUAL and the Northern Ireland hotel sector: A comparative analysis – Part 2. *Managing Service Quality*, *7*(1), 43–49.

Getty, J., & Thompson, K. (1994). A procedure for scaling perceptions of lodging quality. *Hospitality Research Journal*, *18*(2), 75–96.

Getty, J. M., & Getty, R. L. (2003). Lodging quality index (LQI): Assessing customers' perceptions of quality delivery. *International Journal of Contemporary Hospitality Management*, *15*(2), 94–104.

Gronroos, C. (1983). *Strategic management and marketing in the service sector*. Cambridge, MA: Marketing Science Institute.

Hamilton, J. A., Crompton, J. L., & More, T. A. (1991). Identifying the dimensions of service quality in a park context. *Journal of Environmental Management*, *32*(4), 211–220.

Heung, V. C. S., Wong, M. Y., & Qu, H. (2000). Airport-restaurant service quality in Hong Kong: An application of SERVQUAL. *Cornell Hotel and Restaurant Administration Quarterly* (June).

Holbrook, M. B., & Corfman, K. P. (1985). Quality and value in the consumption experience: Phaedrus rides again. In: J. Jacoby & J. Olson (Eds), *Perceived Quality* (pp. 31–57). Lexington, MA: Lexington Books.

Ingram, H., & Daskalakis, G. (1999). Measuring quality gaps in hotels: The case of Crete. *International Journal of Contemporary Hospitality Management*, *11*(1), 24–30.

ISO (2000). *Quality management systems – fundamentals and vocabulary*. Geneva: ISO.

Johns, N., & Howard, A. (1998). Customer expectations versus perceptions of service performance in the foodservice industry. *International Journal of Service Industry Management*, *9*(3), 248–265.

Johns, N., & Tyas, P. (1996). Use of service quality gap theory to differentiate between food service outlets. *Services Industries Journal*, *16*(3), 321–346.

Johnston, C., & Mathews, B. P. (1997). The influence of experience on service expectations. *International Journal of Service Industry Management*, *8*(4), 290–305.

Juwaheer, T. D., & Ross, D. L. (2003). A study of hotel guest perceptions in Mauritius. *International Journal of Contemporary Hospitality Management*, *15*(2), 105–115.

Knutson, B., Stevens, P., Wullaert, C., & Patton, M. (1991). LODGSERV: A service quality index for the lodging industry. *Hospitality Research Journal*, *14*(7), 277–284.

Kozak, M. (2000). A critical review of approaches to measure satisfaction with tourist destinations. *Tourism Analysis*, *5*, 191–196.

Lam, T., Wong, A., & Yeung, S. (1997). Measuring service quality in clubs: An application of the SERVQUAL instrument. *Australian Journal of Hospitality Management*, *4*(1), 7–14.

LeBlanc, G. (1992). Factors affecting the evaluation of service quality in travel agencies: An investigation of customer perceptions. *Journal of Marketing Research*, *30*(4), 10–21.

Lee, H., Lee, Y., & Yoo, D. (2000). The determinants of perceived service quality and its relationship with satisfaction. *Journal of the Services Marketing*, *14*(3), 217–231.

Lee, Y. L., & Hing, N. (1995). Measuring quality in restaurant operations: An application of the SERVQUAL instrument. *International Journal of Hospitality Management*, *14*(3/4), 293–310.

Llosa, S., Chandon, J. L., & Orsingher, C. (1998). An empirical study of SERVQUAL dimensionality. *The Services Industries Journal*, *18*(2), 16–44.

Lovelock, C. H. (1981). Why marketing needs to be different for services. In: J. Donnelly & W. George, W. (Eds), *Marketing of Services* (pp. 5–9). Chicago: American Marketing.

Luk, S. T. K., de Leon, C. T., Leong, F., & Li, E. (1993). Value segmentation of tourists' expectations of service quality. *Journal of Travel and Tourism Marketing*, *2*(4), 23–38.

Miller, J. A. (1977). Exploring satisfaction, modifying models, eliciting expectations, posing problems, and making meaningful measurements. In: H. K. Hunt (Ed.), *Conceptualisation and Measurement of Customer Satisfaction and Dissatisfaction* (pp. 72–91). Cambridge, MA: Marketing Science Institute.

O'Neill, M., & Charters, S. (2000). Service quality at the cellar door: Implications for Western Australia's developing wine tourism industry. *Managing Service Quality, 10*(2), 112–122.

O'Neill, M., Getz, D., & Carlsen, J. (1999). Evaluation of service quality at events: The 1998 Coca-Cola Masters Surfing event at Margaret River, Western Australia. *Managing Service Quality, 9*(3), 158–166.

O'Neill, M., & Palmer, A. (2001). Survey timing and consumer perceptions of service quality: An overview of empirical evidence. *Managing Service Quality, 11*(3), 182–190.

O'Neill, M., & Palmer, A. (2003). An exploratory study of the effects of experience on consumer perceptions of the service quality construct. *Managing Service Quality, 13*(3), 187–196.

O'Neill, M. A., Palmer, A. J., & Beggs, R. (1998). The effects of survey timing on perceptions of service quality. *Managing Service Quality, 8*(2), 126–132.

O'Neill, M. A., Williams, P., MacCarthy, M., & Groves, R. (2000). Diving into service quality – the dive tour operator perspective. *Managing Service Quality, 10*(3), 131–140.

Oliver, R. L. (1980). A cognitive model of the antecedents and consequences of satisfaction. *Journal of Marketing Research, 17*, 460–469.

Oliver, R. L. (1981). Measurement and evaluation of satisfaction process in retail settings. *Journal of Retailing, 57*(Fall), 25–48.

Oliver, R. L. (1993). A conceptual model of service quality and satisfaction: Compatible goals, different concepts. *Advances In Services Marketing and Management, 2*, 65–85.

Parasuraman, P. A., Zeithaml, V. A., & Berry, L. L. (1985). A conceptual model of service quality and its implications for future research. *Journal of Marketing, 49*(Fall), 41–50.

Parasuraman, P. A., Zeithaml, V. A., & Berry, L. L. (1988). SERVQUAL: A multiple-item scale for measuring consumer perceptions of service quality. *Journal of Retailing, 64*(1), 14–40.

Parasuraman, P. A., Zeithaml, V. A., & Berry, L. L. (1994). Reassessment of expectation as a comparison standard in measuring service: Implications for future research. *Journal of Marketing, 58*(January), 111–124.

Patton, M., Stevens, P., & Knutson, B. J. (1994). Internationalising LODGSERV as a pilot study. *Journal of Hospitality and Leisure Marketing, 2*(2), 39–55.

Pizam, A., & Ellis, T. (1999). Customer satisfaction and its measurement in hospitality enterprises. *International Journal of Contemporary Hospitality Management, 11*(7), 326–339.

Qu, H., & Tsang, N. (1998). Service quality gap in China's hotel industry: A study of tourist perceptions and exceptions. *Journal of Hospitality and Tourism Research, 22*(3), 252–267.

Rust, R. T., & Oliver, R. L. (1994). Service quality insights: Management implications from the frontier. In: R. T. Rust & R. L. Oliver (Eds), *Service Quality: New Directions in Theory and Practice*. Thousand Oaks, CA: Sage.

Rust, R. T., & Zahorik, A. J. (1993). Customer satisfaction, customer retention and market share. *Journal of Retailing, 69*(2), 193–215.

Ryan, C. (1999). From the psychometrics of the SERVQUAL to sex – measurements of tourists satisfaction. In: A. Pizam & Y. Mansfeld (Eds), *Consumer Behavior in Travel and Tourism* (pp. 267–286). Binghamton, NY: Haworth Press.

Ryan, C., & Cliff, A. (1997). Do travel agencies measure up to customer expectation? An empirical investigation of travel agencies' service quality as measured by SERVQUAL. *Journal of Travel and Tourism Marketing, 6*(2), 1–27.

Saleh, F., & Ryan, C. (1991). Analyzing service quality in the hospitality industry using the SERVQUAL model. *The Services Industry Journal*, *11*(3), 324–343.

Spreng, R. A., & Olshavsky, W. (1993). A desires congruency model of consumer satisfaction. *Journal of the Academy of Marketing Science* (Summer), 169–177.

Stevens, P., Knutson, B., & Patton, M. (1995). DINESERV: A tool for measuring service quality in restaurants. *Cornell Hotel and Restaurant Administration Quarterly*, *36*(2), 56–60.

Suh, S. H., Lee, Y. H., Park, Y., & Shin, G. C. (1997). The impact of consumer involvement on the consumers' perception of service quality – focusing on the Korean hotel industry. *Journal of Travel and Tourism Marketing*, *6*(2), 33–52.

Sureshchandar, G. S., Rajendran, C., & Anantharaman, R. N. (2002). The relationship between service quality and customer satisfaction – a factor specific approach. *Journal of Services Marketing*, *16*(4), 363–379.

Swarbrooke, J. (1995). *The development and management of visitor attractions*. Oxford: Butterworth-Heinemann.

Taylor, S., & Baker, T. L. (1994). An assessment of the relationship between service quality and customer satisfaction in the formation of customer purchase intentions. *Journal of Retailing*, *70*(2), 163–178.

Taylor, S. A., Sharland, A., Cronin, J. J., Jr., & Bullard, W. (1993). Recreational service quality in the international setting. *International Journal of Service Industry Management*, *4*, 68–86.

Teas, R. K. (1993). Expectations, performance evaluation, and consumer perceptions of quality. *Journal of Marketing*, *57*(4), 18–34.

Tribe, J., & Snaith, T. (1998). From Servqual to Holsat: Holiday satisfaction in Varadero, Cuba. *Tourism Management*, *19*, 25–34.

Wisniewski, M. (2001). Assessing customer satisfaction with local authority services using SERVQUAL. *Total Quality Management*, *12*(7/8), 995–1002.

Wong, A., Mei, O., Dean, A. M., & White, C. J. (1999). Analyzing service quality in the hospitality industry SERVQUAL model. *Managing Service Quality*, *9*(2), 136–143.

Zeithaml, V. A., Berry, L., & Parasuraman, A. (1993). The nature and determinants of customer expectations of service. *Journal of the Academy of Marketing Science*, *21*(1), 1–12.

MARKETING TO LODGING, FOOD SERVICE AND CLUB CONSUMERS IN THE FUTURE: A DELPHI STUDY TO PREDICT MARKETING MANAGEMENT IN 2007

Bonnie J. Knutson, Jeffrey A. Beck, Arjun J. Singh, Michael L. Kasavana and Ronald F. Cichy

ABSTRACT

This article presents findings of a Delphi study that predicts events most likely to impact marketing to consumers in lodging, food service and clubs segments for year 2007. Two rounds of questionnaires were mailed to panels of industry experts within each sector, with an overall response rate of 42%. Findings suggest that the two overarching marketing trends will be convenience as a driver of consumer choice and marketing to an aging population.

INTRODUCTION

In 2002, The School of Hospitality Business at Michigan State University celebrated its 75th anniversary. As part of this diamond jubilee, the faculty launched a benchmark Delphi study among business leaders in three segments of

Advances in Hospitality and Leisure
Advances in Hospitality and Leisure, Volume 1, 25–41
Copyright © 2004 by Elsevier Ltd.
ISSN: 1745-3542/doi:10.1016/S1745-3542(04)01002-1

the hospitality industry: lodging, food service, and clubs. The overall purpose of the project was to combine expert faculty and industry knowledge and opinions to reach a consensus on future issues of importance to the three respective hospitality industry segments. Leaders were asked about the likelihood of occurrence of multiple future events in five general categories in their respective segments: (1) size and structure of the industry; (2) human resources; (3) operations and information technology; (4) marketing; and (5) finance. This article presents the findings from the marketing category.

LITERATURE REVIEW

The Delphi Technique

Delphi forecasting is a business research technique used to determine the likely occurrence of future events. Developed by the Rand Corporation in the 1950s, the Delphi technique elicits opinions from a small selected group of experts. An architect of the technique, Norman Dalkey says, "Delphi is the name of a set of procedures for eliciting and refining the opinions of a group of people . . . with a group of experts or especially knowledgeable individuals" (Dull, 1988, p. 17). The process has several advantages. First, each member of the panel can be involved in each step of the process; second, no member is ever required to defend his position; and third, the process allows for natural development of a trend or consensus (Cone, 1978). The Delphi method also produces dissent so not all viewpoints of individual panel members are reflected in the final outcome. Although the goal is consensus, "Where no agreement develops, the Delphi still helps clarify the issue, crystallize the reasoning process, and increase the accuracy of participants' understanding of the position of others" (Buckly, 1995).[1]

Since its inception, the Delphi technique has been used by organizations in both the public and private sectors. In the beverage industry, for example, conventional research studies did not sufficiently explain industry conditions and declining sales of alcohol for a leading beverage company. The Delphi process showed that the decreasing consumption of alcoholic beverages was related to behavioral factors in an aging population. This technique provided results that helped the beverage company redesign business strategies and redefine markets (Dull, 1988).

Trending and Forecasting

Beginning in the 1990s, changes taking place in society have been exponential. There have been transformations in demographics, communications, economics, technologies, and consumer lifestyles that have bombarded organizations with challenges and opportunities never before experienced. For instance, in 1993, only 23% of Americans owned a computer; in 2003, ownership exceeded 50%. The 12 million Internet users making travel bookings on the Internet in 1998 have grown to more than 64 million in 2003. Growth in cell phone usage, wireless internet, advances in home entertainment systems, such as Plasma and HDTV, technology driven multi-modal communication channels, are some examples of changing consumer lifestyles, which marketers are watching (Cain, 2003). These rapid changes have made organizations increasingly concerned about their futures (Alexander, 1998).

Hospitality marketers are not comfortable making strategic decisions in times of rapid and uncertain changes. Most decision-makers have some feel about the occurrence of future events ranging from a high degree of confidence to a vague and ill-defined level of discomfort (Pyhrr et al., 1989). Sinkley (1992) states that actual change can be segmented into an anticipated component and an unanticipated component. If change consisted only of anticipated components, then there would be little or no risk involved. It is the unanticipated component that is clearly the source of risk. It is also the focus of this Delphi project. A hunter knows that to capture a moving target, he must aim in front of his prey; marketing professionals also know that to capture a target market, they must focus their marketing plan ahead of where the market is moving. In other words, they must anticipate consumer lifestyle trends before they occur. Marketers must also know and understand industry trends that will forge the strategies and tactics used to protect market share and enhance brand position with consumers.

Trends are simply the general direction in which things tends to move (www.dictionary.com). Trends are predictive because they start small then gather momentum. If marketers can connect the dots between the inception of a trend and the impact it will have on their business, they can fine-tune their marketing strategies to fit the trend. Because trends last an average of ten years, the momentum of current trends can propel the business ahead for a decade or more (Popcorn, 1991). The purpose of this study, then, was to identify and predict the key events and issues that will define marketing trends in 2007 in the lodging, food service and club segments of the industry. By successfully predicting the likelihood with which these key trends will occur, some marketing uncertainty can be mitigated.

METHODOLOGY

The faculty of The School of Hospitality Business at Michigan State University developed the prediction issues and event statements. Based on numerous brainstorming sessions among faculty, discussion with and input from hospitality industry leaders in each of the five functional areas represented in the questionnaire, and a literature review, three separate questionnaires were developed representing the three major segments of the hospitality industry: Lodging, Food Service, and Clubs. Each questionnaire was divided into five sections to match the categories named earlier.

In total, over 100 future event statements were developed for the categories in the questionnaire and assigned a 5-point likelihood of occurrence scale with 5 indicating "very likely to occur" and 1 indicating "not likely to occur." In the marketing section of the questionnaire, there were 26 statements each for lodging and food service and 23 statements for clubs. It also provided space at the end of each category where respondents could write open-ended predictions about future events.

Letters inviting them to participate in the Delphi project were mailed to a panel of experts in each industry segment. If they agreed to take part in the study, a questionnaire was then mailed to each expert. For purposes of this project, an expert is defined as someone who has a broad view understanding of their industry segment (lodging, food service and clubs), with specific expertise in at least one functional area. The expert had to be either in a top management or ownership position and directly involved in making strategic decisions for his or her organization.

The School of Hospitality Business at Michigan State University's alumni database and the Club Managers of Association America (CMAA) provided a rich list for the selection of the expert panels. Seventy-four lodging, 47 food service, and 41 club industry executives were selected as experts using the above criteria. Due to a limited number of MSU alumni in the Club Industry, the CMAA list was used to augment the list of experts in that sector of the hospitality industry. Table 1 illustrates the profile of the three expert panels.

The three separate Delphi questionnaires, along with a self-addressed postage-paid return envelope, were mailed as Round 1 to the appropriate hospitality segment experts. Each panelist received two phone calls, first to verify the receipt of the questionnaire and the second to encourage him to complete and mail the questionnaire.

In Round 1, 80 completed questionnaires were received, for a response rate of 49.4%: 38 responses were from the lodging panel, 21 from the food service panel, and 21 from club panelists. In Round 2, 68 completed questionnaires were returned for a second round response rate of 85%: 25 from lodging, 20 from food service, and 23 from clubs. The overall response rate, then, from the original wave of 162 panelists was 42.0%.

All data were entered into the SPSS program for analysis. A 20% verification check was performed; no errors were found. Frequencies and descriptive statistics were run for analysis.

Table 1.   Profile of Respondents.[2]

Industry Sector	Panel Expertise	Round 1 Respondents N	Round 2 Respondents N
Lodging	Lodging panel consists of Presidents, CEOs, Vice Presidents, Owners, General Managers and Senior Hotel Development executives with major U.S. and international hotel companies	38	25
Food Service	Food service panel consists of Presidents, CEOs, Vice Presidents, Owners, General Managers of Food service companies to include full service and fast food restaurants, contract food service firms, independent restaurants, institutional food services, vending companies, specialty food service, food service company vendors, and food service consulting firms.	21	20
Clubs	Club panel consists of CMAA members and members of the board. Most panelists are club general managers, with a few vice presidents and CEOs.	21	23
Response Rate		49.4%	87%
Overall Response Rate	Of the original 162 questionnaires mailed.	42.0%	

FINDINGS AND DISCUSSION

As expected, there was a wide range in the experts' stance on the likelihood of various marketing events happening within the next few years. Since major interest would be in those areas judged most likely to occur, the following discussion focuses on the "top five" probabilities in each segment. In the case of lodging, each of these five events has a probability level of at least 84%, for the food segment sector the probability levels are in the 90s range, while those in clubs span 78–91%.

The Future for Marketing in the Lodging Sector

There is wide consensus among lodging experts that marketing in their segment will be primarily driven by the power of an aging U.S. population. See Table 2.

Table 2.   Events Most Likely to Impact Marketing to Lodging Consumers in 2007.

Variable	Mean[a] 2007	Event Probability 2007[b] (%)
Marketing to an aging population will become increasingly important.	4.3	96
Personalization/customization will be a driving force in marketing.	4.2	96
Consumer databases will lead to more target marketing.	4.0	92
Consumers will be more sophisticated and knowledgeable.	4.2	88
Convenience will increasingly drive consumer choices.	4.0	84
Consumers will increasingly look for price promotions/discounting.	3.9	83
Consumers will want unique hospitality experiences.	3.9	80
Consumers will be more value-driven.	4.0	76
Product differentiation will become increasingly important in growing the business	3.8	75
Word-of-mouth will still be the most influential form of advertising.	3.9	73
Strategic management of brand portfolios and/or brand equity will become increasingly important.	3.9	72
Loyalty programs will become more valuable in developing strategic marketing programs.	3.6	72
Marketing in many international cultures will become more complex.	3.8	71
Hospitality marketing will become more experience oriented.	3.7	71
The largest area of business growth will come from the creation of new markets and product offerings.	3.8	70
Changing demographics will lead to more ethnic-driven market.	3.7	68
"24/7" will be the norm for hospitality organizations (on demand marketing).	3.8	67
The Internet will be the primary marketing channel for the hospitality industry.	3.5	54
Consumer health/wellness will be an integral part of a hospitality product offering.	3.4	52
Consumers will measure "value" in terms of time rather than money.	3.4	52
Operations will increasingly be seen as a valuable marketing tool.	3.5	50
The largest area of business growth will come from product extension on existing brand/product offerings.	3.3	46
Hospitality marketers will be increasingly challenged, as consumer behavior will become difficult to predict.	3.3	38
Environmentalism will be a dominant marketing strategy in hospitality.	2.5	13
The primary components of a company's marketing efforts will focus on local store marketing.	2.4	8
Themed experiences will dominate new concepts.	2.9	4

[a] Scale: 5 = Very likely to occur; 1 = Not at all likely to occur.
[b] Cumulative percent of "Very likely to occur (5)" and "Likely to occur (4)."

People have become familiar with the demographic fact that the U.S. population is aging. Figures from the U.S. Census Bureau (2002) indicate that the older population (65+) numbered 35.0 million in 2000, an increase of 3.7 million or 12.0% since 1990. About one in every eight, or 12.4%, of the population is an older American, over the age of 65. The number of Americans aged 45–64 – those who will reach 65 over the next two decades – increased by 34% during this period. In 2000, persons reaching age 65 had an average life expectancy of an additional 17.9 years (19.2 years for females and 16.3 years for males). By year 2030, the population of older Americans will more than double to about 70 million (Moufakkir et al., 2004).

It is no wonder, then, that the panelists see marketing to this older consumer base growing in importance. According to Dychtwald (1999) the business of travel will go through enormous changes as the population ages. Older Americans are major customers for both luxury travel and budget excursions. With the most money of any major age cohort and the flexibility to schedule their time as they wish, they can be targeted for special off-season promotions designed to fill hotel rooms that would otherwise be empty. They can also be targeted for three-generational packages. A growth in *Grand travel*, grandparents taking grandchildren, is an indication of this trend. Twenty-one percent of grandparents take grandchildren on at least one leisure trip without the parents, now called, "grand trips" (Cain, 2003; Stringer, 2004). But tomorrow's older travelers are not the older travelers of yesterday. They are healthier, more active, and more demanding. In the future, older travelers will be looking for experiences that are more individualized, intimate, unusual, stimulating, informative, and challenging (Dychtwald, 1989).

The second ranked probability event identified by these panelists is personalization or customization. The mantra of the old songs, *I Did It My Way* and *I Gotta Be Me* is quickly becoming a mainstay of the lodging industry. This "me-ness" is not consumer narcissism; it's the need for a little special attention is a very hectic world. It is at the heart of customization and means that "there is profit to be reaped in providing for the consumer's need for personalization – whether it be in product concept, product design, 'customability,' or personal service" (Popcorn, 1991, p. 44). Personalization is niche marketing carried to its ultimate end. From a new product development perspective, the proliferation of boutique hotels illustrates the successful combination of design and service elements to address marketing to a particular lifestyle. At the property services level, we are already seeing the trend develop with such offerings as specially tailored cruises, vacations, and spa retreats, pet friendly hotels, customized vacation packages, online concierges, and experience specialists who customize trips (Stringer, 2004). On an individual guest level, hotels provide welcome baskets filled with favorite candies and fruits to personalized bathrobes (Strauss, 2004). This trend offers significant opportunities for lodging businesses to add "lagniappe" (*Creole for an extra or unexpected gift or benefit*) to their guest's experience and increase perceived value.

The third marketing event judged very likely to occur in 2007 is the use of consumer databases that will lead to more target or niche marketing, and, in turn, to more personalization. There is an old adage in marketing that a business can never know too much about its customers. Some advocate a *20-characteristic rule*, which simply states that, if a business cannot name at least 20 characteristics of its target market(s), it doesn't really know those customers (Do It Yourself Marketing, 1994). As the number of properties expands within the hotel brand, it becomes more difficult for the staff to really be familiar with each guest and understand his/her individual needs and wants. A comprehensive guest database, accessible to each hotel, can be a tool that enables employees at individual properties to better "know" – and, in turn, serve – their guests. There is a paradoxical component here, however; that is, what Naisbitt (1982) coined "high tech-high touch." He developed this formula to describe the way consumers respond to technology: ". . . whenever new technology is introduced . . . there must be a counterbalancing human response – that is *high touch* – or the technology is rejected. The more high tech, the more high touch" (p. 39). Thus, while consumer databases may provide an effective and efficient tool for understanding consumers, hotels will have to be vigilant so as not to diminish the human aspect of hospitality. The evidence that consumer databases will be critical elements of all future marketing efforts is evidenced by the growth in the number of Customer Relationship Management (CRM) software vendors. These products allow hotel marketers to store customer information in "data warehouses" and then drill down using sophisticated "data mining" algorithms. As we learn more about the customer our measure of success will move from revenue per available room (RevPAR) to Revenue per available customer (RevPAC).

The word "sophisticated" can be defined as "having acquired worldly knowledge or refinement; lacking . . . naiveté . . . very complex or complicated having or appealing to those having worldly knowledge and refinement and savoir faire" (www.dictionary.com). These definitions certainly apply to today's – and tomorrow's hotel guests. Based on a survey conducted by the consumer research firm, Yesawich, Pepperdine, Brown & Russell, 60% of the American consumers stated that their IQ is higher than average and 70% said that they depend on their own opinions versus those of the experts. The Internet is their primary source of information to keep them better informed (Cain, 2003). This translates into consumers who demand better service, and are informed negotiators. From a marketer's perspective, this is shifting the locus of control from the seller (hotel) to the consumer (buyer).

Even with the drop in travel caused by the economic downturn of the past few years and the events surrounding 9/11/01, the overall propensity is towards more travel – both nationally and internationally. And as people travel more, they experience more, they expect more, and they demand more. Such an upward spiral in expectations makes it increasingly difficult for hotels to meet and exceed guests' expectations. Hotel marketing is clearly a case of today's luxuries become tomorrow's necessities. This not only applies to products and services, but to advertising as well. Forty years ago, advertising was the most creative business around. The consumer world was new, wide open, and somewhat naive. But as consumers bought more, experienced more, and became inundated with advertisements, they became more knowledgeable about the market place. Couple these smarter consumers with the skyrocketing number of promotional messages and the exploding number of media channels, and it is easy to understand why the lodging panel cited the sophisticated and knowledgeable consumer as a significant trend.

The final trend in the top five relates to the reality of 24/7 lifestyles – convenience. The wise owner of a small, neighborhood Italian grocery store used to always say: *Make it easy for the customer to spend money*. The lodging experts who participated in this study apparently agree. Increasingly, they see convenience driving consumer choices. Whether it is wireless Internet connection, easy check-in and checkout, or a 24-hour fitness center, hotel guests will want properties to make their stay easier for them. Americans live busy, fragmented, multi-tasking lives. In coming years, this trend is expected to accelerate. Consequently, consumers will "continue to rely on (and even demand) things that save us time, keep us terminally in touch and over-connected. Time is measured not in minutes, but in nonoseconds" (Popcorn & Marigold, 1996, p. 209).

The Future for Marketing in the Food Service Segment

A 1999 National Restaurant Association (NRA) Delphi panel looked at the future industry structure in 2010. The results for 2007, presented in Table 3, echo findings from the NRA study. As might be expected, the most important trend cited by food service experts is the power of word-of-mouth (WOM) – or radial – advertising as the most influential form of promotion. For nearly a half of century, research has documented the pervasive influence and importance of WOM on consumer behavior. This is generally thought to be because WOM is perceived as credible and custom-tailored, and generated by people who are seen as having no self-interest in pushing a particular brand (Arndt, 1967; Silverman, 1997). It has also been recognized as among the most effective form of communication in the hospitality industry (Lazer & Layton, 1999). Word of Mouth has taken on an added dimension

Table 3.   Events Most Likely to Impact Marketing to Foodservice Consumers
in 2007.

Variables	Mean[a] 2007	Event Probability 2007[b] (%)
Word-of-mouth will still be the most influential form of advertising.	4.4	95
Marketing to an aging population will become increasingly important.	4.2	95
Convenience will increasingly drive consumer choices.	4.1	95
Consumers will want unique hospitality experiences.	4.1	90
Consumer databases will lead to more target marketing.	4.0	90
"24/7" will be the norm for hospitality organizations (on demand marketing).	3.9	90
Consumers will be more value driven.	4.2	85
Strategic management of brand portfolios and/or brand equity will become increasingly important.	3.9	84
Changing demographics will lead to more ethnic- driven market.	3.8	80
Consumers will be more sophisticated and knowledgeable.	4.0	75
Marketing in many international cultures will become more complex.	3.8	75
The largest area of business growth will come from the creation of new markets and product offerings.	3.3	70
Hospitality marketing will become more experience oriented.	3.7	65
Hospitality marketers will be increasingly challenged, as consumer behavior will become difficult to predict.	3.5	55
Consumers will increasingly look for price promotions/discounting.	3.5	50
Consumer health/wellness will be an integral part of a hospitality product offering.	3.5	50
Personalization/customization will be a driving force in marketing.	3.5	47
Product differentiation will become increasingly important in growing the business.	3.5	40
Loyalty programs will become more valuable in developing strategic marketing programs.	3.4	35
The largest area of business growth will come from product extension on existing brand/product offerings.	3.8	25
Operations will increasingly be seen as a valuable marketing tool.	3.3	25
Themed experiences will dominate new concepts.	3.3	25
Consumers will measure "value" in terms of time rather than money.	3.2	20
The primary component of a company's marketing efforts will focus on local store marketing.	3.1	20
The Internet will be the primary marketing channel for the hospitality industry.	2.6	10
Environmentalism will be a dominant marketing strategy in hospitality.	2.5	0

[a] Scale: 5 = Very likely to occur; 1 = Not at all likely to occur.
[b] Cumulative percent of "Very likely to occur (5)" and "Likely to occur (4)."

as the Internet becomes ubiquitous and related communication and dissemination tools are no longer evanescent. These include: e-mails, chat rooms, and blogs (web logs). Viral marketing is recognized for its ability to encourage individuals to pass on a marketing message to others, creating the potential for exponential growth in the message's exposure and influence. More importantly, it gives the marketer a list of potential targets for further marketing efforts (Hughes, 2002). It's not surprising, then, that the food service panel sees WOM as still being the most influential marketing tool five years into the future. See Table 3.

As stated earlier, it is no secret that America is getting older. Fueled by a declining birth rate, improved medical services leading to longevity, and an aging Baby Boomer generation, the median age of the U.S. population is 35.3 years, the highest in history (Kavaliunas, 2001; U.S. Census Bureau, 2000). This older cohort is a viable market for restaurants. Households headed by persons between the ages of 55–64 spent the most per capita on food away from home in 2000 – $999. Households headed by persons 65 years or older allocated an average of $1205 – or $709 per capita – on food away from home in 2000 (National Restaurant Association, 2000a). For those age 55–65, 42.2% of their food dollar is spent away from home; for those 65 and older, 35.5% of their food expenditures are outside the home too (National Restaurant Association, 2000b). So it is no wonder that virtually all food service experts named marketing to an aging population as increasingly important as the number two probable marketing event.

The third food service event named – convenience – is a direct result of changing demographic trends. The number of single parent and duel-income households with children continues to grow. One-fifth of all meals are consumed in a car and the production of handheld foods has grown 8% per year since 1995 (Trends shaping the food industry, 2002). Since Domino's 30-minutes or less delivery guarantee, the restaurant industry has evolved towards greater levels of convenience for the consumer. From drive-thru to prepared food-to-go to take-and-bake, all segments are looking to increase simplicity in the purchase process. Operational tactics, such as valet parking, Wi-Fi hotspots, and vibrating/lighting buzzers given to patrons to notify them when their table is ready have been added. But convenience is a two-edged sword. With the rise of C-stores, co-branding partnerships, and supermarkets with gourmet delis, the line between retail and restaurants has blurred, thereby increasing the scope of competitors for traditional restaurants. In an industry that is highly competitive already, this is not necessarily good news.

The fourth food service marketing trend cited is the consumers desire for unique hospitality experiences. A stroll through most urban centers gives testimony to this finding. Whether one of the many "eatertainment" venues (such as Rain Forest Café), an intimate bistro tucked along side of a private winery, or having breakfast with the Sesame Street characters at their theme park in Pennsylvania, the growth of the experience economy is rampant. Discretionary needs and choices best describe the growing myriad of hospitality products and services available to consumers. This growth reflects psychic, rather than essential survival needs and focuses marketing attention on *authentic* experiential aspects in order to position the brand (product/services) from its competitors. This fuels the growth of the entire experience economy (O'Sullivan & Spangler, 1998; Pine II & Gilmore, 1999). A recent *Wall Street Journal* article cites the desire for many diners to have culturally authentic foods and service (Bernard, 2004). Acknowledging the prediction of an increasingly sophisticated and knowledgeable consumer, the successful food service company will enhance the overall customer experience by feeding the "magen" (German, for stomach) and the mind through offering authentic experiences.

Through an ambitious new segmentation program called LifeSTYLING, Sodexho Marriott uncovered groups of college students whose lifestyles and backgrounds strongly suggested that they would enjoy more innovative dining options. Creating LifeSTYLING required finding a database of student information that would provide a deep enough picture of student activities and brand preferences; crunching the numbers to create the segments; and injecting data on food and beverage tastes into those segments (Lipke, 2000). This is but one example of how food service operators are turning to complex databases to identify new market opportunities. And, like the hotel panel, the food service experts predict the use of consumer databases to find, attract, and retain more customers as one of the major trends over the next five years.

The Future of Marketing in the Club Segment

Like their counterparts in the other two Delphi groups, experts on the club panel see their marketing strategies being driven by an aging population and more sophisticated members who are looking for unique, convenient experiences. Refer to Table 4.

Older members die or leave the club, forcing clubs to attract a younger, active member. At the same time, the influence of technology, ease of travel, and the transient lifestyle has repositioned club membership from a *yes* to a *maybe* for this segment. Tomorrow's members will not join or remain members of a club for the same reasons members did 20 years ago because their needs and lifestyles have changed. With the proliferation of quality upscale restaurants, the explosion of high-end daily fee golf courses, and a myriad of options for their leisure time and money, clubs will increasingly be challenged to recruit and retain a new cadre of active, loyal members.

Table 4. Events Most Likely to Impact Marketing to Club Members in 2007.

Variables	Mean[a] 2007	Event Probability 2007[b] (%)
Convenience will increasingly drive member choices.	4.3	91
Members will be more sophisticated and knowledgeable.	4.2	91
Members will be more value driven.	3.9	83
Members will want unique hospitality experiences.	4.5	78
Marketing to an aging population will become increasingly important.	4.2	78
Member health/wellness will be an integral part of a club product offering.	3.9	78
Personalization/customization will be a driving force in marketing.	3.8	74
Member databases will lead to more target marketing.	3.9	74
Word-of-mouth will still be the most influential form of advertising.	3.8	74
Members will measure "value" in terms of time rather than money.	3.7	57
Operations will increasingly be seen as a valuable marketing tool.	3.6	52
Product differentiation will become increasingly important in growing the club's business.	3.6	48
The largest area of business growth will come from the creation of new markets and product offerings.	3.4	39
Club marketers will be increasingly challenged, as consumer behavior will become difficult to predict.	3.1	39
Club marketing will become more experience oriented.	3.4	39
Loyalty programs will become more valuable in developing strategic marketing programs.	3.3	35
The Internet will be the primary marketing channel for clubs.	3.0	30
Changing demographics will lead to more ethnic-driven market.	3.1	26
Themed experiences will dominate new concepts.	3.1	26
Increases in cultural diversity will make marketing more complex.	3.1	26
Members will increasingly look for price promotions/discounting.	3.2	22
"24/7" will be the norm for club organizations (on demand marketing).	2.2	9
Environmentalism will be a dominant marketing strategy in clubs.	2.6	4

[a] Scale: 5 = Very likely to occur; 1 = Not at all likely to occur.
[b] Cumulative percent of "Very likely to occur (5)" and "Likely to occur (4)."

In addition to these four trends, club panelists also see another compelling movement: members will be more value driven. Members believe perceived value ought to be greater in their own club because of the ownership and entitlement philosophy that goes with paying dues and initiation fees. They expect their club to provide the highest quality food and beverage, a level of personalized attention not found in the public sector, and good value. If value can be defined as the experience divided by the price ($V = E/P$), where price includes time and hassle as well as money, then the only way clubs can maintain or increase value is to give members a better experience. The key realization in a value-orientated world is that "command and control" marketing – i.e. this is what we're offering, take it or leave it – is over. Every member has similar wants – products, services, programs, facilities and a sense of community – but the expression of those wants change with time (Fornarno, 2004).

SYNERGY ACROSS INDUSTRY SEGMENTS

There are both similarities and differences in how these three panels of experts view the probability of various marketing events in 2007. By far the overarching trends are convenience and marketing to an aging population. They are both named in the top five by all three groups. Using consumer databases for marketing unique experiences to a more sophisticated consumer is in the top five for two groups. One panel each cited customization, word-of-mouth marketing communication, and more value-driven members.

This Delphi project produced several other interesting findings. One that is particularly intriguing is the relatively low ranking of themed experiences – particularly in light of the strong belief that consumers will want unique hospitality experiences. We speculate that one reason for this anomaly is the belief that the novelty of theme venues (as exemplified by the Las Vegas strip) may be waning as a point of differentiation. Similarly, the participants may see an experience as more of an intangible – driven by service – than a tangible. Another interesting variation is in the "on-demand marketing" item. Food service is clearly more driven by the need to be open 24/7. Nine out of ten panelists believe this will be the norm in the near future. Only two-thirds of the hoteliers agree. Since hotels are virtually open 24-hours a day now, the panelists could have been thinking more in terms of facilities, such as fitness centers or business centers, being open 24/7. Fewer than one in ten club experts see their industry being driven by on-demand marketing.

While the tendency may be to micro-analyze the similarities and differences found in each event measured, it is also valuable to view all the events taken together. Therefore, another overarching story is not in the individual differences/similarities themselves, but in their intensity. From item to item, the panelists in the lodging sector are the most fervent in their attitudes. Their percentages are generally higher; their mean scores are generally higher. Furthermore, as shown in Table 5, they are higher on more items.

In other words, hoteliers are more intense about more things – i.e. they appear to have a more complex view of what it will take for effective marketing in 2007. This suggests that, from a marketing perspective, they will have to handle more things at one time – i.e. have "more balls in the air." As expected, the club panelists were the least intensive of the three groups. We speculate that this diminished level may be

Table 5.   Intensity of Belief in Event Probability in All Segments for 2007.

Industry Segment	Number of Events Cited By Respondents Within Each Percentage Range					
	90%	80%	70%	60%	50%	Total (≤50%)
Lodging	3	4	8	2	4	21
Food Service	6	3	3	1	3	16
Clubs	2	1	6	0	2	11

somewhat caused by the industry perception that clubs are built on tradition and heritage, have a captive market and are therefore less susceptible to consumer trends.

CONCLUSIONS

A Delphi study is premised on expectations, which are personal intervening variables that mediate between changes in the environment (stimuli) and a people's responses to these changes (behavior or action). They are a class of attitudes that point to the future and reflect the degree of probability of an event happening. They are acquired and modified by past experiences. Expectations also tend to be directionally stable as well as directionally consistent; that is, they tend to remain favorable or unfavorable over time. The formation of new expectations is not always based on a careful consideration of all facets of a situation (Katona, 1972; O'Connor et al., 1997).

Given this premise, we can consider the findings of this Delphi project to have merit. While the projections found in this study may not be perfect, the considered opinions of experts in three hospitality segments is probably the clearest crystal ball the industry can have. Their outlook can only be validated in 2007.

NOTE

1. For a more in-depth discussion of the Delphi Technique, see: G. H. Moeller and E. L. Shafer, "The Delphi Technique: A Tool for Long Range Travel and Tourism Planning," in J. R. Brent Richie and C. R. Goeldner (Eds), *Travel, Tourism and Hospitality Research: A Handbook for Managers and Researchers* (New York: John Wiley & Sons). 473–480, and H. A. Linstone and M. Turoff, *The Delphi Method* (Addison Wesley, 1979).

ACKNOWLEDGMENTS

The authors would also like to acknowledge the contribution of the other faculty who were members of the Delphi Study Team: Dr. Jeffrey Elsworth; Dr.

Raymond Schmidgall, and Dr. Jack Ninemeier. We also want to give a special acknowledgment to Dr. Arjun J. Singh, who was the team leader on this project and guided the process through to a successful conclusion.

REFERENCES

Alexander, W. (1998). Beyond vision: Creating and analyzing your organization's quality future. *Quality Progress, 31*(7), 31–36.

Arndt, J. (1967). Word-of-mouth advertising and informal communication. In: D. F. Cox (Ed.), *Risk Taking and Information Handling in Consumer Behavior*. Boston, MA: Division of Research, Harvard University.

Bernard, T. (2004). Ethnic food lures restaurateurs to cross over – Chinese food no longer means a Chinese owner as popularity directs menu. *The Wall Street Journal*, January 6, p. D1.

Buckly, C. (1995). Delphi: A methodology for preferences more than predictions. *Library Management, 16*(7), 16–19.

Cain. G. C. (October, 2003). *Travel marketing in the 21st century-A look ahead*. Yesawich, Pepperdine, Brown & Russell, www.YPB&R.com.

Cone, J. C. (1978). Delphi: Polling for consensus. *The Public Relations Journal, 34*(2), Retrieved October 20, 2003, from ProQuest database.

Do It Yourself Marketing (1994). Video. Inc. Magazine. Goldhirsh Group, Inc. http://www.dictionary.com.

Dull, R. (1988). Delphi forecasting: Market research method of the 1990s. *Marketing News, 22*(18), 17.

Dychtwald, K. (1999). Age *power: How the 21st century will be ruled by the new old*. Putnam, New York: Jeremy T. Tarcher.

Fornarno, J. (2004). Make a buck or please members? *Boardroom Magazine*. http://www.boardroommagazine.com.

Hughes, A. M. (2002). *Journal of Database Marketing,10*(2).

Katona, G. (1972). Theory of expectations. *Human Behavior in Economic Affairs*. Amsterdam, Netherlands: Elsevier.

Kavaliunas, J. (2001, Fall). The aging of America. *Marketing Research, 13*(3), 6.

Lazer, W., & Layton, R. A. (1999) *Contemporary hospitality marketing*. Lansing, MI: Educational Institute, American Hotel & Motel Association.

Lipke, D. J. (2000, October). You are what you eat. *American Demographics, 22*(10), 42–46.

Moufakkir, O., Singh, A. J., Holecek, D., & Van der Woud, A. (2004), Impact of light, medium and heavy spenders on casino destinations. *UNLV Gaming Research and Review Journal*, in press.

Naisbitt, J. (1982). *Megatrends*. New York, NY: Warner Books.

National Restaurant Association (1999). *Restaurant industry 2010: The road ahead*. Washington, DC: National Restaurant Association.

National Restaurant Association (2000a). http://www.restaurant.org/research/magarticle.cfm?ArticleID=797.

National Restaurant Association (2000b). http://www.restaurant.org/research/spending.cfm.

O'Connor, M., Remus, W., & Griggs, K. (1997). Going up-going down: How good are people at forecasting trends and changes in trends? *Journal of Forecasting, 16*(3), 165–176.

O'Sullivan, E. L., & Spangler, K. J. (1998). *Experience marketing*. State College, PA: Venture Publishing, Inc.

Pine II, B. J., & Gilmore, J. H. (1999). *The experience economy*. Boston, MA: Harvard Business School Press.

Popcorn, F. (1991). *The Popcorn report*. A Currency Book. New York: Doubleday.

Popcorn, F., & Marigold, L. (1996). *Clicking*. New York: HarperCollins.

Pyhrr, S. A., Cooper, J. R., Wooford, L. E., Kapplin, S. D., & Lapides, P. D. (1989). *Real estate investment*. New York: Wiley.

Silverman, G. (1997). How to harness the awesome power of word of mouth. *Direct Marketing*, November, 32–27.

Sinkley, J. F. (1992). *Commercial bank financial management*. New York: Macmillan.

Strauss, K. (2004). Packaging gets personal. *Hotels*, February, 12–13.

Stringer, K. (2004). Clicks, Perks and cheap cruises. *The Wall Street Journal Online: Journal Report Trends*, February, pp. 1–7. nline.wsj.com.

Trends shaping the food industry (2002). *Growth Strategies*, March, 3–4.

U.S. Census Bureau (2002). http://factfinder.census.gov/servlet/QTTable?_bm=y&-geo_id=01000US&-qr_name=DEC_2000_SF1_U_DP1&-ds_name=DEC_2000_SF1_U.

CONSTRAINTS TO PARTICIPATION IN THE ARTS BY THE YOUNG OLD, OLD AND OLDEST OLD

Francis A. McGuire, William C. Norman and Joseph T. O'Leary

ABSTRACT

This study examined constraints to participation in the arts by three sub-populations of older Americans: the young old (60–69), the old (70–79) and the oldest old (80+). Health, poor performance quality and lack of companions were identified as constraints more frequently by the oldest old than by the younger respondents. The oldest old were five times more likely to be constrained by health than the young old and twice as likely as the old. The oldest old were over two times more likely to be constrained by performance quality and lack of companionship than the young old.

INTRODUCTION

Perspectives on aging have shifted from deficit models focusing on loss to success models focusing on optimum aging and the enhancement of daily life (Rogers et al., 1998). Markides and Black (1996) indicated that the most popular dependent variable in gerontological research may be successful aging. Fry (1996) acknowledged the relative nature of successful aging but indicated that a central

Advances in Hospitality and Leisure
Advances in Hospitality and Leisure, Volume 1, 43–58
ISSN: 1745-3542/doi:10.1016/S1745-3542(04)01003-3

theme from comparative aging research indicates that individuals experiencing a "favorable old age are those who can control their environment socially and materially" (p. 128). However, successful aging is more than control of one's environment. It is also an active process marked by the avoidance of disease, maintenance of high cognitive and physical functioning and engagement with life (Rowe & Kahn, 1998). According to Everard et al. (2000) active engagement has received the least research attention of the three.

One group for whom successful aging may be difficult is the oldest old. This age group, defined as those in the ninth decade of life, experience physical and social losses greater than those of their younger cohorts. As a result, remaining actively engaged in life may be more problematic and therefore the oldest old may face obstacles to successful aging which are different from those experienced by younger individuals. Baltes and Baltes' (1998) belief that the key to successful aging lies in the ability to adjust to its physiological constraints may indicate that increasing physical decline will mitigate the likelihood of successful aging.

According to Horgas et al. (1998) the focus of research examining the oldest old's everyday activities has been on "assessing difficulties in activities of daily living (ADLs) and instrumental activities of daily living (IADLs), and demonstrating when one requires assistance or when one's performance level is insufficient for daily living" (p. 56). This approach is congruent with a view of later life as a period of time when many experience increased dependence on others, new challenges such as impending death and loss of family and friends, and a diminution of physical and cognitive abilities (Femia et al., 1997; Hilleras et al., 1998).

The juxtaposition of increasing debilitation in the oldest old with the evidence of the importance of active engagement to successful aging results in a clear need to identify methods to assist the oldest old in remaining active in the face of barriers to doing so. This group has the potential for leading independent, successful lives; however, the increasing likelihood of disability may require increased efforts to help them maintain involvement and autonomy (Dontas et al., 1996).

Femia et al. (1997) found the oldest old to be a heterogeneous group, marked by both decline and stability. They identified a sense of control as a crucial factor in continued involvement with life. Mastery may lead to an increased ability to "compensate for losses, conserve resources, or cash in on available physical or environmental resources" and therefore result in higher levels of activity (p. 301). A crucial step in increasing perceived mastery in the older population is the identification of barriers to active engagement; however, little is known about what constrains the oldest old.

LITERATURE REVIEW

Active Engagement by the Oldest Old

Examination of the characteristics of individuals identified as the oldest old has focused primarily on cognitive and physical functional changes. For example, Zarit et al. (1995) studied changes in a sample of the oldest old in Sweden using a cohort sequential design over a 4-year period. They conducted interviews, focusing on cognition and activities of daily living, with 324 individuals between the ages of 84 and 90 at the time of the original interview. They found that 30% of the participants had cognitive impairment, 23% had disabilities in personal activities of daily living (including getting out of bed, taking a shower, and grooming) and 61% had significant deficits in instrumental activity of daily living (including heavy household work, cooking, shopping, and using the telephone).

The researchers found that the proportion of individuals with deficits in functioning increased over the four years of the study and concluded that there were high rates of disability in this age group. Similar findings of functional disability in the oldest old were consistent throughout the literature.

Very old age and concomitant losses in functional ability do not necessarily result in reduction in active engagement in life. Garfein and Herzog (1995) examined data from 1644 older respondents to a nationwide survey, Americans' Changing Lives, to examine robust aging in the young old, old and oldest old. Robust aging was defined as exhibiting high levels of functional status, affective status, cognitive status, and productive involvement. High productive involvement was defined as 1500 hours or more of work for pay, unpaid work, and helping activities in the year preceding the study, an average of 30 or more hours of involvement per week. Although the authors found engagement at all ages, they also found a significant decrease in robust aging as age increased. For example, 53% of the young old (aged 60–69), 29% of the old (70–79) and 13% of the oldest old (80+) were in the high productive involvement category. Thirty-five percent of the young old was involved at the second level of productive involvement (10–29 hours per week), 47% of the old and 54% of the oldest old. The findings indicated that even though they were less active than the younger respondents, the oldest old remained vital and capable of staying actively engaged in life.

Horgas et al. (1998) also examined successful aging within the context of activity involvement. They used data from the Berlin Aging Study to describe the daily life of the very old and to examine the effects of background variables such as gender, education and marital status on daily activities. Using the Yesterday Interview to assess daily activity of individuals aged 70 and over, Horgas et al. (1998) found that the elderly spent much of their time in leisure activities. About one-half of a typical day was marked by leisure engagement and most of this was spent watching television or reading. Age was related to leisure, with those in their 90s involved significantly less than people in their 70s and 80s. The authors concluded there was a need for to identify compensatory mechanisms that would support successful aging.

Silverstein and Parker (2002) provided evidence that participation in leisure activities is an effective adaptive strategy used by older adults to compensate for physical and social declines in later life. They used data from the Swedish Panel Study of Living Conditions of the Oldest Old to measure changes in quality of life and participation in 15 different leisure activities over a ten-year period. The authors found that although many individuals did withdraw from activity engagement with increasing age, many actually increased involvement, most notably increasing numbers adopted walking as a leisure activity. They also found a strong relationship between activity involvement and quality of life. Individuals who increased participation in leisure viewed their life situation as having improved over the ten years covered in the study. This relationship was present even in individuals experiencing physical and social losses. The authors viewed leisure as a buffering factor in individuals' lives.

Recent work by Timmer et al. (2003) reaffirmed the importance of an active lifestyle in the later years. They examined anticipated gains as age increased in a nationally representative survey of Germans aged 47–85. They found that the anticipation of enjoying life or retirement, being aware of how to live, taking part in educational activities and cultural events, and socializing were as important to people in old age (77–85) as they were to younger people (47–76). These findings support the importance of active engagement even at the latest stages of adulthood.

Seccombe and Ishii-Kuntz (1991) investigated how perceptions of the problems faced by older individuals differed among older age cohorts. They used data from the 1981 Aging in the Eighties survey conducted with a nationally representative sample of adults. They divided the sample into middle aged (55–64), young old (65–74), middle old (75–84), and oldest old (85+). The respondents were asked to indicate what they perceived to be problems for people over the age of 65. It was found that money, loneliness, housing, fear of crime, and lack of jobs differed across the age groups. The oldest old viewed these areas as less of a problem than the younger age cohorts. The oldest old had a sense of optimism exceeding that of the younger groups. However, caution is needed in interpreting these findings since only non-institutionalized individuals were included in the survey and therefore only the healthiest of the oldest cohort were included. Nevertheless, the findings indicated the oldest old did not necessarily view old age as a life stage marked by problems.

Freund and Smith's (1999) examination of older persons' self-definition found a similarly optimistic perspective toward later life. They asked subjects in their study to generate 10 answers to the question "who am I." Their answers were then coded into idea units based on 24 content domains. Respondents were also measured on functional health constraints and emotional well-being. Data were analyzed to identify differences between the old (70–84) and the very old (85–103) in self-definition. The findings supported a conclusion that more similarities than differences existed between the two groups. Both groups exhibited a broad spectrum of domains in self-definition and shared an activity-oriented lifestyle as their central defining theme. Interests/hobbies at home was the prevalent domain for both groups. The very old were more likely to mention negatively evaluated domains (for example, "it's so sad I cannot get around in the city anymore") and less likely to identify positively evaluated domains ("I am a very good cook") than the younger cohort. Both groups, however, reported more positive than negative components in their self-definition. The importance of this study to the present research was the implication that activities remained important to the very old. Opportunities to remain actively involved were crucial to a positive self-regard. Barriers to continued involvement, therefore, need to be identified and addressed through counseling, programming and policy changes.

Leisure Constraints in Later Life

Mannell and Kleiber (1997) view a constraint as any factor that either blocks engagement in an activity or limits interest in engagement. Although there has been increased focus in the gerontological literature on the oldest old, the leisure constraint literature has paid little attention to this group. Leisure researchers have studied the effect of constraints on a variety of specific population segments, including: women's leisure (Henderson & Allen, 1990; Henderson & Bialeschki, 1993), adolescents (Hultsman, 1991, 1993; Raymore, 1992), the elderly (Mannell & Zuzanek, 1991), ethnic differences (Dergance et al., 2003), immigrants (Stodolska, 1998), and members of Alcoholics Anonymous (McCormick, 1991). Although several publications have included age as a variable when examining leisure constraints, none examined the oldest old as a discrete group. For example, Jackson (1993), Jackson and Witt (1994) and Iso-ahola, Jackson and Dunn (1994) included age as a variable in their analyses of constraints but aggregated all individuals in their mid-sixties or over into one group.

The leisure constraint literature has been largely atheoretical. However, a framework derived from the work of Crawford and Godbey (1987) who categorized constraints as intrapersonal, interpersonal, or structural, provides a structure for interpreting the results of this study. Intrapersonal constraints are conditions, including perceived self-skill, stress, attitudes and personal evaluations of activity appropriateness, and moods, that interact with leisure preferences. Interpersonal constraints are limitations resulting from relationships with others, such as the ability to find companions, and obligations to friends and family, typically influencing leisure preferences and participation. Structural constraints are external to the individual and include lack of opportunity, financial considerations and the weather, and impinge on participation. Crawford and Godbey's framework continues to guide the study of leisure constraints. (Auster, 2001; Little, 2002).

This study will examine the constraints to involvement using these three categories. Some of the concomitants of aging may themselves function as constraints. Many of these age related characteristics would be categorized as intrapersonal constraints. In fact, much of the research examining leisure constraints in the later years (Bruce et al., 2002; Fleisher & Pizam, 2002; Grant, 2001; Jackson, 1993; Jackson & Witt, 1994; Rogers et al., 1998; Strain et al., 2002) has identified intrapersonal constraints, including poor health, fear of injury, and perceived lack of ability, as primary factors limiting later life leisure, typically increasing in importance with age. The gradual decline in physical ability and physiological resources with increasing age is suggestive of the utility of such an approach. In fact, Alexandris et al. (2003) reviewed the literature and found that the importance of intrapersonal constraints significantly increases with increasing age.

There is also evidence that interpersonal constraints, primarily lack of leisure companions, may limit leisure involvement in the later years. For example, Utz et al. (2002) identified having no living children as a constraint to social participation by elderly widows. Similarly, Strain et al. (2002) found that not losing a marital partner was related to continuation in some leisure activities, indicating the importance of companions in engagement in activities. Jackson's (1993) extensive examination of leisure constraints indicated that family commitment exhibited an inverted U shaped relationship to leisure involvement, with relatively few younger and older respondents identifying its as a constraint compared to individuals in their middle ages. However, lack of a partner for leisure and social isolation were more important as a constraint to the youngest and oldest respondents than to those middle aged.

Structural constraints such as lack of facilities or the cost of activities, also constrain older individuals. For example, Alexandris et al. (2003) found that cost and transportation were important factors limiting participation by older individuals in physical activity programs. However Jackson and Witt (1994) found that admission fees and charges, while important constraints to all age groups, were less important to the respondents aged 65+ than to younger respondents. Jackson (1993) also found that cost and accessibility declined in importance with age in one analysis but that accessibility and awareness showed a U shaped distribution, with older and younger respondents significantly more likely to be in this cluster than their middle-age counterparts in a second analysis.

The research examining constraints in later life yields expected results. Factors viewed as concomitants of aging, such as reduced income, physical decline, loss of friends, and uncertainty over ability to keep up, function as brakes on behavior. However, the importance of structural constraints such as money and availability of activities may decline in later years. Although these studies are of interest, and provide foundations for further work, it is also useful to look elsewhere for insight into the leisure-aging-constraint link, particularly because no previous research focused on the oldest old.

The potential range of activities providing opportunities for active engagement is vast. However, for the purposes of this study, we limited our focus to one type of activity, the arts. This was done since participation in the arts is pervasive and therefore a significant arena for engagement by the elderly. Data indicate that half of the adult population in the United States attended at least one of seven art activities (opera, jazz, classical music, plays, ballets, art museums, or musical plays) in 1997 (National Endowment for the Arts, 1998). In addition, arts activities are diverse, requiring varying amounts of skill, energy, time and resources. Therefore, they provide an appropriate context for studying constraints to active engagement.

Study Objectives

The importance of active engagement for successful aging, along with the dearth of knowledge about factors limiting that engagement by the oldest old, led to this study. The identification of barriers faced by the oldest old will ultimately aid in identifying compensatory mechanisms that will assist in continuing engagement. Specifically, the following questions were addressed: Are the oldest old more likely to experience intrapersonal constraints to active engagement than the young old or the old? Are the oldest old more likely to experience interpersonal constraints to active engagement than the young old or the old? Are the oldest old more likely to experience structural constraints to active engagement than the young old or the old?

METHODS

Sample and Design

Data for this study came from the 1997 Survey of Public Participation in the Arts (SPPA) (National Endowment for the Arts, 1998). This nationwide survey of 12,349 individuals focused on involvement in a variety of cultural activities and was completed by Westat for the National Endowment for the Arts using telephone interviews. A random sample of phone numbers was selected from all exchanges in all the area codes within the United States. Any household with at least one resident 18 or over was eligible for the survey. Within each selected household the responding adult was chosen through the "birthday method" wherein the household member who had the most recent birthday was interviewed. For the purposes of this study all respondents aged 65 and over were included in the analysis. (For a complete report of the methods used in SPPA see Loomis et al., 1998).

MEASURES

This study focused on the section of the SPPA examining eleven potential constraints to participation in the arts. Respondents indicated whether each of the 11 was a reason they were not able to participate in activities as often as they wished. Two questions were asked in order to identify the activity used to determine barriers to involvement:

(1) "Now I am going to read a list of events that some people like to attend. If you could do any of these event as often as you wanted, which ones would you go to more often than you do now?" This was followed by a list of eight activities: jazz performances, classical music performances, operas, musical plays or operettas, non-musical plays, ballet performances, dance performance other than ballet and art museums or galleries.
(2) "Of the events you just mentioned, which would you like to do most?" The subsequent barrier question was then built around this activity.

Respondents were asked to indicate which of 11 barriers had kept them from attending the activity more often. The barriers, along with our categorization included: tickets sell out before you have a chance to purchase them (structural); tickets are too expensive (structural); there are not many performances in your area (structural); you think you may feel uncomfortable or out of place (intrapersonal); there is no one to go with (interpersonal); child care responsibilities (interpersonal); health problem or disability (intrapersonal); location is not convenient (structural); location is not in a safe area (intrapersonal); the quality of the performance is poor (structural); it is difficult to make time to go out (structural).

Since the purpose of the study was to examine the relationship of age to constraints respondents were categorized as either young old, old or oldest old for this study. There are various chronological definitions of the oldest old. In this study individuals 80 years of age or over were categorized as oldest old. The young old were defined as between 60 and 69 years of age and the old included individuals between 70 and 79. These categories match those used by Garfein and Herzog (1995) in their examination of active engagement in later life.

Several characteristics of respondents were included as variables in this study in order to provide a more complete overview of constraints in the later years. These included: health, income, marital status and education. Respondents rated their health as either excellent, good/very good, or fair/poor. Household income in the 12 months preceding the study was measured. Income was categorized as under $20,000, $20,000 to $40,000 and over $40,000. Respondents were categorized as either married or not married at the time of the study. Finally, education was coded as either no high school degree, high school degree, some college, or college degree.

Data Analysis

The researchers computed the frequency and percentage of respondents within each age group identifying each constraint as a reason for limiting involvement in order to provide a description of the nature of constraints experienced by each age group. Since the dependent variables were dichotomous in this study, the presence or absence of each constraint, logistic regression was then used to examine the relationship of age and the control variables to constraints. This was done to determine the effect of age on constraints within the context of the other variables used in this study. The Wald statistic was used to determine the significance of the regression coefficients in the logistic model. Odds ratios, and the corresponding 95% confidence intervals, were then computed. The odds ratio for a variable "tells you the change in odds for a case when the value of that variable increases by 1" (SPSS, 1999, p. 41). Demaris (1993) indicated odds ratios, which have a "times as likely" interpretation, are suited to studies where "how much the response variable changes as the predictors change" is the focus. Since the purpose of this study was to examine differences in the nature of constraints in individuals of different ages, the odds ratio was appropriate to use for analytic purposes. The categorical variables were transformed into dummy variable for the logistic regression analysis. In every case, the highest coded value for a variable became the reference category in creating the dummy variables.

RESULTS

Constraints to Engagement

Table 1 displays the percentage of respondents within each age group identifying each constraint as a barrier to participation in the activity they like to do most.

Table 1. Percentage of Respondents Experiencing Each Constraint to Involvement.

Constraint	Young Old (%)	Old (%)	Oldest Old (%)
Location not convenient	51.3	56.4	65.2
Not many performances in area	54.1	55.7	58.1
Health problems/disability	19.1	37.0	56.4
Tickets too expensive	51.6	52.8	46.7
No one to go with	17.4	30.0	38.7
Location not in safe area	21.5	29.6	31.0
Difficult to make time	37.9	25.3	25.8
Poor quality of performances/exhibits	9.7	12.0	21.0
May feel out of place	8.7	7.8	9.7
Tickets sell out	15.0	15.1	6.5
Child care responsibilities	2.3	2.7	1.1

The two most frequently identified constraints were inconvenient locations for the activity and not many performances in the area. The next most common constraint for the young old and old was ticket cost. The oldest old identified health problems as the third most common constraint to attending arts activities.

Multivariate Analysis of the Relationship between Age and Constraints
Eleven logistic regression analyses were completed to examine the link between age and constraints. There were slight variations in the number of respondents included in each analysis because of missing data. For example, the analysis of the constraint "poor quality of the performance" included the smallest number of respondents, 266 individuals aged 60–69, 171 aged 70–79 and 56 respondents aged 80 or over. The constraint "health problems" included the largest number of respondents, 285 between the ages of 60 and 69, 193 between 70 and 79, and 65 aged 80 or over. Examination of all the analyses indicated the participants included more females (58%) than males. Approximately 78% of the respondents rated their health as at least good, 55% had attended college, and 66% had incomes of $40,000 or less. Slightly over half the respondents were between the ages of 60 and 69 and 12% were over 80 years of age. Approximately half of the respondents were married.

Results of the logistic regression analysis for each constraint are presented in Table 2. Only significant relationships are reported in the table. A significant relationship was found between the variables used in the analysis and seven of the constraints: health, unsafe location, feel out of place, tickets sell out, cost, poor performance quality, and no one to go with. However, age was related to the occurrence of only three constraints: health, poor performance quality and lack of someone to go with.

Table 2.   The Relationship Between Constraints and Selected Demographic Variables.

Constraint[a]	Variable (Values[b])	*P* Value	95% CI
Health	Age (60–69 vs. 80+)	<0.01	2.720–10.394
	(70–79 vs. 80+)	<0.05	1.376–3.650
	Health[c] (ex. vs. f/p)	<0.01	0.033–0.156
	Health (g/vg vs. f/p)	<0.01	0.061–0.175
Unsafe location	Education[d] (nhs vs. cd)	<0.01	1.548–6.171
	(hsd vs. cd)	<0.05	1.065–3.373
	Health (ex vs. f/p)	<0.05	0.201–0.864
Feel out of place	Gender (m vs. f)	<0.05	1.017–3.719
	Income (20 vs. >40)	<0.05	1.109–13.346
	(20/40 vs. >40)	<0.01	1.694–16.571
	Married[5] (m vs. nm)	<0.05	0.231–0.969
Tickets sell out	Education (nhs vs. cd)	<0.05	1.142–5.958
	Income (20/40 vs. >40)	<0.05	0.239–0.868
Cost of tickets	Income (<20 vs. >40)	<0.01	1.496–4.476
	(20/40 vs. >40)	<0.05	1.000–2.465
Poor quality	Age (60–69 vs. 80+)	<0.05	1.052–5.673
	Education (nhs vs. cd)	<0.05	1.015–6.210
No one to go with	Age (60–69 vs. 80+)	<0.05	1.257–4.466
	Gender (m vs. f)	<0.01	0.273–0.724
	Health (g/vg vs. f/p)	<0.05	0.344–0.942
	Income (20/40 vs. >40)	<0.05	1.019–3.332
	Married (m vs. nm)	<0.05	0.321–0.846

[a] Constraints were coded as 1 – yes, 0 – no.
[b] Values were coded as (1 vs. 0).
[c] ex – excellent; g/vg – good/very good; f/p – fair/poor.
[d] nhs – no high school degree; hsd – high school degree; cd – college degree m – married; nm – not married.

The young old and the old were significantly less likely to identify health as a constraint than the oldest respondents. The oldest old respondents were approximately five times (OR = 5.31, CI = 2.720–10.394) more likely to be constrained by health than the young old and approximately twice (OR = 2.37, CI = 1.230–4.577) as likely as the old to be constrained by health.

Poor performance quality was significantly related to age. The oldest old were over twice as likely as the young old to identify performance quality as a constraint (OR = 2.45, CI = 1.052–5.673). The final difference between the oldest old and the young old was lack of companionship. The oldest old were over twice as likely to identify lack of companions as a constraint than the young old (OR = 2.36, CI = 1.257–4.466).

DISCUSSION

The constraints experienced by the participants in this study reflected the range of constraints identified by Crawford and Godbey (1987). The three cohorts of elderly were more similar than different in the nature of the barriers limiting their involvement. Structural constraints, including activity cost, location and frequency of performances, were the most frequently identified by all the respondents. However, these were shared cross the age groups studied and were not influenced by age.

The only barrier significantly different across all three age cohorts was health. This supports previous research findings related to the importance of health as a constraint to later life involvement in leisure. The oldest old were more likely to be limited by poor health than either the young old or the old. The importance of health to the oldest old reflects the reality of aging; health does decline and will impact involvement. Summer (1999) indicated 34% of all Americans aged 65–74 limit activities because of chronic conditions. This percentage increases to 45% of all individuals aged 75 or over. Declining health appears to be an overriding reality, noticed and noted, by the oldest old.

Performance quality and lack of companionship were significantly more likely to constrain the oldest old than the young old. The finding about lack of companionship mirrors previous research. Increasing age is typically accompanied by the death of one's spouse and friends. Therefore, it is expected that the number of companions available is fewer for the oldest old than for the young old. The finding related to quality of the performance was not found in previous research and has multiple interpretations. It may be that the effort required to go out to a performance is greater for the oldest old, as a result of health problems, and therefore only the highest quality performance is sufficient justification to attend. An alternate explanation is that the oldest old, as a result of their experience, are more critical of artistic offerings than the younger cohorts. The importance of performance quality may reflect the use of arts activities in this research. Quality may not have been an issue with other types of activities, such as exercise, socialization or volunteer work. It is also possible that concerns about the quality of a performance are related to physical losses of aging. For example, sensory decline may make it more difficult to hear or see a performance and therefore result in a negative evaluation of the quality of the performance. Indeed the categorization of performance quality will change from structural to intrapersonal if health issues are the cause of perceived quality.

It is interesting that the oldest old were more likely to experience one intrapersonal constraint, poor health, one interpersonal constraint, lack of companionship, and a structural constraint, poor performance, than younger cohorts. However, results of the logistic regression indicated age, in most cases, was not a salient factor in understanding the constraints experienced by the elderly. Even the oldest old appeared able to cope and adapt to the physiological concomitants of reaching the outer limits of the lifespan. It may be that older individuals, including the oldest old, have the resources to negotiate constraints, particularly those within their control such as interpersonal and intrapersonal constraints, and are not prisoners to barriers. It is possible older people successfully negate constraints by allowing their circle of activities to shrink and thereby focus remaining efforts of what remains. The selective optimization with compensation model proposed by Baltes and Baltes (1990) would predict such an occurrence. Further research is needed to evaluate the efficacy of this model in explaining leisure in later life.

The findings of this study indicate the need to go beyond the provision of leisure activities when working with older adults. Participation is shaped by many factors in addition to availability of activities. Service providers should also identify and ameliorate constraints limiting involvement. In many cases this may require awareness of the constraints identified in this research. Activities should be held in convenient locations, limiting the impact of factors such as lack of transportation. In addition, the cost of activities may limit involvement. It may be necessary to subsidize activities if the costs are too high. Costs may also be less of a factor if individuals are aware of activities far enough in advance to include the costs into their budget. Health constraints may require creativity in programming. Using technology to bring programs to people may be an effective intervention for individuals whose health limits their mobility. In addition, arts related activities, such as traveling museums, could be brought to people rather than requiring people go to the activity. In many cases the constraints to activities may be removed if activity planning includes consideration of barriers to involvement and ways to limit those barriers.

Study Limitations

Several cautions are necessary when interpreting the results of this study. The low number of respondents aged 80 or over must be noted. In addition to the low number of respondents, it is also necessary to note that the sample consisted entirely of non-institutionalized individuals. The 80 and over population is disproportionately represented among long term care facility residents. The failure of the SPPA to include members of this group, while not lessening the importance of our findings, does require further caution in interpretation. The data used in this study were cross-sectional in nature. Therefore, the conclusions relate only to age differences since examination of age change requires longitudinal data. Lastly, the constraints questions related to attendance at art activities and focused on those activities individuals wanted to do more often. Therefore, the findings are limited to this one area of engagement.

FUTURE STUDY

More research examining the leisure behavior of the oldest old is needed. This segment of the population is not only one of the fastest growing groups in America, they are also among the least understood by leisure researchers. Future research related to involvement, motives, benefits, and functions of leisure will help maximize leisure in the later years and provide service-providers with information needed to attract and serve older consumers. In addition, the data in this study were cross-sectional and therefore useful in examining age differences. However, there is a need for longitudinal research tracking changes in engagement over time. As society ages it is crucial to understand the trajectory of life experienced by individuals as they move through their later years.

REFERENCES

Alexandris, K., Barkoukis, V., Tsorbatzoudis, H., & Grouios, G. (2003). A study of perceived constraints on a community-based physical activity program for the elderly in Greece. *Journal of Aging and Physical Activity, 1*, 305–318.

Auster, C. J. (2001). Transcending potential antecedent leisure constraints: The case of women motorcycle operators. *Journal of Leisure Research, 33*, 272–299.

Baltes, P.B., & Baltes, M.M. (1990). Selective optimization with compensation. In: P.B. Baltes & M.M. Baltes (Eds), *Successful Aging: Perspectives from the Behavioral Sciences* (pp. 1–34). Cambridge University Press.

Baltes, P. B., & Baltes, M. M. (1998). Savoir vivre in old age: How to master the shifting balance between gains and losses. *National Forum, 78*(2), 13–19.

Bruce, D. G., Devine, A., & Prince, R. L. (2002). Recreational physical activity levels in healthy older women: The importance of fear of falling. *The Journal of the American Geriatrics Society, 50*, 84–89.

Crawford, D., & Godbey, G. (1987). Reconceptualizing barriers to family leisure. *Leisure Sciences, 9*, 119–127.

Dergance, J. M., Calmbach, W. L., Dhanda, R., Miles, T. P., Hazuda, H. P., & Mouton, C. P. (2003). Barriers to and benefits of leisure time physical activity in the elderly: Differences across cultures. *Journal of the American Geriatrics Society, 51*, 863–868.

Demaris, A., (1993) *Odds versus probabilities in logic equations: A reply to Roncek Social Forces, 71*, 1057–1066.

Dontas, A. S., Toupadaki, N., Tzonou, A., & Kasviki-Charvati, P. (1996). Survival in the oldest old: Death risk factors in old and very old subjects. *Journal of Aging and Health, 8*, 220–237.

Everard, K. M., Lach, H. W., Fisher, E. B., & Baum, M. C. (2000). Relationship of activity and social support to the functional health of older adults. *Journal of Gerontology: Social Sciences, 55B,* S208–S212.

Femia, E. E., Zarit, S. H., & Johansson, B. (1997). Predicting change in activities of daily living: A longitudinal study of the oldest old living in Sweden. *Journal of Gerontology: Psychological Sciences, 52B,* P294–P302.

Fleisher, A., & Pizam, A. (2002). Tourism constraints among Israel seniors. *Annals of Tourism Research, 29,* 106–123.

Freund, A. M., & Smith, J. (1999). Content and function of the self-definition in old and very old age. *Journal of Gerontology: Psychological Sciences, 54B,* P55–P67.

Fry, C.L. (1996). Age, aging, and culture. In: R.H. Binstock & L.K. George (Eds), *Handbook of Aging and the Social Sciences.* San Diego: Academic Press.

Garfein, A. J., & Herzog, A. R. (1995). Robust aging among the young-old, old-old, and oldest-old. *Journal of Gerontology: Social Sciences, 50B,* S77–S87.

Grant, B. C. (2001). 'You're never too old': Beliefs about physical activity and playing sport in later life. *Aging and Society, 21,* 777–798.

Henderson, K.A., & Allen, K. (1990). The ethic of care: Leisure possibilities and constraints for women. Paper presented at the Sixth Canadian Congress on Leisure Research, University of Waterloo, Waterloo, Ontario.

Henderson, K. A., & Bialeschki, M. D. (1993). Negotiating constraints to women's physical recreation. *Losir et Societe', 16,* 389–412.

Hilleras, P. K., Jorm, A. F., Herlitz, A., & Winblad, B. (1998). Negative and positive affect among the very old: A survey on a sample age 90 or older. *Research on Aging, 20,* 593–611.

Horgas, A. Z. L., Wilms, H., & Baltes, M. M. (1998). Daily life in very old age: Everyday activities as expression of successful living. *The Gerontologist, 38,* 556–568.

Hultsman, W.Z. (1991). Barriers to participation among youth: An extension. Paper presented at the Leisure Research Symposium, National Recreation and Park Association Annual Congress, Baltimore, MD.

Hultsman, W. Z. (1993). The influence of others as a barrier to recreation participation among early adolescents. *Journal of Leisure Research, 25,* 150–164.

Iso-ahola, S., Jackson, E., & Dunn, E. (1994). Starting, ceasing, and replacing activities over the life-span. *Journal of Leisure Research, 26,* 227–250.

Jackson, E. (1993). Recognizing patterns of leisure constraints: Results from alternative analyses. *Journal of Leisure Research, 25,* 129–150.

Jackson, E., & Witt, P. (1994). Change and stability in leisure constraints: A comparison of two surveys conducted four years apart. *Journal of Leisure Research, 26,* 322–337.

Little, D. E. (2002). Women and adventure recreation: Reconstructing leisure constraints and adventure experiences to negotiate continuing participation. *Journal of Leisure Research, 34,* 157–178.

Loomis, L., Rizzo, L., & Krawchuk, S. (1998). 1997 Survey of public participation in the arts (SPPA): Report on data collection experiences, response rates, and weighing procedures.

Mannell, R.C., & Kleiber, D.A. (1997). *A social psychology of leisure.* State College, PA: Venture Publishing.

Mannell, R. C., & Zuzanek, J. (1991). The nature and variability of leisure constraints in daily life: The case of the physically active leisure of older adults. *Leisure Sciences, 13,* 337–351.

Markides, K.S., & Black, S.A. (1996). Race, ethnicity, and aging: The impact of inequality. In: R.H. Binstock & L.K. George (Eds), *Handbook of Aging and the Social Sciences.* San Diego, CA: Academic Press.

McCormick, B. (1991). Self-experience as leisure constraint: The case of Alcoholics Anonymous. *Journal of Leisure Research, 23,* 345–362.

National Endowment for the Arts (1998). *1997 survey of public participation in the arts: Summary report.* Washington, DC: National Endowment for the Arts.

Raymore, L.A. (1992). The perception of constraints on leisure among adolescents: Support for the Crawford, Jackson, and Godbey model. Paper presented at the Leisure Research Symposium, National Recreation and Park Association, Baltimore, MD.

Rogers, W. A., Meyer, B., Walker, N., & Fisk, A. D. (1998). Functional limitation to daily living tasks in the aged: A focus group analysis. *Human Factors, 40,* 111–126.

Rowe, J.W., & Kahn, R.L. (1998). *Successful aging.* New York: Pantheon Books.

Seccombe, K., & Ishii-Kuntz, M. (1991). Perceptions of problems associated with aging: Comparisons among four older age cohorts. *The Gerontologist, 31,* 527–533.

Silverstein, M., & Parker, M. G. (2002). Leisure activities and quality of life among the oldest old in Sweden. *Research in Aging, 24,* 528–547.

SPSS (1999). *SPSS regression models,* 9.0. Chicago: SPSS.

Stodolska, M. (1998). Assimilation and leisure constraints: Dynamics of constraints on leisure in immigrant populations. *Journal of Leisure Research, 30,* 521–551.

Strain, L. A., Grabusic, C. C., Searle, M. S., & Dunn, N. J. (2002). Continuing and ceasing leisure activities in later life: A longitudinal study. *The Gerontologist, 42,* 217–223.

Summer, L. (1999). *Chronic conditions: A challenge for the 21st century.* Washington, DC: National Academy on an Aging Society.

Timmer, E., Bode, C., & Dittmann-Kohl, F. (2003). Expectations of gains in the second half of life: A study of personal conceptions of enrichment in a lifespan perspective. *Aging & Society, 23,* 3–24.

Utz, R. L., Carr, D., Nesse, R., & Wortman, C. B. (2002). The effect of widowhood on older adults' social participation: An evaluation of activity, disengagement, and continuity theories. *The Gerontologist, 42,* 522–533.

Zarit, S. H., Johansson, B., & Malmberg, B. (1995). Changes in functional competency in the oldest old. *Journal of Aging and Health, 7,* 3–23.

AN IN-DEPTH COMPARATIVE REVIEW OF BURNOUT, PLATEAU, AND DERAILMENT: CONCEPTS THAT THREATEN THE SUCCESS OF HOSPITALITY INDUSTRY MANAGERS

John A. Williams

ABSTRACT

This research paper provides an in-depth look at the concepts of burnout, plateau, and derailment for managers. It has become increasingly important to be able to spot these types of impediments to success for management of hospitality organizations before they happen. Differentiations are made between the three concepts as well as the subtle characteristics that may bind them together or cause one to lead to another in a manager's career. Key insights are provided so that organizations can proactively approach burnout, plateau, and derailment.

INTRODUCTION

Many events in recent decades have changed the dynamics of a career path for hospitality managers. For example, structural changes, technological progress, reduced levels of supervision, and changes in organizational demographics have

Advances in Hospitality and Leisure
Advances in Hospitality and Leisure, Volume 1, 59–70
ISSN: 1745-3542/doi:10.1016/S1745-3542(04)01004-5

combined to exercise strong pressure on anticipated career paths. As the demands of leadership in these environments have changed, so has what these leaders need to meet those demands. As noted by Williams et al. (2001), hospitality managers are dealing with far more complex, ambiguous leadership situations; moving from independence to interdependence and team-building; and from dominance over subordinates to more interactive awareness.

Hospitality literature has produced several articles focusing on the subject of burnout of managers. When managers have prematurely failed in their positions, it has often been erroneously attributed simply to burnout. The concept of burnout is not the only contributor to management's failure to succeed over time. This paper will address the issues of plateau and derailment in comparison to the concept of burnout.

BURNOUT

Herbert Freudenberger (1975) was one of the first to use the term "burnout" in the literature to describe a state of physical and emotional depletion experienced by his colleagues and himself while working intensively during the late 1960s and 1970s. During this time, burnout literature was primarily anecdotal, and interest in the subject was predominantly among practitioners in various human service fields rather than researchers (Daley, 1979; Forney et al., 1982; Kremer & Owen, 1979).

More recently, burnout has been defined as "a state of mental and/or physical exhaustion caused by excessive and prolonged stress" (Girdino et al., 1996). Burnout is a multidimensional construct of emotional exhaustion, depersonalization, and reduced personal accomplishment that can occur among individuals who work extensively with others under considerable time pressures. In addition, burnout is particularly relevant to individuals when working with people in emotionally charged situations (Maslach & Jackson, 1986). Long work hours are generally considered contributing factors to managerial burnout (Porter & Steers, 1972; Rizzo et al., 1970; Terkel, 1974).

The hospitality industry is one that affords a great amount of stress with extreme time constraints. Stress is a major cause of low productivity, high absenteeism, poor decisions, and low morale. People become physically and psychologically weakened from trying to combat it. When they become burned out, they are more likely to complain, attribute their errors to others, and become highly irritable. As a result, turnover, decreased productivity, absenteeism etc. have become far more predominant in society. Often, the resulting alienation they feel drives them to think about quitting their jobs (Yuen & Martin, 1998). Hogan (1992) reports estimations of the cost of an individual case of management turnover in the hospitality industry at $17,000–20,000.

It has become increasingly important to be able to spot these types of stressful conditions and subsequently prevent burnout before it occurs. The National Institute for Occupational Safety and Health (NIOSH) states that early signs of job stress are headaches, short tempers, trouble sleeping, and low morale. Also, according to the American Psychological Association, 60% of work absences are from psychological problems that result in a cost of $57 billion annually.

CAREER PLATEAU

The career plateau has been defined as the "point in a career where the likelihood of additional hierarchical promotion is very low" (Ference et al., 1977). While burnout can have dire consequences for managers, it is just one of the many possible contributors to plateau. Although the phenomenon of career plateauing is not new, it has received increased attention in recent years. It is therefore essential to understand how plateau can develop and what the consequences are for managers who plateau.

Stoner et al. (1980) divided individuals who plateau into four categories:

(1) *Learners or comers* – individuals who are seen as having high potential for advancement but who are presently performing below standard. The most obvious examples are trainees who are still learning the ropes. Longer service managers who recently were promoted to new positions which they have not yet mastered would also be included.
(2) *Stars* – individuals presently doing outstanding work. The combination of economic, social, and demographic pressures is causing career plateaus to occur to a greater extent for managers who are considered stars.
(3) *Solid Citizens* – individuals whose present performance is rated satisfactory to outstanding but who are seen as having little chance for future advancement. They are, perhaps, the largest group in most organizations and perform the bulk of organizational work.
(4) *Deadwood* – individuals who are seen as having little potential for advancement and whose performance has fallen to an unsatisfactory level. These people have become problems, whether for reasons of motivation, ability, or personal difficulty. They are often the recipients of considerable attention, either for rehabilitation or for removal.

As can be seen by these categories, some groups of individuals were viewed favorably, however, they still plateaued. Organization's personal and professional development efforts have typically focused on either the high performers or the low performers. As a rule, high performers will have opportunities to participate in management development programs and to receive mentorships from senior management. Low performers are usually sent to programs designed to improve performance before demotion or dismissal. The major portion of employees, known as "solid citizens," are performing good to outstanding work but are not identified as promotables. Solid citizens may be left in positions well beyond the point where the job is challenging and meaningful, thereby laying the groundwork for future stagnation and ineffectiveness (Stoner et al., 1980).

The consequences of ignoring career plateau can harm the employee and the organization. The ineffective plateauee can be a source of difficulty for superiors, peers, and subordinates. In addition to direct costs of poor job performance, the ineffective plateauee may provide inadequate support to superiors; create additional work for peers and subordinates who must pick up the slack and work around the plateaued employee; block the promotional opportunities of others, and provide inadequate support to subordinate and/or peers. Because of the reluctance of many organizations to dismiss or demote long-service employees, the problem can persist over long periods of time. This can produce a negative effect on others in the organization. In contrast, the effective plateauee or solid citizen often receives little or no attention (Stoner et al., 1980).

In addition to the conditions previously mentioned above, there are several key circumstances that may exist in an organization that cause plateau for both effective and ineffective employees that include the following:

Slow Organizational Growth

Many organizations have restructured and downsized their management and labor forces in order to enhance their competitive edge. These changes have closed off promotion opportunities, forcing many people into plateaued careers. Such restructuring, moving away from the traditional hierarchy to a much flatter model, has been a common feature of many large organizations in the last ten years. Therefore, the number of people who are likely to receive future promotions has decreased dramatically, highlighting the need to better understand both individual and organizational approaches to those in career plateaus (Williams & DeMicco, 1998).

When organizations experience restricted growth, there are fewer opportunities for potential candidates to assume more responsibility (Ference et al., 1977). The slow growth is more likely to eliminate positions and thereby slow down pay raises and promotions (Anderson et al., 1981). The result is a condition where managers cannot rise up in the organization by promotion nor receive appropriate reimbursement for their efforts.

In large organizations, the organizational pyramids become the foundation of structural plateauing. As employees move upward along the organizational pyramids, the number of available positions become fewer and fewer, whereas employees continue to expect endless promotion possibilities. In addition, no one can predict with any degree of certainty whether or not a specific career path will be available five or ten years down the road (Parker, 1989).

Job tenure and plateau research among managers has shown that employees who remain in the same jobs for a number of years are less satisfied with their careers than those who are more mobile (Viega, 1981). Therefore, as job tenure increases, unrealistic expectations of rapid promotions are replaced with more precise expectations of career opportunities based on experience in searching for better positions. The longer people are unsuccessful in advancing within their organizations, the lower their expectations about career mobility will be. Dalton et al. (1977) reported that professional workers employed by relatively large, complex organizations get lower performance ratings after age 35. As a result of their interviews with 550 professional men, four distinct stages of a career were identified:

(1) Stage I: Apprentice – The individual works under the direction of others, helping and learning from one or more mentors.
(2) Stage II: Colleague – The individual has become an independent contributor.
(3) Stage III: Mentor – The individual focuses on assuming responsibility for others.
(4) State IV: Sponsor – The individual exercises power in shaping the direction of the organization.

The Dalton et al. (1977) model has been very useful in providing professional workers an understanding of the career stages and what occurs in each stage. Employees who remain in the colleague stage indefinitely may eventually plateau and may require career development strategies that will maintain and enhance their technical competence.

Perceived opportunity for intraorganizational mobility has implications for work motivation and attitudes. Often, employees will only work hard to get promoted if they perceive that appropriate positions are available and that promotion decisions are based on work performance. Promotions aid talented people to move up, motivate the ambitious to perform well, reconcile mediocre performers to a lesser career path, and exert pressure on poor performers to improve or leave the organization (Conner & Fjerstad, 1979; London & Stumpf, 1982; Martin & Strauss, 1956; Peter & Hull, 1969). Organizations use promotions to motivate employees to advance in their present jobs, aspire to more challenging work, and remain committed (Edwards, 1979; Martin & Strauss, 1956; Rosenbaum, 1984). Studies have found that employees who perceive few opportunities for advancement have negative attitudes towards work and their organizations (Kanter, 1977; Kippnis, 1964).

Organizations do not hire all employees with the expectation that they will at sometime receive promotions. Some jobs are what is referred to as the secondary labor market (Althauser & Kelleberg, 1981; Edwards, 1979; Reich et al., 1973). They require limited education, training, or commitment to enter and are often characterized by intense conditions, rapid turnover, and absence of unionization. The hospitality industry has many positions like this at the lower level, however, management positions are increasingly demanding more and more expertise at entry level positions (Williams et al., 2000).

If they see that alternatives exist, these employees may leave their present situations. If perceived ease of movement is low because alternatives are not available, employees may adjust their aspirations or contributions to their organizations downward. It would be ideal to manage one's career so that plateauing happens at the very same time as retirement. This is rarely the case. But, there are steps that should be initiated. Addressing the realities of career plateauing can force employees to ask what they are going to do with the rest of their lives. Plateaued managers who are still satisfied employees can function as mentors to younger people in the organization. In situations like these, it becomes paramount for the plateaued employee to feel as though they have worth.

Stress and Burnout Leading to Career Plateau

When stress increases up to moderate levels, individuals may become energized and may become more motivated to perform up to their potential. In contrast, if the amount of stress becomes too great or prolonged over time, work effort declines, work performance suffers, and job attitudes become more negative (McGrath, 1976).

With mass layoffs, pay cuts, seemingly endless workdays and disappearing vacations, managers are coping with an incredible amount of job stress. Feeling unable to keep up with the demands of their jobs, many are reaching burnout levels. Employees, who plateau due to stress and burnout, experience decreased performance and job attitudes. The stress can impede a manager's perceptual and decision-making skills. Plateaued managers are far more likely to procrastinate, forget important pieces of information; and fail to seek additional information (Janis & Mann, 1977). Stress and burnout lead to poorer mental health and general dissatisfaction (Brief et al., 1981).

Lack of Training

Managers plateaued due to insufficient skills and abilities eventually become poor performers and develop negative job attitudes. Their performance suffers due to low levels of skills and abilities. In addition, absenteeism and turnover may increase (Anderson & Milkovich, 1980; Porter & Steers, 1973). As Ellen Nash, vice president of communications for the National Restaurant Association Educational Foundation (NRAEF) in Chicago relates, managers must not only learn the technical skills they need to oversee an efficient, well-run operation, but their training must also cover the more personal "soft skills" that turn good managers into great leaders (Restaurants & Institutions, 2004).

An important distinction should be made between plateauing and performance. The two should be considered as independent. A person who has reached a "terminal level" in an organization can be a good performer or a poor one. Similarly, people with continued advancement potential can also show strong or weak performance. The critical point is not that there will be an increase of plateauing in the future, but that growth and learning can be maintained when a person has plateaued (Hall, 1985).

Williams (1999) looked at plateau for hospitality managers of managed service companies working in acute care hospitals in the United States. The research found that there is little opportunity for management to advance without appropriate training for their positions. For multi-department managers, this is compounded by the fact that there are shifts in expectations as managers take on more departments and responsibilities. Learning in the face of change then takes on a new dynamic. Organizational intervention then becomes necessary for managerial growth, whether through structural training programs, feedback, coursework, coaching or placing young managers with advanced well-trained role models.

The hospitality industry is well-known for the broad expanse of diverse areas within its organizations. Hotels and restaurants, in addition to managed service positions, have many separate areas of expertise that a manager must be highly knowledgeable in prior to achieving the role of general manager. Hotels, for example, have front desk, concierge, food & beverage, housekeeping, room service, catering, sales & marketing, etc.

The incidence of plateaued managers seems likely to increase in future years owing to demographic trends and sporadic economic growth. Retaining managers with critical skills, creating career paths to help more senior managers break out of career plateaus, and retraining managers whose skills have become outdated will pose unique challenges to hospitality organizations.

DERAILMENT

Derailment in a managerial or executive role is defined as being involuntarily plateaued, demoted, or fired below the level of anticipated achievement or reaching that level only to fail unexpectedly (Lombardo et al., 1988). Managers of hospitality operations oversee several diverse areas within their organizations. As the demands of leadership in these environments have changed, so has what these leaders need to meet those demands. Leadership skills required are different, even from five years ago. Managers can no longer rely on the power of their position to accomplish the job. Followership is critical, particularly in downsizing organizations.

McCall and Lombardo (1983) conducted research that explored reasons for success before derailment for executives. They found that the average executive had two or three of the following characteristics:

(1) Outstanding track record – identified early as having high potential and had a string of successes.
(2) Outgoing, well liked, charming.
(3) Technically brilliant.
(4) Loyal and helpful to management; willing to make sacrifices.
(5) Ambitious; managed career well.
(6) Moved up during reorganization or merger.
(7) Excellent at motivating or directing subordinates.

They were identified as "having it" and ran up a string of successes. McCall and Lombardo also looked at executives who were perceived as having great potential to be very successful in their careers, however, were transferred, demoted, opted for early retirement, plateaued, or fired. These were viewed as better than the competition and about half of them were viewed as technical geniuses, or brilliant problem solvers. In examining the reasons for their derailment, the average executive had at least two of these characteristics:

(1) Cold, aloof, arrogant.
(2) Insensitivity to others; an abrasive, intimidating, bullying style.
(3) Specific performance problems with the business.
(4) Betrayal of trust.
(5) Overmanaging – failing to delegate, or build a team.
(6) Overly ambitious – thinking of the next job, playing politics.
(7) Failing to staff effectively.
(8) Unable to think strategically.
(9) Unable to adapt to a boss with a different style.
(10) Overdependent on an advocate or a mentor.

Findings of the Lombardo et al. (1988) quantitative study on derailment supported earlier qualitative studies. The results of their research included several areas showing differences between derailees and those considered to be in the midst of a promising career:

(1) Concerning derailment and the leadership of others, scores on the leadership of subordinates and staffing scales were different for successful and derailed and those considered to be in the midst of a promising career.

(2) Scores on the integrity, composure, drive, and sensitivity scales were different for successful and derailed managers. This indicated that personal flaws led to derailment. Derailed managers were much more likely to be seen as unstable, lack drive, be abrasive, or more untrustworthy than were the successful.

(3) With regard to derailment and managerial skills, the study found that derailed managers were much more likely to be seen as lacking the cognitive capabilities or skills to handle complex business ventures, think strategically, make high-quality decisions in ambiguous circumstances, and demonstrate needed political skills than were the successful.

Lombardo and Eichinger (1992) looked at derailment from the perspective of how it plays out over time. They noted that standards of excellence change as managers who were first rewarded for standout individual contributions are later expected to perform tasks as building networks and team building. As a result, tolerance for mistakes and lack of management flexibility decreases dramatically as the stakes change:

• A strength no longer matters.
• A strength becomes a weakness.
• An untested area becomes a weakness.
• A flaw now matters.
• A blind spot becomes a flaw.

Derailment can only be prevented if managers are willing to look at some very tough developmental issues. Understanding why it may be difficult to relate to others, or to let go of personal achievements in favor of team-building may involve facing issues around trust, security, self-confidence or power (Drath, 1993). The learning that is involved can be highly emotional, demanding an elevated level of readiness or maturity on the part of managers.

Williams et al. (2000) research results showed that hospitality organizations and their management must realize that as the demands of leadership have changed, so has what is needed of leaders to meet these demands. Their study found that successful managers must have the ability to change managerial style to fit the occasion, be creative, and have the ability to develop new ideas. A unique finding of the research was that a high degree of tenure is not necessarily an indicator of the amount of authority and supervision given to managers. As managerial stakes increase, managerial flaws can have an increased impact. Exposing managers early to varied leadership challenges before the stakes become insurmountable is therefore vital.

CONCLUSION

Burnout, plateau, and derailment will continue to be factors that impede management success and restrict organizational growth. This paper has provided an understanding of the distinctions between these concepts. In many instances, when the signs of these three problem areas are noticed, it may already be too late. A more proactive stance is needed. Organizations and top management share the responsibility of working together to minimize the risks for management. It becomes vitally important to move from broad definitions of burnout, plateau, and derailment to the identification of more defined sub patterns and from general identification of symptoms to the discovery of specific problems. The organization is the manager's classroom, and as in a classroom, the proper learning environment must be developed to prevent burnout, plateau, and derailment.

REFERENCES

Althauser, R. P., & Kalleberg, A. L. (1981). Firms, occupations and the structure of labor markets: A conceptual analysis. In: I. Berg (Ed.), *Sociological Perspectives on Labor Markets* (pp. 119–149). New York: Academic Press.

Anderson, J. C., & Milkovich, G. T. (1980). Propensity to leave: A preliminary examination of March and Simon's model. *Relations Industrilles, 35,* 279–292.

Anderson, J. C., Milkovich, G. T., & Tsui, A. (1981). A model of intraorganizational mobility. *Academy of Management Review, 6,* 529–538.

Brief, A. P., Schuler, R. S., & Van Sell, M. (1981). *Managing job stress.* Boston: Little, Brown.

Connelly, R. D., & Fjerstad, R. L. (1979). Internal personnel maintenance. In: D. Yoder & H. G. Heneman (Eds), *APSA Handbook of Personnel and Industrial Relations* (pp. 4–244). Washington, DC: Bureau of National Affairs.

Daley, M. R. (1979). Burnout: Smoldering problems in protective services. *Social Work, 24,* 375–379.

Dalton, G. W., Thompson, P. H., & Price, R. L. (1977). The four stages of professional careers: A new look at performance by professionals. *Organizational Dynamics, 6,* 19–42.

Drath, W. (1993). *Why managers have trouble empowering: A theoretical perspective based on concepts of adult development.* Technical Report No. 155. Greensboro, NC: Center for Creative Leadership.

Edwards, R. C. (1979). *Contested terrain.* New York: Basic.

Ference, T. P., Stoner, J. A., & Warren, E. K. (1977). Managing the career plateau. *Academy of Management Review, 2*(4), 602–612.

Forney, D. S., Wallace-Schutzman, F., & Wiggens, T. T. (1982). Burnout among career development professionals: Preliminary findings and implications. *Personal and Guidance Journal, 61,* 435–439.

Freudenberger, H. J. (1975). The staff burnout syndrome in alternative institutions. *Psychotherapy Theory, Research and Practice, 12*(1), 73–82.

Girdino, D. A., Everly, G. S., & Dusek, D. E. (1996). *Controlling stress and tension.* Needham Heights, MA: Allyn & Bacon.

Hall, D. T. (1985). Project work as an antidote to career plateauing in a declining engineering organization. *Human Resource Management, 24*(3), 271–292.

Hogan, J. J. (1992, February). Turnover and what to do about it. *The Cornell Hotel and Restaurant Quarterly,* 40–45.

Janis, I. L., & Mann, F. (1977). *Decision making: A psychological analysis of conflict, choice, and commitment.* New York: Free Press.

Kippnis, D. (1964). Mobility expectations and attitudes toward industrial structure. *Human Relations, 17,* 57–71.

Kremer, B. J., & Owen, W. A. (1979). Stress in the life of the counselor. *School Counselor, 26,* 40–45.

Lombardo, M., & Eichinger, R. (1992). *Preventing derailment: What to do before it's too late.* Charlotte, NC: Center for Creative Leadership.

Lombardo, M. M., Ruderman, M. N., & McCauley, C. D. (1988). Explanations of success and derailment in upper-level management positions. *Journal of Business and Psychology, 2*(3), 199–216.

London, M., & Stumpf, S. A. (1982). *Managing careers.* Reading, MA: Addison-Wesley.

Martin, N. A., & Strauss, A. L. (1956). Patterns of mobility within industrial organizations. *Journal of Business, 22,* 101–110.

Maslach, C., & Jackson, S. E. (1986). *Maslach Burnout Inventory manual* (2nd ed., p. 1). Palo Alto, CA: Consulting Psychologists Press.

McCall, M. W., & Lombardo, M. M. (1983). What makes a top executive? *Psychology Today, 17*(2), 26–31.

McGrath, J. E. (1976). Stress and behavior in organizations. In: M. D. Dunnette (Ed.), *Handbook of Industrial and Organizational Psychology* (pp. 1351–1396). Chicago: Rand McNally.

Parker, C. S. (1989). *Management information system.* R. R. Donnelly & Sons Company.

Peter, L. J., & Hull, R. (1969). *The Peter principle.* New York: William Morrow.

Porter, L. W., & Steers, R. M. (1973). Organizational work and personal factors in employee turnover and absenteeism. *Psychological Bulletin, 80*(2), 151–176.

Reich, M., Gordon, D. M., & Edwards, R. C. (1973). Dual labor markets: A theory of labor market segmentation. *American Economic Review, 63,* 359–365.

Rizzo, J. R., House, R. J., & Lirtzman, S. I. (1970). Role conflict and ambiguity in complex organizations. *Administrative Science Quarterly, 15,* 150–163.

Rosenbaum, J. E. (1984). *Career mobility in a corporate hierarchy.* New York: Academic Press.

Staff (2004, April 15). Movin' on up. *Restaurants & Institutions.*

Stoner, J. A. F., Ference, T. P., Warren, E. K., & Christensen, H. K. (1980). *Managerial career plateaus.* New York: Center for Research in Career Development, Columbia University.

Terkel, S. (1974). *Working.* New York: Pantheon Books.

Viega, J. F. (1981). Plateaued versus nonplateaued managers: Career patterns, attitudes and path potential. *Academy of Management Journal, 24,* 566–578.

Williams, J. A. (1999). The challenge of multi-department management: A vital step in addressing career plateau. *The Bottomline, 14*(7), 16–24.

Williams, J. A., & DeMicco, F. J. (1998). The challenge of multi-department management for future hospitality graduates. *Journal of Hospitality & Tourism Education, 10*(1), 13–17.

Williams, J. A., DeMicco, F. J., & Shafer, E. L. (2000). Attributes associated with success as perceived by managers in three levels of multi-department management in acute care hospitals. *Journal of Hospitality & Tourism Research, 24*(1), 36–48.

Williams, J. A., DeMicco, F. J., & Shafer, E. L. (2001). Derailment: An impending dilemma for management as they assume expanded roles. *Florida International University Hospitality Review, 19*(2), 60–72.

Yuen, J., & Martin, M. (1998). Creative ways for managing work-place tension. *Communication World, 15*(18, August), 18.

PRICE-ENDING PRACTICES AND CONSUMER BEHAVIOR IN THE HOSPITALITY INDUSTRY: A RECIPROCAL PHENOMENON PART II

Sandra Naipaul and H. G. Parsa

ABSTRACT

The current study investigates odd-even psychological pricing with the aid of a Price endings and Consumer Behavior (PCBM) Model *for the hospitality industry. The PCBM proposes that a reciprocal relationship exists between hospitality marketers and consumers with reference to 00 and 99 price ending practices. Theoretical support for the posited model is provided by signaling theory, a persuasion knowledge model (PKM), and learning by analogy from marketing and psychology literatures. Results indicate that consumers use intuition and knowledge gained from interacting in the retail marketplace to respond to the intentions of hospitality marketers' odd-even psychological pricing strategy. After repeated exposures to odd-even pricing, consumers learn to accept the 00 and 99 pricing endings as extrinsic cues for quality and value and as pricing norms of the hospitality industry.*

Advances in Hospitality and Leisure
Advances in Hospitality and Leisure, Volume 1, 71–87
Copyright © 2004 by Elsevier Ltd.
All rights of reproduction in any form reserved
ISSN: 1745-3542/doi:10.1016/S1745-3542(04)01005-7

INTRODUCTION

In the marketplace, including the hospitality industry $0.00 and $0.99 are two of the most commonly used price endings. This variation of the odd-even psychological pricing strategy is designed to appeal to consumer emotions. It attempts to influence customer decision-making processes by using price endings as a decision-making attribute (Pride & Ferrell, 1997). In addition, it tends to influence buyer perceptions of the price or the product (Nagle & Holden, 1995).

Research provides strong empirical evidence, showing that 00 and 99 price endings are used extensively throughout the general marketplace (Georgoff, 1972; Ginzberg, 1936; Schindler, 1984; Schindler & Kibarian, 1996; Schindler & Warren, 1988; Stiving & Winer, 1997). (Table 1) The above studies indicate that these price endings are manipulated according to market segment, product category, selling price, and price level. High-priced and/or upscale firms selling high-quality products tend to use 00 more than any other price endings whereas low-end, low-priced firms, and/or firms promoting a high-value image tend to use 99 more than any other price endings (Friedman, 1967; Kreul, 1982; Naipaul & Parsa, 2001; Rudolph, 1954; Stiving & Winer, 1997; Twedt, 1965). Interestingly, research also indicates that 00 and 99 price endings are manipulated between regular and sales prices, with regular prices more likely to end in 00 and discounted prices more like to end in 99 (Schindler & Kirby, 1997).

Specific to the hospitality industry, empirical evidence shows that 00 and 99 price- endings practices are well established in the hospitality industry and depend on market segment (Kreul, 1982; Naipaul & Parsa, 2001). Naipaul and Parsa (2001) research comparing the practice of using 00 and 99 price endings on restaurant menus found that fine-dining restaurants tend to use 00 much more (35%) than

Table 1. Selected Price-Ending Studies.

Author	Study	0 (%)	5 (%)	9 (%)	No. of Items
Rudolph (1954)	General merchandise	18	18	37	22,011
Twedt (1965)	Processed meats	1	19	64	30,878
	Grocery items	4	15	57	2,597
Friedman (1967)	Recommended prices <$1.00	3	19	34	3,326
Kreul (1982)	Menu prices <$7.99	6	35	58	246
	Menu prices $7.99–$10.99	15	71	11	345
Schindler & Kirby (1997)	Regular prices	33	20	26	887
	Discount prices	18	16	39	528
Naipaul & Parsa (2001)	Menu price <$5.00	13	24	63	1128
	Menu prices >$10.00	35	62	3	2303

the 99 price endings (3%). On the other hand, quick-service restaurants tend to use the 99 price endings to a greater extent (63%) than fine-dining restaurants (13%). (Table 1) The findings indicate that fine-dining restaurants selling expensive products may be using 00 to signal high quality while quick-service restaurants may be using 99 to promote a high value image.

In addition to the research evidence showing the common practice of odd/even pricing strategies in the marketplace, several studies indicate that 00 and 99 price endings appeal to consumer emotions, influencing their perceptions of the price, product or the store. These studies indicate that due to these common pricing practices, consumers may have learned to interpret 00 to signal high-quality products (Halloway, 1968; Naipaul & Parsa, 2001; Stiving, 2000; Stiving & Winer, 1997; Wingate et al., 1972) and a high level of class or retailer prestige (Alpert, 1971; Feinberg, 1962; Halloway, 1968; Nagle & Holden, 1995; Raphael, 1968; Spohn & Allen, 1977).

On the other hand, the common use of 99 price endings by specific segments throughout the marketplace may have caused consumers to interpret 99 as the lowest price around (Bliss, 1952; Mason & Mayer, 1990); a good deal (Schindler & Kibarian, 1996); a sale price (Quigley & Notarantonio, 1992; Raphael, 1968; Schindler & Kibarian, 1996; Schindler & Kirby, 1997); a reduced price, possibly from the next higher even price (Alpert, 1971; Friedman, 1967; Knauth, 1949; Schindler & Kibarian, 1996); as a discount price or low price (Nagle & Holden, 1995); as a signal of value pricing (Collins & Parsa, 2004) or pricing to the penny.

Based on the phenomenon that 00 and 99 price endings appeal to consumer emotions, experimental research indicates that 00 and 99 affect sales. Schindler and Kibarian (1996) reported that in their sales experiment, 99 pricing yielded 8% higher revenues than the 88 or 00 pricing for the same products. Also, higher price elasticity was realized when prices ended with the digit 9 (Nagle & Holden, 1995) and product demand was also relatively more elastic at the odd-even price points (Georgoff, 1972). In other situations, some product categories experienced greater sales with 99, some product sales increased with 00, and in some cases there were no significant differences (Blattberg & Neslin, 1990; Dalyrimple & Haines, 1970; Ginzberg, 1936). Although results of these studies are mixed and inconclusive, it is important to note that all of the above studies have shown that 00 and 99 price endings do affect sales.

In summary, these findings suggest that the 00 and 99 is a pricing strategy extensively used in the marketplace, including the hospitality industry. More importantly, findings suggest that 00 is predominantly used in the high-price, upscale market segments and 99 is most common with the low-end, high-value market segment. This indicates that 00 and 99 price endings are pricing strategies used to signal quality and value.

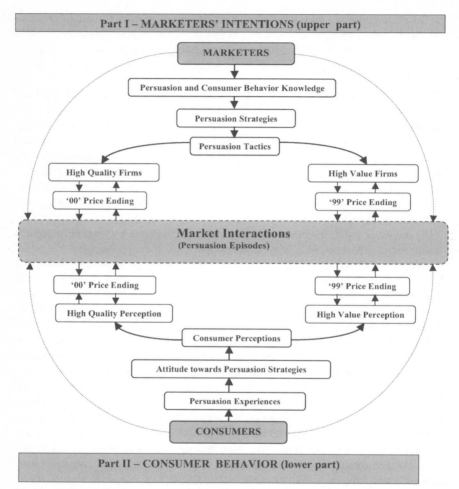

Fig. 1. Price-Ending Practices and Consumer Behavior Model (PCBM): A Reciprocal
Phenomenon (Part I & II).

From a marketing perspective, a plausible explanation for the manipulation
of pricing structures is that marketers are aware that price acts as an indicator
of perceived quality and value (refer to Zeithaml, 1988, for a summary), which
leads them to manipulate 00 and 99 endings. From a psychological perspective,
consumers' repeated exposure to the common use of 00 by upscale firms and 99 by
low-end firms may lead them to construct their own intuitive pricing theories that

associate price endings with product attributes such as quality (00) and value (99). Engaging in such intuitive thinking is a reflection of consumer efforts to conserve time and cognitive resources while maximizing the extrinsic cues found in the marketplace and avoiding risk.

Price endings aren't necessarily the "paramount" vehicle to signal quality and value; however, this common practice in the hospitality industry strongly suggests that they are important channels for signaling quality and value. In view of this, we posit that consumers *respond positively* to marketers' manipulation of 00 and 99 price-endings practices (Naipaul, 2001). To explain this phenomenon and the relevant theoretical rationales, we present the *Price-endings and Consumer-Behavior Model (PCBM – Part II – lower part of the model)* as presented in Fig. 1. (Part I of the PCB Model is presented elsewhere, see reference Naipaul & Parsa, 2004).

It must be noted that the research evidence demonstrates that marketers commonly manipulate 00 and 99 price endings in the marketplace and that 00 and 99 price endings tend to affect consumers' subjective perceptions of the products offered or the store image. To the authors' knowledge, however, only one study (Naipaul & Parsa, 2001) specifically investigated how consumers interpret and use this pricing strategy in their daily interactions with the hospitality industry. The purpose of this article is to determine whether consumers respond to price endings as intended by marketers, and whether they perceive price endings as signals of quality and value respectively (PCBM – Part II – lower part). This article attempts to provide theoretical explanations and empirical evidence for consumer response to marketer manipulation of 00 and 99 price endings, a variation of the odd-even psychological pricing strategy.

PRICE-ENDINGS AND CONSUMER BEHAVIOR MODEL (PCBM)

The Price-endings and Consumer Behavior Model (PCBM) (Fig. 1) attempts to explain the theoretical rationale for 00 and 99 price endings that dominates the restaurant segment of the hospitality industry. The PCBM postulates that a positive relationship occurs in the selling-and-buying game as a result of specific market segments' common use of 00 and 99 price endings and consumer acceptance of these price-endings practices in the intended manner. The PCBM – Part I (upper part of the model) postulates that fine-dining (high-quality) and quick-service (high-value) restaurant marketers develop persuasion episodes using 00 price endings to signal quality and 99 price endings to signal value (Naipaul, 2001). The PCBM – Part II (lower part of the model) posits that exposure to these persuasion episodes leads consumers to develop intuitive theories about the use of price endings and the intentions of restaurant marketers, which they then use to develop certain attitudes towards 00 and 99 pricing, the products involved, and the marketers themselves (Freistad & Wright, 1994).

The PCBM is developed from the *Persuasion Knowledge Model* (PKM) (Freistad & Wright, 1984), which illustrates the interplay in the game of selling and buying in the marketplace. The PCBM offers the following psychological theories to explain the observed the positive relationship between restaurant marketer intentions in using 00 and 99 pricing strategies and consumer acceptance of the intended messages of quality and value: *Signaling Theory* (Boulding & Kirmani, 1993; Spence, 1974), *Intuition in Inference Making* (Broniarczky & Alba, 1994); and *Consumer Learning by Analogy* (Gregan-Paxton & John, 1997). The PCBM follows a systematic study of 00 and 99 price endings based on specific theoretical assumptions that are well-accepted in the marketing literature.

To evaluate whether consumers learn to use 00 and 99 price endings as signals of quality and value, it is important to understand why such "persuasion heuristics" have the potential to influence consumers in their purchasing decisions. According to the Heuristic-Systematic Model (Chaiken, 1987), consumers seeking to improve their knowledge of a product, often learn to conserve cognitive effort on that task by using simple "persuasion heuristics" (Freistad & Wright, 1994). Hence, by integrating psychological base approaches, the PCBM – Part II demonstrates that consumers use persuasion heuristics to interpret "00" and "99" price endings as signals of quality and value respectively, which they are likely to use in their purchasing decisions for hospitality products. Over time, consumers may either perceive persuasion attempts by marketers or may learn to develop appropriate strategies to adapt to such attempts. This phenomenon could be explained by *in Inference Making* (Broniarczky & Alba, 1994) and *Consumer Learning by Analogy* (Gregan-Paxton & John, 1997) theories.

The PCBM – Part II postulates that when consumers are repeatedly presented with persuasion episodes such as 00 and 99 price endings in different market segments, they are more likely to develop certain beliefs about these persuasion episodes. For example, with experience in the marketplace and repeated exposure to 00 price endings in the pricing structure of high-priced, upscale or high-quality stores, consumers may learn to interpret this price ending as a signal of quality (Halloway, 1968; Naipaul & Parsa, 2001; Stiving, 2000; Stiving & Winer, 1997; Wingate et al., 1972); high quality products within the same retail outlet (Nagle & Holden, 1995), and a high level of class or prestige of the retailer (Alpert, 1971; Feinberg, 1962; Halloway, 1968; Raphael, 1968; Spohn & Allen, 1977).

On the other hand, from repeated exposure to 99 price ending in sale/discount situations, low-price or lower quality stores, and/or stores promoting high value, consumers may learn to interpret this price ending as signaling the value of store offerings (Georgoff, 1972; Lambert, 1975; Naipaul & Parsa, 2001, Schindler & Warren, 1988). More specifically, consumers interpret a pricing structure that ends with 99 as a sale price (Quigley & Notarantonio, 1992; Raphael, 1968; Schindler & Kibarian, 1996; Schindler & Kirby, 1997); a reduced price, possibly from the next higher even price (Alpert, 1971; Friedman, 1967; Knauth, 1949; Schindler & Kibarian, 1996); discount price or low-price (Nagle & Holden, 1995); the lowest price around (Bliss, 1952; Mason & Mayer, 1990); or a good deal (Schindler & Kibarian, 1996).

In the marketplace, consumers have the option to accept or reject persuasion episodes initially, but eventually – upon repeated exposure – they may learn to accept them as market norms. This can be illustrated by the example of ubiquitous practice of superscripted 0.99 cents after the normal price for a gallon of gasoline in the USA. Although consumers may rationally reject it initially, after time they learn to accept it as a marketing norm and develop appropriate coping strategies. Similar examples include: the book publishing industry in China where digit 8 is the exclusively used price ending digit for books deliberately avoiding digit 9 as the price ending (Parsa & Hu, 2004; Simmons & Schindler, 2002); the predominant use of 9/99 price ending in the quick-service restaurant industry and deliberate avoidance of 00 price ending; and deliberate avoidance of 9/99 price-ending by the wine industry and fine dining restaurants in Europe and North America.

According to the PCBM – Part II such scenarios are likely to lead consumers to develop their own theories, developing hypotheses about persuasion episodes and about how to improve their bargaining and purchase decisions using these persuasion episodes (Freistad & Wright, 1994; Wright, 1985). Eventually, these beliefs become the basis of persuasion knowledge which strengthens their intuitions (Broniarczyk & Alba, 1994) and shapes their perceptions about the relationship between price endings and the quality and value attributes of a product. That is, they are likely to use these price endings as heuristics to improve their knowledge of a product thus conserving time and cognitive effort (Chaiken, 1987) when making purchasing decisions.

According to Gregan-Paxton and John (1997) *"consumers learn by analogy,"* and may experience a process of internal knowledge transfer, which involves the use of a familiar situation to understand and respond to new or novel domains. From repeated exposure to the common practice of 00 and 99 price endings in the general marketplace consumers are likely to use these heuristics to improve their knowledge of the quality and value of products in the hospitality industry. Hence, when consumers are faced with marketing situations where the quality and/or value attributes of a product cannot be easily discerned, consumers are likely to use knowledge transfer heuristics for pricing strategies most commonly encountered in the marketplace. For example, consumers may use 00 and 99 price endings as possible signals of quality and value – thus maximizing the extrinsic cues found in the marketplace and conserving time and cognitive energy in their shopping experience.

An example of consumer internal knowledge transfer can be found in the early part of the 20th century, in the USA. During that time, retail prices often ended in even numbers. As a differentiation strategy and to communicate high value, some retail firms innovated the just-below pricing (99 cents) practice, which became more popular during the Great Depression. One of the commonly known phrases of the 1930s, "All you can eat under a buck," lends support to the later popularity of 99 price endings in the foodservice industry. Consumers, *by analogy* (Gregan-Paxton & John, 1997), are likely to draw on their knowledge acquired from interaction in the marketplace, associating high value with 99 price endings from the "all you can eat under a buck" diners as well as other high-value retail operations where 99 price endings are used.

In addition, the PCBM – Part II shows that when upscale marketers use 00 in their prices promoting high quality, and the low-priced stores use 99 price endings promoting high value over an extended period, it becomes a part of the marketplace norm. Consequently, consumers expect similar pricing to occur under similar conditions (00 pricing whenever high- quality products are introduced into the marketplace and 99 pricing whenever high-value products are introduced). Such pricing practices may result in consumers developing specific price thresholds. Hence the following hypotheses:

H1. Consumers associate high end, fine-dining restaurants with 00 price endings and not with 99 price endings.

H2. Consumers associate low-end, quick-service restaurants with 99 price endings and not with 00 price endings.

H3. Consumers identify restaurants that use 00 price endings as offering high-quality products.

H4. Consumers identify restaurants that use 99 price endings as offering a high-value products.

METHODOLOGY

To test the PCBM – Part II with the posited four hypotheses, data was collected from the restaurant segment of the hospitality industry. This decision was made for the following reasons: restaurant products are experience goods, where quality and value cannot be discerned easily prior to initial consumption; fine-dining restaurants tend to be promoted as offering high-quality products and services; quick-service restaurants (fast food) tend to be promoted as offering value meals; and, in the past, restaurants and menu prices have been the choice of research context for studying the odd-even psychological pricing strategy (Kreul, 1982; Naipaul & Parsa, 2001; Parsa & Hu, 2004; Schindler & Kibarian,1996). Therefore, the restaurant segment of the hospitality industry is appropriate for testing hypotheses posited by the PCBM – Part II in order to continue adding and building the research surrounding the odd-even psychological pricing strategy.

To test whether consumers respond to 00 and 99 price endings as intended by marketers, data was collected through an experimental design involving faculty and staff at a major Midwestern university. Subjects were limited to faculty and administrative staff only because the pre-testing process indicated that students might not have had enough experience with the fine-dining restaurant segment to effectively participate in the experiment. The experimental design was a between-subject 2 × 3 design consisting of two treatments: *Treatment A* (High-end, Fine-dining restaurants) and *Treatment B* (Low-end, Quick-Service Restaurants). In each treatment, three different cuisines (Italian, American and French) and three price endings (00, 99 and 00/99) were manipulated. Seventy-five subjects participated in each treatment, resulting in a total of 150 subjects.

Treatment A – High-End, Fine-Dining Restaurants

Three different fine-dining experimental menus were developed from a collection of 150 fine-dining restaurant menus (collected over one year) after testing several times for effectiveness, representation, brevity, clarity and price presentation. To control for the confounding variables such as specific restaurant name etc., these restaurant menus were labeled as Restaurant 1, 2 and 3. Three versions of each fine dining menu were developed with the following price endings 00, 99, and mixed 00/99. In each set, menus were labeled as Menu A, Menu B, and Menu C to avoid confounding effects. Subjects were randomly assigned to a menu set, either Restaurant 1, 2 or 3. A pre-tested scenario describing a promotional strategy for a restaurant company accompanied each experimental menu set. The experimental scenarios for Treatment A and B were pre-tested over a one-year period with several experimental groups, and were found to be very effective and reliable.

Treatment B – Low-End, Quick-Service Restaurants

An experimental design similar to fine-dining restaurants was used for the Treatment B. Similar to fine-dining restaurant menus, QSR menus and the accompanying scenario were also pre-tested. It must be noted that no time limits were imposed on the subjects during the experiment because it was not our intention to test for cognitive decision-making under duress. An example of experimental design:

Experimental Design

Restaurant 1	Restaurant 2	Restaurant 3
Menu A 00	**Menu A** 99	**Menu A** 00/99
25 subjects	25 subjects	25 subjects
Menu B 99	**Menu B** 00/99	**Menu B** 00
25 subjects	25 subjects	25 subjects
Menu C 00/99	**Menu C** 00	**Menu C** 99
25 Subjects	25 Subjects	25 Subjects

RESULTS AND DISCUSSION

Demographic Data

In the experimental design investigating consumer response to the marketing strategy 00 and 99 price endings as signals of quality and value, we needed to control for confounding variables. Specifically, consumers might not be clear on the expectation from fine dining and quick service restaurants in reference to quality and value. To control for this confounding variable, subjects were asked about their expectations from fine-dining and quick-service restaurants. Participants responded to statements that fine-dining restaurants are expected to offer unquestionably high-quality products and services and quick-service restaurants emphasize high- value pricing in their product offerings. Participants

Table 2. Consumers Expect Fine Dining Restaurants to Offer Unquestionably Superior Quality Products and Services.

Scale	Unquestionably Superior Quality	
	(*n*)	(%)
Strongly agree	54	72
Agree	20	27
Disagree	1	1
Total	75	100

Note: (*n*) Number of responses; (%) Percent of responses.

rated these statements using a 4-point Likert scale (strongly agree, agree, disagree and strongly disagree). Results indicate that 72% of the participants "strongly agreed" and 27% "agreed" that they expected fine-dining restaurants to offer unquestionably superior quality products (Table 2). Conversely, 35% of the participants "strongly agreed" and 59% "agreed" that quick-service restaurants are more likely to offer high-value products (Table 3). These findings validate that the participants associate fine-dining restaurants with high-quality products and quick-service restaurants with high value products, hence their suitability for the study.

An important goal of this study is to identify whether consumers interpret 00 price endings to signal "quality" and 99 price endings to signal "value" as intended by marketers. Participants were asked to identify the price endings they expected to appear on fine-dining and quick-service restaurant menus. Sixty four percent (64%) of the participants expected to see 00 price endings on fine-dining menus, while only 15% expected 99 price endings. In contrast, 75% of the participants expected

Table 3. Consumers Expect Quick Service Restaurants to Offer More Value-Priced Products and Services.

Price Endings	Value Priced (Quick Service Restaurant Menus)	
	(*n*)	(%)
Strongly agree	26	35
Agree	44	59
Disagree	3	4
Strongly disagree	2	2.7
Total	75	100

Note: (*n*) Number of responses; (%) Percent of responses.

Table 4. Consumers Associate Price-Endings with Quality and Value in
Choosing Restaurant Menus.

Price Endings	Quality Fine Dining Restaurant Menus		Value Quick Service Restaurant Menus	
	(*n*)	(%)	(*n*)	(%)
00 Price ending	48	64	10	13
99 Price ending	11	15	9	75
00/99 Price ending	16	21	56	12
Total	75	100	75	100

Note: (*n*) Number of responses; (%) Percent of responses.

to see 99 price endings on quick-service menus and only 13% expected to see
00 price endings (Table 4). These results overwhelmingly confirm the assumption
that consumers associate fine-dining restaurants with 00 price endings and expect
quick-service restaurants with 99 price endings. These results support H1, that
consumers associate fine-dining restaurants with 00 price endings and not with 99
price endings, and H2, that consumers associate quick-service restaurants with 99
price endings and not with 00 price endings.

Support for H1 and H2 demonstrates that consumers are affected by 00 and 99
price endings as signaling mechanisms commonly used in the marketplace. That
is, through repeated exposure in the marketplace consumers tend to develop their
own intuitive theories about the common practice of 00 and 99 price endings,
which they learn to use as persuasion heuristics to determine quality and value,
conserving time and cognitive efforts.

One may then ask, are marketers' persuasion attempts strong enough to affect
the purchase behavior of consumers? To answer this question, an experiment
was conducted where participants were required to select a restaurant's menu
that would signal the highest quality and highest value. To determine whether
consumers use 00 as a persuasion heuristic to interpret quality when interacting in
the marketplace, Treatment A (Fine-Dining Restaurant) was randomly assigned to
75 participants. A descriptive scenario was provided along with a set of menus. The
participants selected the menu that they believed would signal the restaurant that
offered the highest-quality products. Results from Treatment A show that 53%,
a large majority of the participants chose the menu that carried 00 pricing, while
only 39% chose the menu that carried 99 pricing and 8% chose the menu that
carried the mixed pricing (00/99) (Table 5).

To determine whether consumers use 99 price endings as a persuasion heuristic
to interpret value when interacting in the marketplace, Treatment B (Quick-Service

Table 5. Consumers' Choice of Restaurant Menus is Based on Overall Quality and Value.

Price Endings	Quality Fine Dining Restaurant Menus		Value Quick Service Restaurant Menus	
	(*n*)	(%)	(*n*)	(%)
00 Price Ending	40	53.0	21	28.0
99 Price Ending	29	39.0	30	40.0
00/99 Price Ending	6	8.0	24	32.0
Total	75	100	75	100

Note: (*n*) Number of responses; (%) Percent of responses.

Restaurant) was randomly assigned to 75 participants. A pre-tested scenario was accompanied by a set of menus with three differing price-endings (00, 999, 00/99 mixed). The respondents were asked to select the menu that they believe would signal a restaurant offering the highest value products. Results from Treatment B show that 40% of the participants chose the menu that carried 99, while only 28% chose the menu that carried 00 and 32% chose the menu that carried mixed (00/99) (Table 5). These results present evidence in support of H3 and H4, stating that consumers associate 00 with overall high quality and 99 with overall high value when interacting in hospitality industry.

These findings indicate that consumers who are exposed to high-quality firms' common use of 00 and high-value firms common use of 99 develop heuristics which associate these price endings with high quality and high value in the retail marketplace. Hence the assumption that consumers make analogies in similar situations in the retail marketplace when confronted with new situations and/or different products. These findings are consistent with the results reported by Naipaul and Parsa (2001).

Collectively, the findings from the consumer aspect of the PCBM – Part II (H1–H4) provide evidence that consumers use their intuition about the odd-even psychological pricing strategy when interacting in the retail marketplace. The empirical evidence also supports the idea that the odd-even psychological strategy as a signaling mechanism creates an effective equilibrium condition in the fine-dining and quick-service segments of the restaurant industry. It must be noted that identifying the consumer learning process was not the objective of the current study. However, the learning processes described in the Persuasion Knowledge Model (PKM) and consumer-learning theories provides some basis for how consumers learn to associate 00 price endings with quality and 99 price endings with value.

Theoretical Implications

The findings from this research make a significant contribution to the understanding of the odd-even psychological pricing commonly practiced in the hospitality industry. The evidence strongly supports the theoretical rationale postulated by the Price-endings and Consumer Behavior Model (PCBM – Part II). It supports consumer response to 00 and 99 price endings strategy as intended by marketers (Naipaul, 2001), and that over time consumers learn to use 00 and 99 price endings as persuasion heuristics when the quality and value of products cannot be easily discerned. Implications from this study include:

(1) The current study provides a theoretical explanation for odd-even psychological pricing strategy in the hospitality industry.
(2) Consumers associate 00 price endings with quality and 99 price endings with value.
(3) Consumers use 00 price endings as a signal for quality when intending to purchase fine- dining restaurant products and services.
(4) Consumers use 99 price endings as a signal for value when intending to purchase quick- service restaurant products and service.

Managerial Implications

Managerial implications from the findings of odd-even psychological pricing strategy of the study are straightforward. The evidence suggests that when high-end hospitality firms desire to signal quality, the preferred price endings should be 00 price endings. On the other hand, when low-end hospitality firms want to signal high value, the preferred price endings should be 99 price endings. This is especially true for hospitality products, where quality and value are not easily discerned before consuming a product. Managers should be aware that consumers adapt appropriate response strategies when exposed to persuasion tactics. Managers should be cognizant of the process by which their actions can influence consumer beliefs and eventual purchase decisions. Marketers should keep in mind the process by which consumers' subjective perceptions are formed when exposed to persuasion episodes.

Limitations

The major limitation of the consumer response behavior of the PCBM – Part II is that the experimental design used was a between subjects design, which limited the statistical analysis. Finding an experimental design where subjects can respond to both fine dining and quick service menus without confounding the study may prove more insightful. This will provide a greater understanding as to how consumers respond to 00 and 99 price endings as persuasion heuristics for determining quality and value.

CONCLUSION

The marketing strategy of the odd-even psychological pricing has been an enigma in the marketing literature. For example, during the early 20th century, European wines were priced differently than American wines, denoting their superiority over the developing American wine industry. Similarly, during the Great Depression, diners in the Western USA started advertising "all you can eat under a buck" and "all you can eat for 99 cents" – specials to meet the needs of the new migrants from the Midwestern states. After that, low-end retailers began the just-under-a-buck pricing practice to promote the higher value associated with their merchandise and to differentiate their stores from the high-end retailers emphasizing high quality. Thus, psychological pricing is well established and has been used extensively as a marketing tool for over a century. In spite of its extensive use in business (including e-business), very few studies have explored the theoretical rationale for this ubiquitous phenomenon. The current study offers theoretical explanations and empirical support for how consumers respond to the odd-even psychological pricing practiced by hospitality marketers.

The current study sought to investigate the odd-even psychological pricing strategy through the posited Part II of *Price-endings and Consumer Behavior (PCBM)* developed from the review of literature resulting in four postulated hypotheses. The four hypotheses investigating how consumers respond to the odd-even psychological pricing in the PCBM (Part II) were supported.

Based on the finding of the current study, it appears that after repeated exposure to 00 and 99 price endings practice, consumers adopt these pricing endings as persuasion heuristics, signaling the quality and value of products in the hospitality marketplace. Collectively, findings from the postulated four hypotheses support the presented PCBM – Part II, indicating that consumers respond positively to the odd-even psychological pricing strategy as intended by marketers, resulting in an equilibrium effect. In conclusion, the research supports the findings of Naipaul and Parsa (2001). We recommend that the experimental design be revised and the study repeated to provide more robust evidence using different statistical methods. In addition, further research on the price ending pricing practice is recommended in other segments of the hospitality industry.

REFERENCES

Alpert, M. I. (1971). *Pricing decisions*. Glenview, IL: Scott, Foresman and Company.

Blattberg, R., & Neslin, S. A. (1990). *Sales promotion, concepts, methods and strategies*. Englewood Cliffs, NJ: Prentice-Hall.

Bliss, P. (1952). Price determination at the department store level. *Journal of Marketing, 17*(July), 37–46.

Boulding, W., & Kirmani, A. (1993, June). A consumer-side experimental examination of signaling theory: Do consumers perceive warranties as signals of quality? *Journal of Research, 20*, 111–123.

Broniarczyk, S. M., & Alba, J. W. (1994, January). Theory versus data in prediction and correlation tasks. *Organizational Behavior and Human Decision Processess, 57*, 117–139.

Chaiken, S. (1987). The heuristic model of persuasion. In: Zanna et al. (Eds), *Social Influence: The Ontario Symposium* (Vol. 5, pp. 3–39). Hillsdale, NJ: Erlbaum.

Collins, M., & Parsa, H. G. (2004). Innovative pricing strategies to maximize revenues in the hotel industry. Working Paper, the Ohio State University, Columbus, OH, USA.

Dalyrimple, D. J., & Haines, G. H., Jr. (1970). A study of the predictive ability of market period demand-supply relations for a firm selling fashion products. *Applied Economics, 1*(4), 277–285.

Feinberg, S. (1962). Quiet defiance of psychological pricing. *Women's Wear Daily, 104*(March, 11), 10.

Friedman, L. (1967). Psychological pricing in the food industry. In: P. Almarin & O. E. Williamson (Eds), *Prices: Issues in Theory, Practice, and Public Policy* (pp. 187–201). Philadelphia: University of Pennsylvania Press.

Friestad, M., & Wright, P. (1994). The persuasion knowledge model: How people cope with persuasion attempts. *Journal of Consumer Research, 21*(June), 1–31.

Georgoff, D. M. (1972). Odd-even retail price endings. East Lansing: Bureau of Business and Economic Research, Graduate School of Business Administration, Michigan State University.

Ginzberg, E. (1936). Customary pricing. *American Economics Review, 26*(June), 296.

Gregan-Paxton, J., & John, D. R. (1997). Consumer learning by analogy: A model of internal knowledge transfer. *Journal of Consumer Research, 24*(December), 266–284.

Halloway, R. J. (1968). Experimental work in marketing: Current research and new development. In: F. M. Bass, C. W. King & E. A. Pessemier (Eds), *Applications of the New Sciences in Marketing Management* (pp. 393–394). New York: Wiley.

Knauth, O. (1949). Consideration in setting retail prices. *Journal of Marketing, 14*(July), 1–2.

Kreul, L. M. (1982). Magic numbers: Psychological aspects of menu price. *Cornell Hotel and Restaurant Administration Quarterly, 23*(August), 70–75.

Lambert, Z. V. (1975). Perceived prices as related to odd and even price endings. *Journal of Retailing, 51*(Fall), 13–22.

Mason, J. B., & Mayer, M. L. (1990). *Modern retailing: Theory and practice* (5th ed.). Homewood, IL: BPI/Irwin.

Nagle, T. T., & Holden, R. K. (1995). *The strategy and tactics of pricing: A guide to profitable decision making* (2nd ed.). Englewood Cliffs, NJ: Prentice-Hall.

Naipaul, S. (2001). *The odd-even psychological pricing strategy and consumer response behavior in the restaurant industry*. Ph.D. Dissertation, The Ohio State University.

Naipaul, S., & Parsa, H. G. (2001). Menu price endings that communicate value and quality. *Cornell Hotel and Restaurant Administration Quarterly, 42*(1), 26–37.

Naipaul, S., & Parsa, H. G. (2004). *Odd-even psychological pricing strategy in the restaurant industry and marketers' intentions: A reciprocal phenomenon (PCBM Part I).* unpublished manuscript.

Parsa, H. G., & Hu, H. H. (2004). Price-ending practices and cultural differences in the foodservice industry: A study of Taiwanese restaurants. *Foodservice Technology, 4,* 21–30.

Pride, W. M., & Ferrell, O. C. (1997). *Marketing concepts and strategies* (10th ed.). Houghton-Mifflin.

Quigley, C. J., Jr., & Notarantionio, E. M. (1992). An exploratory investigation of perception of odd and even pricing. In: V. L. Crittenden (Ed.), *Developments in Marketing Science.* Chestnut Hill, MA: Academy of Marketing Science.

Raphael, M. (1968). Is 99 sense more than a dollar? *Direct Marketing, 76*(October).

Rudolph, H. J. (1954). Pricing for today's market. *Printers' Ink, 247*(May, 28), 22–24.

Schindler, R. M. (1984). Consumer recognition of increase in odd and even prices. In: T. C. Kinnear (Ed.), *Advances in Consumer Research* (Vol. 11, pp. 459–462). Provo, UT: Association for Consumer Research.

Schindler, R. M., & Kibarian, T. M. (1996). Increased consumer sales response through use of 99-ending prices. *Journal of Retailing, 72*(Summer), 187–199.

Schindler, R. M., & Kirby, P. T. (1997). Patterns of rightmost digits used in retail price advertising: Implications for consumer effects. *Journal of Consumer Research, 24*(September), 192–201.

Schindler, R. M., & Warren, L. S. (1988). Effect of odd pricing on choice of items from a menu. In: M. J. Houston (Ed.), *Advances in Consumer Research* (Vol. 15, pp. 348–353). Provo, UT: Association for Consumer Research.

Simmons, L., & Schindler, R. (2002). Cultural superstitions and the price endings used in Chinese advertising. *Journal of International Marketing, 11*(3), 101–111.

Spohn, R. F., & Allen, R. Y. (1977). *Retailing.* Englewood Cliffs, NJ: Prentice-Hall.

Stiving, M. A. (2000, December). Price-endings when prices signal quality. *Management Science, 46*(12), 1617–1629.

Stiving, M. A., & Winer, R. S. (1997). An empirical analysis of price endings with scanner data. *Journal of Consumer Research, 24*(June), 57–67.

Twedt, D. W. (1965). Does the 9 'fixation' in retail pricing really promote sales? *Journal of Marketing, 29*(October), 54–55.

Wingate, J. W., Schaller, E. O., & Miller, F. L. (1972). *Retail merchandise management.* Englewood Cliffs, NJ: Prentice-Hall.

Wright, P. (1985). Schemer schema: Consumer's intuitive theories about marketers' influence tactics. In: J. L. Richard (Ed.), *Advances in Consumer Research* (Vol. 13, pp. 1–3). Provo, UT: Association for Consumer Research.

Zeithaml, V. A. (1988). Consumer perceptions of price, quality, and value: A means-end model and synthesis of evidence. *Journal of Marketing, 52*(July), 2–22.

USES OF HOSPITALITY AND LEISURE SERVICES: VOICES OF VISITORS WITH DISABILITIES

Rachel J. C. Chen

ABSTRACT

There are more than 40 million Americans with disabilities. If U.S. hospitality and leisure professionals are keen to attract customers with disabilities, then the particular services in line with the needs of those individuals have to be addressed, given the lack of clear actions toward the service delivery to individuals with disabilities. This study attempts to discover the issues pertaining to the perceptions of the services and facilities offered to visitors with disabilities. A total of three thousand questionnaires are distributed to visitors with disabilities. Cross-tabulations, chi-square, and ANOVA are deployed to determine the differences among visitors with different disabilities. Promotion strategies, suggestions regarding accessibility issues, and the benefits associated with a visit to various destinations are also presented.

INTRODUCTION

Historically, people with disabilities were categorized by their medical condition or the level of self-sufficiency (Burnett & Baker, 2001). According to the American Disabilities Act of 1990 (ADA, 1990), individuals who are considered disabled

Advances in Hospitality and Leisure
Advances in Hospitality and Leisure, Volume 1, 89–102
ISSN: 1745-3542/doi:10.1016/S1745-3542(04)01006-9

under the act are "those individuals with physical or mental impairments that substantially limit one or more of the major activities of life, such as walking, talking, caring for oneself, or working" (ADA, 1990). The term also applies to someone who has a history of impairment, such as someone recovering from cancer or with a history of lower-back problems, as well as people who are regarded as having a disability, such as a person with disfiguring injury such as a burn or scar, even though the individual does not have any physical limitations. The physical conditions that are temporary, such as a broken leg, are not considered as disabilities (Burnett & Baker, 2001).

There are differences between the way disability is seen between Eastern and Western cultures. This is attributed to psychological and religious differences or due to political inequalities. In addition, the economic backgrounds of people with disabilities vary from one country to the other. According to United Nations projections, about 14% of the population of the Asia-Pacific region, by the year 2025 will be 60 years or older, and the region will be home to 56% of the world's older persons. For instance, in Western Australia more than 50% of the people over 60 years of age have a disability (Miles, 1982). Cameron (2003) reported that the senior population of developed countries (including North America, parts of Europe, Australia and New Zealand) is rising at an alarming rate and those countries have already started looking at barrier-free tourism offerings for people with disabilities.

It is estimated that the disabled traveler segment is a potential market of million individuals. This group with disabilities is expected to double by the year 2030 (Lach, 1999). It is now widely recognized that people with disabilities along with their assistants, family, and friends constitute a large potential consumer market segment. However, the development of this niche market would depend on how tourism industry addresses the issues of the accessibility to tourism opportunities. The European Disability Forum (2001) has supported the idea that the "tourism for all" approach makes good business sense. The European Commission handbook has estimated the clientele of consumers with disabilities to be a strong 35 million overnight travelers plus other accompanying friends and families. It is believed that by improving the quality of service for disabled people, the quality of services to those tourists without disability could also be improved accordingly.

Cavinato and Cuckovich (1992) found that the nature of the travel decision and travel choice is primarily governed by: (1) the available information specific to accessibility; and (2) the constraints faced by the nature of the disability. In last few years, the relevant efforts has been made in improving the accessibility to transportation for individuals with disabilities (Cameron, 2003). Abeyratne (1995) reported that the U.S. legislature and the United Nations have adopted measures to facilitate international travel by the elderly and the persons with disabilities.

Especially, aircraft manufacturers have contributed notably to achieve this agenda. Although the above progresses have helped increase the mobility of disabled travelers, there is a clear lack of systematic efforts of providing the necessary travel assistances and services dear to the individuals with disabilities (Cameron, 2003).

The National Council on the Handicapped estimated that in 1986 there were 36 million persons with disabilities in America. Over 6.5 million people used some specific aid for mobility (Cavinato & Cuckovich, 1992). Burnett and Baker (2001) reported that 60–70% of those classified as disabled in the United States are 65 and older. According to the Census 2000 Supplementary Survey (C2SS), about 14% of the total U.S. population has a long-lasting physical, emotional, or mental disability. The largest population segment of individuals with disabilities is between the ages of 21 and 64 that is in the work force, while more than 60% of seniors age 65 and above have a disability. Plausibly, the Americans with Disabilities Act stipulates that all businesses and services should be accessible to persons with disabilities. However, the problems of accessibility for the disabled have not been addressed sufficiently and effectively. If tourism and hospitality professionals are meant to provide leisure opportunities for all, serving the needs of persons with disabilities should be a top priority (Chen, 2002).

To supply the current deficiencies in visitor studies in connection with disabled customers, this research is to identify the perceptions of people with disabilities on the physical accessibility to various tourist attractions in Tennessee. The specific objectives of this research are twofold: (1) to collect data regarding physical accessibilities to hospitality and tourism services (e.g. accommodations, restaurants, and information centers); and (2) to render suggestions and recommendations that help consummate disabled visitors' trip experiences

METHOD AND FINDINGS

In general, the data were gathered from Tennessee households having at least one member with disabilities. In particular all participants in this study were: (1) adults who used mobility devices (e.g. manual chair, power chair, cane, walker, scooter, and crutches), personal assistants, service animals, or communication devices; (2) adults with hearing impairments; or (3) parents/caregivers of an individual with developmental disabilities and kids with disabilities.

Households that have an individual with disabilities were invited to participate in the study and asked to fill out the survey if they had have visited any attractions (traveled more than 100 miles away from home) in Tennessee during the previous 12 months. The questionnaires with postage-paid envelope were resent to those having not responded within two weeks after the first mail survey. A total of three thousand questionnaires were distributed to Tennessee households in 2001 and 2002. Of these questionnaires, 625 usable questionnaires were collected.

Cross-tabulations, frequency distributions, chi-square, and ANOVA tests were used to exam the differences among visitors with different disabilities by using a Statistical Analysis System (SAS) software package. The following sections report the key findings from the study.

Characteristics of Visitors with Disabilities

The study analyzed three groups of respondents that represent different types of persons with disabilities: (1) people with physical disabilities, for example, individuals who use mobility devices (wheelchairs, scooters, walkers, cane, crutches); (2) people with hearing impairments, for example, individuals who use the hearing aids; and (3) people with developmental disabilities. People with disabilities visiting Tennessee ranged between the ages of 3 and 100 with a mean age of 46 for all participants; with a mean age of 50 for the visitors with physical disabilities ($n = 495$); with a mean age of 59 for the visitors with hearing impairments ($n = 51$); and with a mean age of 12 for the individuals with developmental disabilities ($n = 79$).

Types of Assistances and Devices

The three most common assistances/devices used by the visitors with disabilities were canes (46%), manual wheelchairs (31%) and power wheelchairs (15%). The visitors with disabilities also used personal assistants (21%), walkers (20%), hearing aids (9%), communication devices (4%), animal assistance (1%), and other devices (16%).

Visitor Expectations/Perceptions of Physical Accessibility in the State of Tennessee

Participants were asked to rate their perceptions and experiences concerning the accessibility to those Tennessee attractions they visited. The above measurements were based on a seven-point scale, where 1 = not a problem, and 7 = major problem. The physical accessibility problems replied by *visitors with physical disabilities* ($n = 495$) were rough path/walkway surface (mean of 3.44 on a

1–7 scale, 1 = not a problem & 7 = major problem), and followed by narrow path/walkway width (mean = 3.29), lack of accessible restrooms (mean = 2.93), lack of curb cuts (mean = 2.66), lack of accessible drinking water (mean = 2.39), lack of accessible transportation (mean = 2.29), lack of accessible lodgings (mean = 2.09), lack of accessible eating places (mean = 2.05), lack of visibility (mean = 2.01), lack of appropriate telephone system (mean = 1.92), and lack of appropriate print media (mean = 1.82). As for visitors with hearing impairments, the problems on the Tennessee attractions were similar to the perceptions/experiences of visitors with physical disabilities.

The physical accessibility problems in Tennessee attractions to *visitors with hearing impairments* ($n = 51$) were rough path/walkway surface (mean = 3.29), and followed by narrow path/walkway width (mean = 2.87), lack of accessible restrooms (mean = 2.8), lack of accessible drinking water (mean = 2.74), lack of accessible transportation (mean = 2.55), lack of curb cuts (mean = 2.48), lack of visibility (mean = 2.23), lack of appropriate telephone system (mean = 2.12), lack of appropriate print media (mean = 2.05), lack of accessible eating places (mean = 2), and lack of accessible lodgings (mean = 1.76).

The physical accessibility problems in Tennessee attractions to *parents/ caregivers of kids with disabilities* ($n = 79$) were narrow path/walkway width (mean = 3.1), rough path/walkway surface (mean = 3.07), lack of accessible restrooms (mean = 2.8), lack of curb cuts (mean = 2.54), lack of accessible drinking water (mean = 2.04), lack of visibility (mean = 1.9), lack of accessible eating places (mean = 1.78), lack of accessible lodgings (mean = 1.73), lack of accessible transportation (mean = 1.7), lack of appropriate telephone system (mean = 1.69), and lack of appropriate print media (mean = 1.67). Differences in the "lack of accessible transportation" ($p < 0.052$) category for people with physical disabilities, people with hearing impairments and people with developmental disabilities were statistically significant at the 0.1 level (Table 1).

Trip Characteristics

Sources of Information Used
The four most important sources of information used while planning trips for visitors with physical disabilities were previous experience (49.9%), friends (37.87%), attraction brochures (36.27%), and relatives (35.49%). The four most common sources of information used while planning trips for visitors with hearing impairments were the previous experiences (48.98%), friends (48.94%), relatives (44.9%), and attraction brochures (32.65%). The four most important sources of information used while planning trips for visitors with developmental

Table 1. Visitors' Perceptions of Physical Accessibility in the State
of Tennessee.

Physical Accessibility	Physical (n = 495)	Hearing (n = 51)	Developmental (n = 79)	P
Lack of visibility	2.01	2.23	1.90	0.566
Lack of restroom	2.93	2.80	2.80	0.820
Lack of transportation	2.29	2.55	1.70	*0.052**
Lack of accessible drinking water	2.39	2.74	2.04	0.125
Lack of accessible lodgings	2.09	1.76	1.73	0.125
Lack of accessible eating places	2.05	2.00	1.78	0.387
Lack of appropriate print media	1.82	2.05	1.67	0.362
Lack of appropriate telephone system	1.92	2.12	1.69	0.318
Lack of curb cuts	2.66	2.48	2.54	0.787
Rough path/walkway surface	3.44	3.29	3.07	0.420
Narrow path/walkway width	3.29	2.87	3.1	0.454

Note: 1 = not a problem, 7 = major problem (reported with average grade).
* = Significant at the 0.1 level.

disabilities were previous experience (49.35%), attraction brochures (39.47%), friends (33.78%), and relatives (27.4%). The results indicated that the three types of visitors with disabilities using the sources of information [automobile clubs ($P < 0.018$), travel agents ($P < 0.001$)] may be considered as different (statistically different at the 0.05 level) (Table 2).

When the Trip was Planned
Differences in the trip plans of visitors with physical disabilities, visitors with hearing impairments, and visitors with developmental disabilities were not statistically significant ($p < 0.78$). Most people with physical disabilities planned their trips less than 3 months (89.35%) in advance, with 8.47% planning to go today, 16.71% planning less than one week in advance, and 16.71% planning between one and two weeks, 18.16% planning between 2 weeks and one month, and 29.30% planning between one and 3 months. Regarding visitors with hearing impairments and developmental disabilities, their trip plans were similar to the plans of people with physical disabilities (Table 3).

Types of Group
People with physical disabilities (88.75%), people with hearing impairments (85.42%) and people with developmental disabilities (97.19%) traveled with their families and friends ($P < 0.21$). At the 0.05 level, the results indicate that the three types of travelers were similar in the kinds of groups with which they traveled (Table 3).

Table 2. Sources of Information Used.

Sources of Information	Physical	Hearing	Developmental	P
Automobile clubs	n = 471	n = 50	n = 74	
Yes (%)	10.4	24	12.16	
No (%)	89.6	76	87.84	0.018**
Travel agents	n = 467	n = 49	n = 73	
Yes (%)	4.71	8.16	16.44	
No (%)	95.29	91.84	83.56	0.001**
Previous experience	n = 481	n = 50	n = 77	
Yes (%)	49.9	48.98	49.35	
No (%)	50.1	51.02	50.65	0.991
Attraction brochures	n = 477	n = 49	n = 76	
Yes (%)	36.27	32.65	39.47	
No (%)	63.73	67.35	60.53	0.737
Relatives	n = 479	n = 49	n = 73	
Yes (%)	35.49	44.90	27.40	
No (%)	64.51	55.10	72.60	0.137
Friends	n = 478	n = 50	n = 74	
Yes (%)	37.87	48.94	33.78	
No (%)	62.13	51.06	66.22	0.231
State maps	n = 474	n = 47	n = 73	
Yes (%)	19.83	21.28	13.70	
No (%)	80.17	78.72	86.30	0.432
Magazines	n = 470	n = 48	n = 74	
Yes (%)	14.47	14.58	14.86	
No (%)	85.53	85.42	85.14	0.996
Television	n = 471	n = 47	n = 74	
Yes (%)	15.07	21.28	14.86	
No (%)	84.93	78.72	85.14	0.527
Newspaper	n = 475	n = 48	n = 73	
Yes (%)	12.84	14.58	12.33	
No (%)	87.16	85.42	87.67	0.931
Radio	n = 468	n = 47	n = 72	
Yes (%)	7.69	8.51	11.11	
No (%)	92.31	91.49	88.89	0.613

**Significant at the 0.05 level.

Table 3.   Trip Planning.

	Physical	Hearing	Developmental	P
When the trip was planned	$n = 413$	$n = 45$	$n = 70$	
Planning to go today (%)	8.47	6.67	4.29	
Less than a week in advance (%)	16.71	17.78	25.71	
One – two weeks (%)	16.71	20.00	14.29	
2 weeks but less than 1 month (%)	18.16	13.33	21.43	
1 month but less than 3 months (%)	29.30	28.89	28.57	
Above 3 months (%)	10.65	13.33	5.71	0.78
Types of group	$n = 413$	$n = 45$	$n = 70$	
Family (%)	50.24	62.5	57.75	
Friends (%)	8.61	6.25	4.23	
Family and friends (%)	29.90	16.67	35.21	
Groups (church, tour, school) (%)	3.83	8.33	1.41	
Visited alone (%)	5.26	6.25	0	
Others (%)	2.15	0	1.41	0.21
Types of lodging	$n = 343$	$n = 41$	$n = 57$	
Hotel (%)	24.49	19.51	50.88	
Motel (%)	33.24	39.02	26.32	
Campground (%)	8.75	19.51	12.28	
With friends or relatives (%)	11.08	7.32	3.51	
Condominium/ resort (%)	5.54	7.32	3.51	
Others (cottage, cabin) (%)	16.91	7.32	3.5	0.002[**]

** Significant at the 0.05 level.

Types of Lodging

The three most common types of lodging used during the trips for visitors with physical disabilities were motels (33.24%), hotels (24.49%), and with friends or relatives (11%). The three most common types of lodging used during the trips for visitors with hearing impairments were motels (39.02%), hotels (19.51%), and with friends or relatives (19.51%). The three most common types of lodging used during the trips for visitors with developmental disabilities were hotels (50.88%), motels (26.32%), and with friends or relatives (12.28%). Differences in the types of lodging for three types of visitors with disabilities were statistically significant ($p < 0.002$) (Table 3).

Nights Away from Home

Most people with disabilities indicated that their trips did include an overnight stay away from home. No statistically significant difference ($p < 0.59$) was found in the nights/miles away from home of people with physical disabilities ($n = 413$, 2.2 nights, 261 miles), people with hearing impairments ($n = 45$, 2.3 nights, 279 miles), and people with developmental disabilities ($n = 70$, 1.9 nights, 190 miles).

Who Handled the Trip Expenses

The visitors with physical disabilities reported their trip expenses were handled by themselves (93.1%), shared with relatives/friends (5.17%) and paid by someone else (1.72%). The visitors with hearing disabilities reported their trip expenses were handled by themselves (96.97%) and paid by someone else (3.03%). The parents/caregivers of visitors with physical disabilities reported their trip expenses were handled by themselves (98.11%) and shared with relatives/friends (1.89%). The results indicated that the ways of handling the trip expenses for the three types of people with disabilities could not be considered statistically different at the 0.05 level.

Visibility Issues vs. Destination Choices

Differences in the destination choice of three types of people with disabilities were statistically significant ($p < 0.0001$). When asked if "lack of visibility" were one of the major problems in the surrounding communities of the attraction, would they like to revisit the place next time, nearly 85% of people with physical disabilities, 82% of people with hearing impairments and 60% of parents/caregivers of people with disabilities said "yes" respectively.

Good Places for Future Visits

When asked what would be good places for people with disabilities to visit in the future, the six most mentioned places for visitors with physical disabilities were zoos/aquariums (62%), mountain (61%), museum (58%), national parks (57%), beaches (51%), and theme parks (45%); the six most mentioned places for visitors with hearing disabilities were national parks (61%), beaches (61%), zoos/aquariums (59%), museum (58%), mountain (55%), and theme parks (54%); the six most mentioned places for visitors with developmental disabilities were national parks (60%), zoos/aquariums (55%), theme parks (53%), beaches (45%), mountain (41%), and museum (36%). Differences in the "museum" ($P < 0.032$) and "mountains" ($P < 0.048$) categories for three types of visitors with disabilities were statistically significant.

Motivation

The benefits important to visitors with physical disabilities were to relax (mean = 6.23 on a 1 to 7 scale), to increase fun/joy/enthusiasm (mean = 5.86), and to learn knowledge (mean = 5.30). The least important benefits to visitors with physical disabilities were to increase appropriate behaviors (mean = 3.67), and to improve attitudes toward school (mean = 3.42). For visitors with hearing impairments, the most important benefits were to relax (mean = 6.30 on a 1 to 7 scale), to increase fun/joy/enthusiasm (mean = 6.10), and to learn knowledge (mean = 5.60). The least important benefits to visitors with hearing impairments were to increase

Table 4.   Trip Motivations.

Motivations	Physical (n = 495)	Hearing (n = 51)	Developmental (n = 79)	P
To explore a new area	4.93	5.17	4.86	0.614
To learn/increase knowledge	5.30	5.60	5.11	0.648
To relax	6.23	6.30	6.32	0.790
To increase fun/joy/enthusiasm	5.86	6.10	6.18	0.143
To increase cooperation/trust	4.31	4.89	4.61	0.136
To gain knowledge from park/outdoor classrooms	4.20	4.65	4.29	0.315
To enhance self-esteem	4.40	4.77	4.62	0.407
To enhance social interactions	4.28	4.46	4.64	0.322
To increase appropriate behaviors	3.67	4.15	4.53	*0.0041***
To improve attitudes toward school	3.42	4.09	3.82	*0.092**
To improve physical health and fitness	4.96	5.60	4.88	*0.095**
To reduce anger, tension, frustration	5.16	5.48	5.13	0.602
To decrease sleep disturbance	4.54	4.17	3.70	*0.015***

Note: 1 = not at all important, 7 = very important (reported with average grade).
* Significant at the 0.1 level.
** Significant at the 0.05 level.

appropriate behaviors (mean = 4.15), and to improve attitudes toward school (mean = 4.09). For visitors with developmental disabilities, the most important benefits were to relax (mean = 6.32 on a 1 to 7 scale), to increase fun/joy/enthusiasm (mean = 6.18), and to reduce anger/tension/frustration (mean = 5.13). The least important benefits to visitors with developmental disabilities were to improve attitudes toward school (mean = 3.82) and to decrease sleep disturbance (mean = 3.70). Differences in the "increase appropriate behaviors" ($p < 0.0041$) and "to decrease sleep disturbance" ($P < 0.015$) categories for three types of travelers with disabilities were statistically significant. In addition, differences in the "improve attitudes toward school" ($P < 0.092$) and "to improve physical health and fitness" ($P < 0.095$) categories were also statistically significant at the 0.1 level (Table 4).

Socio-Demographic Characteristics

Education
Nearly 32% of visitors with physical disabilities had attended some college and 27% obtained a high school diploma. Twenty eight percent of visitors with hearing impairments had attended some college and 28% obtained a high school diploma. Twenty five percent of parents/caregivers of kids with disabilities had a four years college degree, 22% had attended some college and 23% obtained a high school

Table 5. Socio-Demographic Characteristics of the Respondents.

	Physical	Hearing	Parents/Caregivers	P
Education	n = 489	n = 50	n = 79	
Grade school (%)	2.04	4.00	1.27	
Some high school (%)	5.73	10.00	3.80	
High school diploma (%)	26.58	26.00	22.78	
Some college (%)	31.49	28.00	21.52	
Two years college (%)	13.50	8.00	13.92	
Four years college (%)	9.00	4.00	25.32	
Some graduate school (%)	6.54	8.00	5.06	
Master degree (%)	4.09	10.00	3.80	
Ph.D. Degree (%)	1.02	2.00	2.53	*0.011***
Income	n = 441	n = 46	n = 68	
Under $10,000 (%)	20.41	17.39	7.35	
$10,000–$19,999 (%)	21.54	17.39	10.29	
$20,000–$29,999 (%)	12.24	15.22	8.82	
$30,000–$39,999 (%)	12.02	10.87	23.53	
$40,000–$49,999 (%)	11.56	6.52	10.29	
$50,000–$59,999 (%)	8.84	8.70	24.71	
$60,000–$69,999 (%)	4.99	6.52	4.41	
$70,000–$79,999 (%)	2.72	6.52	7.35	
$80,000–$89,999 (%)	0.91	4.35	5.88	
$90,000–$99,999 (%)	1.81	2.17	2.94	
$100,000 or more (%)	2.95	4.35	4.41	*0.018***

**Significant at the 0.05 level.

diploma. Differences in the education categories were statistically significant at the 0.05 level ($p < 0.011$) (Table 5).

Income

Forty two percent of travelers with physical disabilities reported earning incomes totaling under $19,999. Of households of visitors with hearing impairments, 35% had income under $19,999 and 41% had income between $20,000 and $59,000 per year. Of households of visitors with developmental disabilities, 18% had income under $19,999 and 57% had income between $20,000 and $59,000 per year. Differences in the incomes of three types of travelers with disabilities were statistically significant ($p < 0.018$) (Table 5).

Age

The average age of people with physical disabilities (average age = 50.3) was significantly different ($p < 0.0001$) from that of people with hearing impairments (average age = 59) and developmental disabilities (average age = 12).

Occupation

Nearly 20% of the travelers with physical disabilities indicated that they were retired and 21% were homemakers. More travelers with hearing impairments appeared (39%) to be retired than general travelers with physical disabilities and parents/caregivers of kids with disabilities (19%). Nearly 33% of the parents/caregivers of kids with disabilities indicated that they were in the professional/managerial field. Differences in the occupation status of different types of travelers with disabilities were statistically significant ($p < 0.001$).

The results indicated that six of the ten trip characteristics for the three groups of travelers were statistically significantly different. These include: sources of information used, problems of the accessibilities, good places for future visits, visibility issues vs. destination choices, motivations, and the uses of types of lodging places. The results also summarized the demographic characteristics of the three groups of travelers and indicated that age, education, income, and occupation were statistically significantly different at the 5% level.

DISCUSSIONS AND SUGGESTIONS

The key findings of this study are that the differences in travel motivations, perceptions, trip-related characteristics, and socio-demographics exist among three types of visitors with disabilities. The parents/caregivers of visitors with developmental disabilities are more likely to be employed in professional occupations, and less likely to be retired. Visitors with physical disabilities and visitors with hearing impairments are more likely to plan their trips to the attractions in Tennessee between one weeks to three months in advance, more likely to stay away from home during their trips, and more likely to use previous experiences, friends, relatives, and attraction brochures for making their trip plans.

According to Cavinato and Cuckovich (1992), a disabled traveler has three options for making her/his travel plans – s/he can use the services of a regular travel agent; look for a tour agency that caters to travelers with disabilities; or plan the trip individually with the help of books and government publications on accessibility for tourists with disabilities. Marketers of tourism and hospitality products may consider using strategic marketing implications based on the key findings of this study. For example, the chambers of commerce and tourism operators which promote Tennessee as a vacation destination may add relevant information that helps create a positive image of Tennessee in regard to its accessibility to visitors with disabilities.

Since parents/caregivers of visitors with disabilities are using various sources of information (e.g. automobile clubs and travel agents) for their trip plans, marketers of tourism organizations may provide those parents/caregivers with specific travel information for visitors with disabilities on the internet to bring up the awareness of potential travel offerings in Tennessee. It is unarguable that sustaining travel business in Tennessee, tourism planners and service providers ought to understand visitors' motivations toward the tourism attracitions. This study finds that the motivations critical to visitors with both physical disabilities and hearing impairments are to relax, to increase fun/joy/enthusiasm, and to learn knowledge; for individuals with developmental disabilities, the most important motivations are to relax, to increase fun, and to reduce anger/tension/frustration. Since Tennessee has significant natural features (e.g. the Great Smoky Mountains National Park) and man-made attractions (e.g. the DollyWood amusement park), to position Tennessee as a regional scenic and recreational destination for travelers with disabilities could be a feasible marketing objective. For instant, marketers may create relevant slogans such as "enjoy the beauty of nature," "escape the humdrum of daily life," or "family-based destination" to the first-time visitors to Tennessee.

While traveling within the State of Tennessee, travelers with physical disabilities and hearing impairments both are apt to visiting zoos/aquariums, visiting mountains, museums, national parks, and theme parks. Burnett and Baker (1992) stated that pricing decisions are important to the individuals with disabilities. Strategically, while developing joint promotions mixing with nature sites, theme parks and museums, the marketers may reveal the special rate offered to travelers with disabilities.

The problems on the Tennessee attractions identified by visitors with disabilities are narrow path/walkway width, rough path/walkway surface, lack of accessible restrooms, and lack curb cuts. In order to increase the satisfaction of visitors with disabilities and provide an optimal visitor experience, the sites with high attendance (e.g. visitor centers) may consider adding more accessible restrooms, or providing maps showing all the nearest facilities that are open for visitors with disabilities in the surrounding communities of the tourism sites.

Surveys that help tourism practitioners identify destination problems as well as grasp the core segments of visitors would be a viable research agenda. Also, future studies may focus on the benefits sought by visitors with disabilities. Because of the budget constraints, this study could only focus on the travelers with disabilities in the State of Tennessee. It is plausible that future studies evaluate the motivation, perception and preferences issues that relate to travelers with disabilities from the state other than Tennessee.

REFERENCES

Abeyratne, R. I. R. (1995). Proposals and guidelines for the carriage of elderly and disabled Persons by Air. *Journal of Travel Research*, 34(4), 52–59.

Americans with Disabilities Act of 1990. *U.S. Department of Justice, Civil Rights Division.* [On-line]. Available: http://www.usdoj.gov/crt/ada/pubs/ada.txt.

Burnett, J. J., & Baker, H. B. (2001). Assessing the travel-related behaviors of the mobility-disabled consumer. *Journal of Travel Research, 40*(3), 4–11.

Cavinato, J. L., & Cuckovich, M. L. (1992). Transportation and tourism for the disabled: An assessment. *Transportation Journal, 31*(3), 46–53.

Chen, R. J. C. (2002). Visitor expectations and perceptions of physical accessibility in the Great Smoky National Park (Tech. Report for the National Center on Accessibility and U.S. National Park Service).

European Disability Forum (2001). EDF position paper on tourism: Framing the future of European tourism. (Doc. EDF 01/13 EN). Brussels, Belgium. [On-Line]. Available: http://www.edf-feph.org/Papers/pospaper/01–13/EDF01–13_EDFresponse_European_Tourism.pdf.

Lach, J. (1999, June). Disability ≠ liability. *American Demographics, 2*(2), 21–22.

Miles, M. (1982). Why Asia rejects western disability advice. [On-Line]. Available: http://www.pcs.mb.ca/%7Eccd/disbookl.html.

COLLABORATIVE SUPPLY CHAIN MANAGEMENT IN THE AIRLINE SECTOR: THE ROLE OF GLOBAL DISTRIBUTION SYSTEMS (GDS)

Marianna Sigala

ABSTRACT

Competition had traditionally been highly intense in the airline sector, forcing airlines to continually foster collaborative practices. Although Information & Communication Technologies (ICT) had always been the backbone of any airline collaborative practice, research investigating the role of ICT in supporting collaboration had been solely concentrated on Global Distribution Systems (GDS) and their impact on marketing practices. In this vein, the importance of GDS to support streamlined supply chains in the airline sector has been neglected. This paper aims to show how the functionality and core competences of GDS are exploited to facilitate collaborative supply chain management and enhance airlines' competitiveness.

INTRODUCTION

There are increasing changes and competition in the modern business environment, which features more customized products and services, globalization of markets

Advances in Hospitality and Leisure
Advances in Hospitality and Leisure, Volume 1, 103–121
ISSN: 1745-3542/doi:10.1016/S1745-3542(04)01007-0

and cost efficient production. Firms strive to achieve competitive advantage through satisfying customers effectively and efficiently. Effectiveness requires that firms be equipped with customer-focused common goals among all the related suppliers and partners, while business success now depends largely on the capability of quick response to customer requirements. Both suppliers and producers need to cooperate and coordinate in sharing the common goal of strategy of improving product quality and customer service level. Efficiency demands firms to meet customer requirements economically, which also calls for collaboration between suppliers and producers. Addressing these considerations, supply chain management (SCM) is encountering increased interest in both the academic and professional communities. SCM is a well-established discipline that involves the coordination of an organization's internal planning, manufacturing/production, procurement and distribution efforts with those of its external partners (i.e. suppliers, retailers etc). To reduce inefficiencies in the supply chain, firms are increasingly exploiting Information and Communication Technology (ICT) tools (Serve et al., 2002) to integrate systems and processes throughout their supply chain, as integration and synchronization among partners can eliminate excess inventory, reduce lead times, increase sales and improve customer service (Anderson & Lee, 1999). However, mere coordination amongst trading partners today is no longer enough to maintain a competitive advantage. Instead, companies are moving towards collaborative SCM in an effort to reduce the information imbalances that result in the dreaded "bullwhip effect" (Lee et al., 1997) and increase their responsiveness to market demands and customer service (Mentzer et al., 2000). Collaborative SCM is continually being recognized as an effective tool of survival and maintenance of long-term advantages in global and heavily competitive market (Folinas et al., 2004; McLaren et al., 2002; Rudberg et al., 2002). Indeed, much earlier, Christopher (1992) had advocated that leading-edge companies have realized that the real competition is not company against company, but rather supply chain against supply chain.

The airline sector is not an exception of such developments. Airline collaboration and alliances have been a heavily adopted and effective practice for competing in the global market. Indeed, nowadays, competition in the airline industry has emigrated from the single airline level to the airline supply chain level, whereby three major airline alliances represent the majority of international passengers (Table 1). However, airline collaboration practices have primarily focused on enhancing upstream supply chain processes (e.g. distribution, marketing, customer service etc.) whose coordination and synchronization is being enabled and fostered by Global Distribution Systems (GDS).

In this vein, research has neglected to investigate the role of GDS to streamline both upstream and downstream supply chain processes and foster collaborative

Table 1. The Marketing Power of the Major Airline Alliances.

	Leaders	Members	M Pax	M $ Revenue
One word	AA, BA	8 + Swiss Cathay Pacific Iberia, Qantas etc.	214 (13.3%)	46,541 (14.1%)
Sky team	Delta, AF	6 + KLM Alitalia etc.	202 (12.5%)	37,550 (11.4%)
Star alliance	United, LH	15 + U.S. Air	301 (18.6%)	69,589 (21.1%)

Source: Airline Business 07/03.

practices in the whole airline supply chain. Moreover, although the contribution and impact of operations research on airline management is widely recognized (e.g. Barnhart et al., 2003; Smith, 2000), such arguments and debates have been concentrated on the use of operations management tools for developing and solving statistical models supporting day-to-day airline operational problems, e.g. revenue management – fare mix, optimization of schedule planning etc. On the contrary, the impact of operations management on supporting strategic and tactical airline decisions has been neglected. Thus, the main purpose of this paper is twofold: (a) illustrate the value and role of collaborative SCM operations management theories on the development of competitive airline strategies; and (b) show how airlines use and could also further exploit the functionality and core competences of GDS in order to streamline and synchronize their whole supply chain for achieving collaborative SCM benefits and enhancing their competitive advantage. To achieve these, first a literature review is conducted for identifying and analyzing collaborative business processes with a SCM focus. As there is a lack of research regarding SCM in the airline sector, theories and arguments are borrowed from the generic operations management field, but these are then adopted within the airline context. Overall, based on this analysis, collaborative SCM processes are first identified and then examples and current practices illustrating how GDS functionality supports the former are provided. Finally, some concluding remarks and suggestions for future research are presented.

COLLABORATIVE SCM GOALS AND PROCESSES

Several definitions of SCM exist nowadays. Recently, the globalization of markets has forced research and firms to not only consider material, information and customer flows in the traditional value chain, but rather in a network of facilities. First of all, it is important to include a customer perspective in the supply chain definition. Second, most companies today try to work with processes and not functions. Third, a collaborative environment is starting to grow and it is better to study organizations than linked facilities. A relatively "old" definition encompasses all these issues and so this will be the definition used throughout this paper. So, according to Christopher (1992, p. 12) a supply chain is:

> ... the network of organizations that are involved, through upstream and downstream linkages, in the different processes and activities that produce value in the form of products and services in the hand of the ultimate consumer.

Turning to the management of supply chain, the Global Supply Chain Forum provides a definition of SCM that follows logically from Christopher's definition of supply chain:

> supply chain management is the integration of key business processes from the end user through original suppliers and information that add value for the customer and other stakeholders (Lambert et al., 1998, p. 1).

Managing with a *process* rather than a function focus is quite important as the latter usually leads firms to manage only their part of the supply chain (Lambert et al., 1998). Function based SCM results in detrimental "bullwhip effects" whereby the effects of uncertainty in demand and lead times cause order sizes and times to be inflated the further up the supply chain and away from the end customer you get (Lee et al., 1997). The result is excess and obsolete inventory to be kept along the supply chain. Converting to the airline sector, lack of communication regarding demand patterns among retailers and airlines crucially harm the optimization of seats and fares inventories along the supply chain leading to the negative effects of overbookings and underbookings. Thus, with increased coordination of the supply chain and by making end-customer demand information readily available to the entire supply chain, the bullwhip effect can be reduced and there is limited amplification of uncertainty along the chain (Lee et al., 1997). GDS have been for long gathering demand information through travel agents and other retailers and then pushing it back to airlines. Indeed, GDS had been a crucial tool enabling airlines to exploit this market intelligence for gaining and maintaining competitive advantage and market shares in the hypercompetitive e-marketplaces (Sigala, 2003a).

However, in order to optimize the entire supply network and not just create local optima in one or two partners, the organizations must jointly make supply chain and demand decisions that create sustainable value for all involved. In this vein, collaborative SCM goes beyond mere exchanging and integrating information between suppliers and their customers, and involves tactical decision making amongst the partners in the areas of collaborative planning, forecasting, distribution and product design (Kumar, 2001). Collaboration also involves strategic joint decision making about partnership and network design. The benefits of collaborative SCM is not only the reduction of waste in the supply chain through reduced process costs, inventory levels and product costs that result from the coordination of actual demand with supplier production plans, but also the increased responsiveness, improved customer service and satisfaction, better understanding of end-customer needs throughout the entire chain (market intelligence) and competitiveness amongst all members of the partnership (Mentzer et al., 2000). Thus, collaborative SCM systems allow organizations to progress beyond mere operational-level information exchange and optimization and

Table 2. Supply Chain Business Processes.

VICS (2000)	Norris et al. (2000)	Hoque (2000)	Kalakota & Robinson (1999)	Cooper et al. (1997)
Auction/reverse auction	Supply Chain Replenishment	Demand planning	Order commitment	Customer Relationship Management (CRM)
Request for quotation (RFQ)	e-procurement	Supply planning	Advanced scheduling	Customer Service Management
Request for proposal (RFP)	Collaborative planning	Logistics	Demand planning	Demand Management
Purchase order release	Collaborative product development	Production planning/fulfillment	Transportation planning	Order fulfillment
Collaborative planning, forecast and replenishment (CPFR)	e-Logistics		Distribution planning	Manufacturing flow management
Vendor managed inventory (VMI)			Order planning	Procurement
Transportation and shipment tracking			Replenishment	Product development & commercialization
Demand forecasting			Production planning	Returns channel
Promotion management			Distribution	
Buyer and seller organization				

can transform a business and its partners into more competitive organizations. In summary, as Folinas et al. (2004) illustrated firms can experience a greater level of benefits as, by exploiting ICT advances, their supply chains evolve from an internal focus on business logistics to more collaborative relationships.

However, despite the importance of process management in collaborative SCM, a literature review aiming to identify the critical business processes of collaborative SCM revealed the lack of a universally accepted framework. Indeed, as Table 2 illustrates different authors have identified a series of collaborative SCM processes. On the other hand, the Supply Chain Council has followed a different structure for classifying collaborative SCM processes. Its Supply Chain Operation Reference (SCOR) model categorizes the supply chain processes into five major processes building blocks namely Plan, Source, Make, Deliver and Return. Although the model was initially regarded as an intra-firm activity, recent versions and analysis of the model encompasses inter-firm activity giving it a collaborative nature. However, as the definition of the major process building blocks of the SCOR model is straightforward and easily comprehensive, this structure has been used for classifying the previously identified SCM business processes. Hence, processes presented in Table 2 were classified as Plan, Source, Make or Deliver processes depending on their characteristics (Table 3).

Table 3. Supply Chain Processes (as in Table 2) Categorized with the SCOR Model as Reference.

Plan	Source	Make	Deliver
CPFR	Auction/reverse auction	Production planning/fulfillment	VMI
Collaborative planning	Buyer and seller aggregation	Order commitment	Replenishment
Demand planning	(e)-procurement	Order planning	E-logistics
Demand forecasting	RFQ	Advanced scheduling	Logistics
Supply planning	RFP	Production process	Distribution
Transportation planning	Purchase order release		Transportation and shipment tracking
Promotion management			Customer Relationship Management (CRM)
Collaborative product development			Customer Service Management
Product development & commercialization			Order fulfillment

COLLABORATIVE SCM IN THE AIRLINE SECTOR

Collaboration within the airline sector is widely accepted as a highly beneficial and of strategic importance practice for several reasons (Evans, 2001; Gudmuudsson & Rhoades, 2001; Morrish & Hamilton, 2002). The major services and operations in which airline collaborative alliances mainly concentrate are: joint sales and marketing; joint purchasing; joint insurance; joint flights; improved flight connections; code-sharing; links between FFPs; shared airport facilities (check in, business lounge, gates etc); wet leasing; block seat arrangement. Overall, the major motivation and benefits that push airlines to form such collaborative practices are summarized as follows:

- Increased market reach (including access to new markets via partner airlines and bypassing bilateral restrictions).
- Cost control.
- More efficient supply of capacity.
- Traffic feed, e.g. interline hubbing (particularly between domestic and international flights, i.e. the link with regional airlines, whereby bilateral agreements do not offer opportunities for serving the market/route).
- Economies of marketing.
- Technical advantages.
- Shared Computer Reservation Systems (CRSs) and other ICT applications.
- Retention of independence.
- Economies of scale, scope and learning; e.g. group purchasing, focus on one type of aircraft maintenance:
  - Access to benefits of another firm's assets.
  - Reduced risk by sharing it.
  - Defense of current markets and trends towards globalization.
  - Addressing processes of deregulation and liberalization (for interline and serving different routes which were not possible).
  - Survival.

However, despite the above mentioned arguments, there has not been any systematic and theory-based analysis illustrating the rational, business value and importance as well as impact and interrelationships of such airline collaborative practices. To address this gap, after debating the business importance of collaborative SCM, the framework of collaborative SCM processes (as presented in Table 3) was applied and adapted within the airline sector. Table 4 summarizes the findings of this approach. Table 4 also provides the different and major business/organizations involved in each collaborative practice as well as the way/role in which the GDS functionality and tools support each collaborative

Table 4. Collaborative Processes in Airline SCM and the Role of GDS.

SC Processes	Supply Chain Function	Major Airline (Collaborative) Processes	GDS Functionality and Support for Collaborative SCM	Players Involved
Plan	Product planning and development	Schedule design: identification of routes; number and types of aircrafts (capacity) to serve routes; frequency of routes/schedules; pricing; hub and spoke systems vs. point-to-point flights; purchase, leasing and development of aircrafts	Competitive Information as well as demand data gathered by GDS are used to support such decision-making	Airline manufacturers; Airlines; Governments; Associations; Airports
Source	Procurement	Procurement of major resources: Fuel; Human resources; In flight catering and amenities; Aircrafts; Slots/gates and other airport facilities (business lounges), e.g. slow swapping	"Aero-Xchange" an online marketplace set up by Lufthansa, in cooperation with most of the Star Alliance partners, that offers industry-specific goods and services ranging from special screws to aero-engines. This system is totally supported demand information and forecasts gathered from GDS; GDS demand data and requirements forwarded to in flight caterers for preparing amount and type of meals; GDS demand forecasts and data required for supporting the crew scheduling and pairing functions, as well as the baggage handling processes (delayed, lost baggage),	Suppliers; Airlines; Airports; Airline manufacturers; Airline alliances

Make	Production/operations	Fleet assignment; Aircraft maintenance routing; Crew scheduling, pairing and assignment; Travelers check in, airport services/amenities, in flight entertainment and catering services, airport management, luggage handling	GDS are the corporate systems of major airlines, i.e. the systems that airlines use for handling most of their operating day to day functions, e.g. check in, crew scheduling rotating, yield management, FFP, catering requirements of travelers etc. GDS also support remote check in and other operations (e.g. sms alerts for gates and time changes) through mobile devices	Airlines, Handling companies, In flight catering companies, Insurers, Technicians, Fuel companies, Etc.
Deliver – Marketing	Promotion and pricing	Promotion, information and distribution points of sale, marketing campaigns, campaign management, customer communication, pricing and (network) yield management	GDS are and/or support the different electronic or not point of sales; GDS also gather marketing intelligent; GDS support and enable YM; GDS enable customer communication through their FFP functionalities, e.g. newsletters, e-mail alerts, CRM etc. GDS support web-based airline co-opetition models e.g. opodo.com, orbitz.com (for bypassing the travel agencies); GDS support CRM practices, e.g. FFPs	GDS; Travel agents; Airlines point of sales; Consolidators; Web based distributors
	Distribution	Creation of sales points; Distribution of the paper ticket to the customer; Technological support of the e-tix	GDS support several sales points; GDS are also the backbone of several web-based travel agencies, infomediaries and airlines' websites; GDS are required for printing/issuing tickets; GDS are the backbone of several airlines for enabling their e-tix (electronic ticketing) for by-passing travel agents	Distributors with GDS access/availability; Airlines
	After sale support	Customer communication and support/service: cancellations, changes, delays, confirmation of flights, lost luggage tracing, travel/itinerary information	GDS support online CRM and Customer Service management practices: GDS support services such as checkmytrip.com for online customer services; GDS support online luggage tracing facilities	Travel agents; Airlines; GDS; Web based distributors

process. As discussed below, the major findings of this analysis clearly demonstrate that airlines do not anymore compete amongst each other. Instead, the level of competition has nowadays risen amongst different airline supply chain networks, which by fostering and supporting collaborative SCM practices aim to optimize the value of their whole supply network by enhancing its competitive advantage and the value of its external and internal customers.

Product Planning and Development

Schedule design, i.e. the identification of markets and routes as well as the frequencies airlines will use for serving the needs of the former, is considered as one of the major decisions that airlines should take as concerns their product development process. However, membership in an airline alliance implies that such decisions are taken collaboratively with other airline partners, as the overall aim of the supply chain network is the optimization of the market value and coverage of the network so that resources of each network partner are exploited at a maximum. The purchase, lease of aircrafts and other resources, the introduction of new routes balancing the trade-offs of point-to-point flights and the design of hub and spoke systems, the selection and introduction of new airline partners for optimizing network reach/service are some of the most important decisions in the product development process. For example, the proliferation of hub and spoke systems has forced planning departments to manage their network as a whole by scheduling departure waves and coordinating flights. Critical data required to support such decisions are demand patterns (e.g. historic traffic data, previous load factors, reservations lead times) and forecasts. Planning departments use Integrated Flight Schedule Management Systems to support airlines in planning their schedules. However, such systems need to provide seamless integration with other systems, including Operations Control, Reservations and Revenue Management, Maintenance Control, and Crew Management. Moreover, by collaborating with supply chain members to establish a joint forecast, uncertainty on demand within the supply chain is reduced and so demand amplifications are avoided. In this vein, external integration of such Integrated Flight Schedule Management Systems with other network partners is required.

GDS are the major source of demand data, but as it is revealed (Sigala, 2003b) GDS owner airlines use several techniques (e.g. delays, differential formats and payments for information provision) for inhibiting other airlines obtaining such data on time. As GDS owner airlines also belong to one of the major airline alliances (e.g. Lufthansa is Amadeus owner airline and Star Alliance member, American Airline is Sabre owner airline and Oneword member), it becomes evident that airline membership in one of the airline alliances, i.e. supply chain network, can critically affect their demand forecasting and product development processes. On the other hand, competition among airline supply chain networks at this process is reflected and translated as an ongoing competition to gather, disseminate, analyse and exploit demand data as they are captured from network partners including GDS, business and high street travel agents, online retailers empowered by GDS etc. Moreover, the motivation of airline's networks to create, control and support several sale points is not only driven by their aim to enhance their retail network (as it will be illustrated later), but also by their effort to gather and control as much as possible demand information. The latter has been clearly evident in British Airways' and Lufthansa's decisions to enable the purchase of tickets of other competing airlines in their websites. Of course, their aim was not to divert sales to their competitors (customers would have anyway click on other airline's websites if they could not find a flight), but rather to gather demand data from a sale that could have been lost anyway (Sigala, 2003b).

Other evidence of collaborative product development processes is also the effects that the introduction of A380 would have on the schedule design of airline alliances, whereby national airlines will mainly concentrate on long haul flights while regional airlines will serve as feeder airlines to big hub airports. Enhanced collaborations and cooperation would be needed for aligning flight times, enabling ticket interlining etc., with the overall aim to optimize the customer and assets value of the airlines' network, while differentiating it from other airline networks.

Source – Procurement

Airlines engage in collaborative procurement processes for two major reasons: (a) achieve economies of scale and scope in procurement, e.g. reduce costs of major resources and negotiate better purchase deals regarding maintenance, delivery times etc., through joint purchases; and (b) optimize the utilisation of resources by exchanging, swapping resources such as crew, aircraft, gates with other network airlines. The most remarkable example is the joint purchases of airbus aircrafts by Star Alliance partners, which in turn are operated and shared among Star Alliance airlines according to network needs. Recently, Lufthansa, in cooperation with most of the Star Alliance partners, has also set up the "Aero-Xchange" marketplace which is an airline industry online trading exchange that offers industry-specific goods and services ranging from special screws to aero-engines. Procurement marketplaces have become highly economical for airlines by making markets more transparent and by allowing companies to bundle their procurement volumes. Developing B2B applications and interconnecting extranet systems will support both airlines and their partners to streamline them and reduce their turnaround time at the airport. Moreover, clarity of communication and efficiency chain is critical for both controlling costs and delivering service. Finally, resource management systems such as maintenance control systems, eProcurement systems, technical documentation management systems and crew management systems are integrated with demand forecasting systems and other operational support systems in order to minimize out-of-service periods and service disruptions and maximize fleet and staff utilisation.

Production – Operations

Having planned its schedule, the major tactical operational decisions that an airline would need to consider are the following:

- Fleet assignment: specification of which size of aircraft to assign to each route;
- Aircraft maintenance routing: determination of each aircraft's route to ensure satisfaction of maintenance requirements;
- Crew scheduling: selection and assignment of crews to each flight to minimize crew costs.

To optimize resource performance without violating regulations and reducing service provisions, airlines need to gather and simultaneously analyze a huge amount and variety of information in order to co-ordinate the use of their resources. The latter is more efficiently achieved by the utilization of the following major ICT applications, which would need to be integrated with demand systems in order to coordinate production and resource utilization with actual and/or forecasted demand. So, Operations Control systems that support the automatic calculation and distribution of flight plans as well as other features, such as automatic consideration of all valid aeronautical restrictions, require inputs of demand data. In particular, Flight Watch collects and displays vital information, such as booking figures, passenger transfer information, critical weather conditions, crew rotations, airport limitations, etc. Moreover, as airlines usually have or they are part of a wide network of hubs to support, Station Control Systems monitor all kinds of connections on a hub and report on operational details, such as aircraft turns, crew connections, passengers, baggage, and cargo connections. Thus, all airlines and airports need to collaborate and work together to reduce aircraft turn-around times, shorten passenger connection times and increase resource utilisation. These systems also help station managers plan their operations and ensure that all resources are in place to service each flight. In addition, Maintenance Control systems used to coordinate aircraft maintenance, commercial, and operational requirements, and

Crew Management Systems used for undertaking pairing construction, roster generation, and crew control, also need to be coordinated with all associated activities, such as flight scheduling, network requirements, operations control, crew contact, flight briefing, etc.

Overall, it becomes evident that collaborative demand planning is the starting point and the major process upon which all other collaborative SCM process are developed. However, the role of GDS in production and operations is extended further. For example, GDS are the corporate operating systems (i.e. the systems handling with check in, FFPs) of major airlines (e.g. Amadeus for Lufthansa and Austrian Airlines). GDS technology is also nowadays used for other operational activities and services such as remote check-in and SMS-mobile phone alerts for gates and time changes and flight cancellations.

Promotion and Pricing

GDS technology and systems are the backbone and enabling tool of several airline collaborative promotional initiatives and Customer Relationship Management Programmes (online and offline), such as the Frequent Flyer Programmes (FFPs). The marketing intelligence gathered by GDS is exploited by airlines (collaboratively and/or individually) for developing and implementing campaigns and promotions (e.g. online contests, auctions), facilitating customer communication (e.g. newsletters, SMS and e-mail alerts). The most evident and recent collaborative promotional activity has been the development of the two "co-opetition" e-commerce models of the airline marketspaces opodo.com and orbitz.com. These represent a collaboration among competing airlines (European based airlines in the former website and American based airlines in the latter) along with the support and empowerment of the relative GDS (e.g. Amadeus and Sabre respectively). The motives and benefits of such collaborative practices are several among which the major are: (a) address online competition coming from numerous travel webstores by creating a marketspace that provides flights and fares transparency (e.g. not all websites of airlines can support this); (b) create a marketplace that provides good customer value and service comparable with that of travel agents, so that airlines could collaboratively bypass the travel agents and reduce their distribution costs.

The GDS marketing intelligence also consists an indispensable input of yield management systems that try to optimize airline revenues by determining fare-mixes and overbooking rates. However, nowadays pricing and fare class mixes is frequently done collaboratively among airline network partners with the aim to optimize the network revenue. The concept of yield network management is widely applied, while several models have been developed and implemented in order to maximize yield at a network level.

Distribution

The role and importance of GDS for airline distribution and creation of sale points has been widely discussed and recognised for very long (e.g. Knowles & Garland, 1994). However, the advent of the Internet and the subsequent introduction of several travel webstores, each one implementing different e-commerce business models, have not only challenged but at the same time they have enabled innovation within the airline distribution chain. In particular, as Sigala (2003b) illustrated in her study e-commerce applications not only reduced, but on the contrary they increased the importance of GDS in airline e-distribution. Specifically, the GDS technology is the booking engine behind several webstores belonging to different distribution players such as airlines, online travel agents and tour operators, corporate travel agents, virtual stores, auction websites etc. The case of Amadeus that created e-travel.com, a spin off company selling online airline booking solutions for any type of webstores, clearly illustrates the previous argument. As previous studies also report, around 80% of online airline reservations are supported/empowered by GDS technologies (Connolly & Sigala, 2001). The benefits of this GDS distribution expansion strategy are, apart from the revenue streams coming from the technology support, the increased flight sales and demand data for the network airline partners. Moreover, as GDS also represent airline alliances, it becomes evident how the GDS distribution expansion strategy further supports the collaborative demand planning and so, all its supported collaborative SCM processes, e.g. product development and operational processes.

Thus, overall, instead of creating electronic markets (i.e. increased transparency of products and prices and mobility among webstores), the Internet has created electronic airline hierarchies empowered by GDS that in turn support the development of certain airline supply networks. Sigala (2003b) classified the airline electronic hierarchies that are controlled and empowered by GDS in three major categories of webstores: (a) forward/consumer biased marketplaces, e.g. reversed/auction markets; (b) regional and/or backward (supplier or distributor) biased marketplaces; (c) global marketplaces. Nowadays, most of these marketplaces are personalising their product/services in order to lock-in customers (e.g. my expedia.com), while Sigala (2003b) advocated that soon, Internet ubiquity and accessibility from mobile devices will lead to totally one-to-one personalised marketplaces offering services/products customised to each person, his/her location and circumstances at any time. In such case, airline networks would be able to maximise network yield management by applying one-to-one yield management pricing policies that would differentiate fares based on the reservation date, distribution channel and individual customer.

Airline distribution does not only involve the dissemination of flight schedules and fares but also the distribution of airline tickets. GDS have been the major tool enabling airlines and its distributors issuing/printing tickets. However, the use of travel agents corresponds to commission costs for airlines, while the issue of tickets has been one of the few customer services that online travel agents cannot provide. To address the latter, e-tix (the paperless ticket enabling customers to fly without a physical ticket) has been introduced as a co-operation among GDS and airlines (Christou et al., 2004). However, as the major disadvantage of e-tix nowadays is its limitation to handle complex tickets among different airlines, further collaboration among GDS and all network airlines is required for enabling such interlining possibilities with e-tix.

After Sale Support

Airline alliances and the respective GDS have also collaborated for exploiting the GDS backbone technology and offering after sales support systems. The latter include a series of several CRM and Customer Service management practices of which the most well known are checkmytrip.com by Amadeus and getthere.com by Galileo. These websites offer customers (business and individuals) the possibility to find any information about their flights, itineraries, destinations, airports facilities, destination weather and travel requirements etc by simply entering their PNR number and surname.

Summarizing the Role of GDS in Airline Collaborative SCM Processes

Process collaboration has been found to be the most important element in achieving optimum network performance in the airline supply chain. Specifically, following Chan and Qi (2003) process-based approached for measuring supply chains' benefits, two major types of benefits of collaborative SCM are found in the airline chain:

- Responsiveness to market:
  - Service level gains.
  - Market intelligence gains.

○ Cycle time reduction, i.e. flight scheduling based on demand data, flight sales until the last minute and development of flight product packaging (e.g. special in flight meal etc) in short turns.
- Supply chain cost reduction:
  ○ Process cost reduction, e.g. economies of scope and scale, avoidance of idle resources.
  ○ Increased load factors and enhanced yield rates.
  ○ Reduced aircraft operating costs.

GDS are also found to be one of the major tools for enabling such collaboration along the whole supply chain. Specifically, it was revealed that GDS foster and support supply chain process collaboration through information sharing and logistics coordination/integration (Lee, 2000). Overall, based on the above analysis, it becomes evident that:

- GDS are found and support all the processes in the airline supply chain
- GDS gather *and control* the competitive information that is necessary for enabling decision making and developing competitive strategies.
- Marketing intelligence is primarily available only to GDS owner airlines which are also leading members of major airline alliances. In this vein, airline alliances exploit GDS information for enhancing their collaboration processes in the supply chain and optimizing their network performance. In other words, GDS have fostered and support competition among airline supply networks.

Finally, it can be concluded that GDS and airline alliances are enabling collaboration, control and optimum network performance in the airline industry both vertically (within the airline supply chain, e.g. suppliers, partners) and horizontally (for each individual airline within the airline sector itself).

CONCLUSIONS AND IMPLICATIONS FOR FUTURE RESEARCH

Nowadays, all firms and particularly airlines need to develop effective coordination within and beyond their traditional business boundaries in order to maximize the potential for converting competitive advantage into profitability. In this vein, by applying operations management theories, this paper illustrated the role and importance of collaborative SCM in creating competitive airline strategies at a network level. Specifically, a framework of collaborative SCM processes within the airline supply chain was developed which illustrated how the structure of activities within and between companies is a critical cornerstone of creating unique and superior chain performance. Indeed, competitiveness and profitability increases when internal key activities and processes are linked and managed across multiple network companies. The analysis has also demonstrated the role and importance of GDS in fostering and supporting network collaboration as an information sharing and logistics integration tool among network partners. Overall, findings supported a widely accepted argument that the company that is most closely aligned to consumers or end-users at the point of sales (i.e. the GDS in the airline chain) eventually becomes the channel master and control of its supply chain (Serve et al., 2002). Overall, it becomes evident that studies examining the future role of GDS in the competitive airline sector arena are granted of huge industry and academic interest.

However, although technology is one of the major and enabling factor for supporting supply chain collaboration, other factors such as relationship linkages and trust, culture and strategy integration among network partners have also been recognized as vital determinant collaboration factors. However, limited research has so far aimed to develop the meaning of the coordination concept in the supply chain and then examine its role on supply chain performance as well as investigate the impact of soft organizational factors on the success of coordination (Simatupang et al., 2002). In this vein, it is important that future research would address and investigate the impact and role of factors such as commitment, trust, business understanding, risk sharing and partnership quality on collaborative SCM practices. The role and importance of organizational factors are particularly critical within the airline sector which has been operated for long time under subjective and, not business profitability criteria and strategic aims such as national pride.

Moreover, given the business opportunity costs involved with collaboration practices, future studies should aim to help individual airlines in their decisions on how to assess and select amongst different collaboration proposals. To achieve that, studies should concentrate at developing a framework that would summarize and balance the different collaboration benefits and costs such as partnership opportunity costs, while it would also identify the various environmental parameters that may affect such cost-benefit modeling. Finally, as collaborative SCM result in the reassessment of the way businesses are managed, it is argued that a whole stream of new research directions should be developed that would aim to adopt and investigate the applicability of management strategies at a supply chain level. For example, although most research has focused on the application and role of Total Quality Management (TQM) within one business, future studies should examine and illustrate how TQM practices can expand beyond traditional business borders and be adapted at an inter-enterprise level.

REFERENCES

Anderson, D. L., & Lee, H. L. (1999). Synchronised supply chains: The new frontier. In: D. Anderson (Ed.), *Achieving Supply Chain Excellence Through Technology* (pp. 83–99). San Francisco, CA: Montgomery Research.

Barnhart, C., Belobaba, P., & Odoni, A. R. (2003). Applications of operations research in the air transport industry. *Transportation Science, 37*(4), 368–391.

Chan, F., & Qi, H. J. (2003). Feasibility of performance measurement system for supply chain: A process-based approach and measures. *Integrated Manufacturing Systems, 14*(3), 179–190.

Christopher, M. (1992). *Logistics and supply chain management*. London: Pitman.

Christou, E., Avdimiotis, S., Kassianidis, P., & Sigala, M. (2004). Examining the factors influencing the adoption of web based ticketing: Etix and its adopters. In: A. Frew (Ed.), *Information & Communication Technologies in Tourism 2004* (pp. 129–138). Vienna: Springer Verlag.

Connolly, D., & Sigala, M. (2001). Major trends and IT issues facing the hospitality industry in the new e-economy. *International Journal of Tourism Research, 3*(4), 325–327.

Cooper, M. C., Lambert, D. M., & Pagh, J. D. (1997). Supply chain management: More than a new name for logistics. *The International Journal of Logistics Management, 8*(1), 1–13.

Evans, N. (2001). Collaborative strategy: An analysis of the changing world of international airline alliances. *Tourism Management, 22*, 229–243.

Folinas, D., Vlachopoulou, M., Manthou, V., & Sigala, M., (2004, forthcoming). Modeling the e-volution of supply chain: Cases and best practices. *Internet Research: Electronic Networking Applications and Policy.*

Gudmuudsson, S. V., & Rhoades, D. (2001). Airline alliance survival analysis: Typology, strategy and duration. *Transport Policy, 8*, 209–218.

Hoque, F. (2000). *e-Enterprise: Business models, architecture and components*. New York: Cambridge University Press.

Kalakota, R., & Robinson, M. (1999). *E-Business: Roadmap for success*. Reading, MA: Addison-Wesley.

Knowles, T., & Garland, M. (1994). The strategic importance of CRSs in the airline industry. *Travel and Tourism Analyst, 4*, 4–16.

Kumar, K. (2001). Technologies for supporting supply chain management. *Communications of the ACM, 44*(6), 58–61.

Lambert, D. M., Cooper, M. C., & Pagh, J. D. (1998). Supply chain management: Implementation issues and research opportunities. *International Journal of Logistics Management, 9*(2), 1–19.

Lee, H. L. (2000). Creating value through supply chain integration. *Supply Chain Management Review, 4*(4), 30–36.

Lee, H. L., Padmanabhan, V., & Whang, S. (1997). Information distortion in a supply chain: The bullwhip effect. *Management Science, 43*(4), 546–558.

McLaren, T., Head, M., & Yuan, Y. (2002). Supply chain collaboration alternatives: Understanding the expected costs and benefits. *Internet Research: Electronic Networking Applications and Policy, 12*(4), 348–364.

Mentzer, J. T., Foggin, J. H., Golicic, S. L., (2000) Collaboration: The enablers, impediments and benefits, *Supply Chain Management Review*, September/October, 28–36.

Morrish, S., & Hamilton, R. T. (2002). Airline alliances – who benefits? *Journal of Air Transport Management, 8*(6), 401–407.

Norris, G., Dunleavy, J. R., Hurley, J. R., Balls, J. D., & Hartley, K. M. (2000). *E-business and ERP: Transforming the Enterprise*. New York: Wiley.

Serve, M., Yen, D., Wang, J., & Lin, B. (2002). B2B-enhanced supply chain process: Toward building virtual enterprises. *Business Process Management Journal*, 8(3), 245–253.

Sigala, M. (2003a). Competing in the virtual marketspace: A strategic model for developing e-commerce in the hotel industry. *International Journal of Hospitality Information Technology*, 3(1), 43–60.

Sigala, M. (2003b). Evaluating the electronic market hypothesis in the airline distribution chain. In: A. Frew, M. Hitz & P. O'Connor (Eds), *Information & Communication Technologies in Tourism 2003* (pp. 193–201). Vienna: Springer Verlag.

Simatupang, T., Wright, A., & Sridharan, R. (2002). The knowledge of coordination for supply chain integration. *Business Process Management Journal*, 8(3), 239–308.

Smith. B. (2000). The impact of operations research on the evolution of the airline industry: A review of the airline planning process. Dallas, TX: Research paper, Sabre.

VICS (2000). Collaborative transportation management – A proposal. *Voluntary Interindustry Commerce Standards Association*, available at: www.cpfr.org.

MEASUREMENT ISSUES IN LEISURE RESEARCH: ACCURACY, BIAS, AND RELIABILITY

Tzung-Cheng Huan

ABSTRACT

The study of leisure consumption often involves estimating physical figures such as visits, attendance, and expenditures. However, the accuracy and reliability of such estimates are not adequately determined. It is evident that the misleading statistics arising from random variation may result into management mishaps. To address such a deficiency, this research first proposes that the information of the accuracy of estimation should be available. This study then presents appropriate ways of determining reliability and illustrates misconceptions of reliability measurement.

INTRODUCTION

By reviewing empirical investigations published from 1994 to 2004 in two leisure-related journals (*Leisure Sciences* and *Journal of Travel Research*), the study finds that most studies did not address the *accuracy* of trip estimates such as number of visits and trip expenditures, except by efforts: (a) to prevent non-response bias; or (b) by assuming bias did not exist and treating reliability as accuracy. To illustrate the importance of acquiring accuracy information for estimates, this study presents the following survey scenario involving the measurement of trip expenditures.

Advances in Hospitality and Leisure
Advances in Hospitality and Leisure, Volume 1, 123–132
ISSN: 1745-3542/doi:10.1016/S1745-3542(04)01008-2

Assuming 2500 out of 4000 questionnaires are collected from a visitor survey, the total amount of fees paid (TFP) by a travel party is analyzed. TFP includes event entry fees, lodging expense, parking charges, etc. It was determined that the average TFP by a party was $ü_f = \$185.50$. When data are collected by a survey of 4000 randomly, $û_f$ is equal to $200. The estimated mean-TFP $= û_f$ will generally not be exactly $185.50. This study generates simulation data under the assumption that the similar survey has been repeatedly administrated over 1000 times.

Simulation results are given in Fig. 1 where a curve shows the distribution of mean-TFP $(û_f)$. The points on the distribution curve identify the frequency with which a given rounded mean-TFP occurs. For example, 26 out of 1000 replications show that $û_f$ is rounded to $185. This is seen from 26 being the y-axis corresponding to the point (185,26). By the distribution curve being zero for $157 and $213, there were no replication in which $û_f$ was equal to $157 or $213. It is important to note that 15% of the replications have a $û_f$ equal to $200 or more. In this case, identical surveys may yield an estimate $14.50 more than

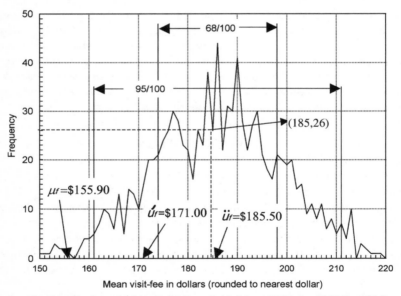

Fig. 1. The Distribution of Mean Total Fees Paid (Mean-TFP) for 1000 Replications of a Survey. *Note:* The biased mean-TFP, $ü_f$, around which rounded estimates for particular replications are distributed, is not the correct mean-TFP, μ_f. In other words, $ü_f$ is biased. The location of a less biased mean is shown by $ú_f$ and as such the location around which estimates based on that less biased survey would vary.

the mean-TFP. It is vital to recognize different values of TFP according to the distribution shown in Fig. 1.

First, although the distribution is shaped like a normal distribution, when going from dollar to dollar, it has large fluctuations. With 250,000 responses the fluctuations would be about one-tenth of the magnitude $[= (250,000/2500)^{1/2}]$ so the curve would look much more like a smooth bell-shaped normal distribution. Regardless of the fluctuations, the distribution tends to form a normal distribution (Devore & Peck, 1986, pp. 199–218) shape. Vertical lines, connected by "arrows" mark out areas of the curve in which 68/100 and 95/100 of $\hat{u}_f$ values are expected to occur. For example, 68/100 of the estimates tend to occur within one standard deviation $[s(\hat{u}_f)]$ of \$185.50 which is between \$173 and \$197. Based on being approximately normally distributed, 95/100 of the estimates occur within $\pm 2s(\hat{u}_f)$ of \$185.50.

So far the discussion on Fig. 1 has focused on sample means distributed around $\ddot{u}_f = \$185.50$. To further refine the statistical notation, let $f =$ TFP. The curve in the figure is for mean values of f so when n responses are received from 4000 interviews $\hat{u}_f = (1/n)\Sigma f$ where the sum of f is for n responses. As for $\ddot{u}_f = \$185.50$, $\ddot{u}_f$ can be though of as the average value of $\hat{u}_f$ that would be obtained based on a very large number of independent surveys. In other words, $\ddot{u}_f$ is the mean value of $\hat{u}_f$. A problem arises because $\ddot{u}_f = \$185.50$ does not imply that the actual mean-TFP is \$185.50. If the actual TFP is calculated by using accurate accounting information is $\mu_f = \$155.90$, then the correct estimate is $\hat{u}_f = \$155.90$ while the survey yields $\ddot{u}_f = \$185.50$.

In other words, the survey could overestimate the mean-TFP by \$29.60 (19%). $[= 100 * (185.50 - 155.90)/155.90]$. The measurement difference between actual and estimated values is referred to as bias. Recognizing the potential threats to the research findings, unlike most academic institutes, some statistics bureaus often attempt to address the bias issues. For example, a bias of 15% under estimation has occurred in the Canadian Travel Survey, which is administered by Statistics Canada (Beaman et al., 2001). Moreover, such an excessive bias is also found in the Fishing Hunting and Wildlife Relate Activity Survey executed by the U.S. Bureau of Census (Chu et al., 1992; FHWAR, n.d.).

However, the study is not to discuss the possible reasons creating bias. For relevant information, readers may review the works of Burton and Blair (1991) and a recent study by Krosnick (1999). Now, it is assumed a travel survey draws random "individuals but treats" a travel group as the unit of analysis. Individuals from a larger travel group have a higher probability of being selected than those from smaller parties. Logically, the total TFP tends to be higher for travel groups having more people. In this case, mean-TFP computed by $\hat{u}_f = (1/n)\Sigma f$ is expected to be overestimated. However, weighting methods can be deployed to eliminate bias. For example, in Canadian Travel Survey, a particular weighting scheme was adopted (Statistics Canada, 1997).

Alternatively, to correct such a problem, the following weighting procedure (w_i) can be introduced to reduce the contribution of those over sampled to the mean. The unbiased mean is computed as $\hat{u}_f = (1/\Sigma w_i)\Sigma f_i\, w_i$ where the sums are for the n responses received. In the case where bias relates to the number of respondents in the party, r_i, $w_i = 1/r_i$ where i refers to a particular party. Lastly, those biases that can be removed by weighting are considered as *estimation bias*. Unfortunately, not all kinds of bias are estimation bias. For instance, if a bias is caused by the respondents who underestimate/overestimate their travel expenditures, the problem can only be solved through further research which involves establishing a *standard* for TFP that has to be accurately determined and could be used for comparisons against the estimates.

In sum, there are reasons for introducing $\ddot{u}_f$, $\acute{u}_f$, and μ_f. It has been illustrated that bias can arise from different sources that influence the strategies of correct bias. Estimation bias can be eliminated by such methods as using weighting in making estimates. An estimate tending to be high by 20% can certainly lead to poor decisions. When bias is large, collecting a relatively large sample to get "accurate" results can be a waste of resources. If a sample size of about 2500 is being obtained so that the estimate of mean-TFP has a 68/100 chance of being within about 5% of its correct value, it could create a problem. Figure 1 shows that while 68/100 estimates are within about 6% ($= 100 \times 12/185$) of $185.50, bias of $29.60 with less than 10/100 of estimates are within 5% of $155.90. Why pay for such bias results from a large survey? Would it not have been better to spend money on a survey that gave less biased results?

While bias occurrence in leisure-related studies is not widely documented, a variety of studies have dealt with its presence (Beaman et al., 2002; Chase & Harada, 1984; Chu et al., 1992; Hwang et al., 2002; Lindblom et al., 1992; Tarrant & Manfredo, 1993). Recently, Crompton and Tian-Cole (2001) argued that common practices for bias reduction, such as those endorsed by Dilman (1978), might not be effective.

In physical sciences, accuracy is assessed by comparison to measurable standards (e.g. time, distance, and mass). Such an approach works because standards for time, distance, etc. can be established. For leisure studies, psychological constructs are often used that are subjective and abstract. However, trip estimates such as travel expenditures and number of participation can be observed, so that adopting the standard for estimates is feasible. Therefore, bias can theoretically be measured. However, to establish a standard (e.g. TFP) that only applies to a particular period of time (e.g. two years) is costly. Alternatively, a standard for TFP could be determined every 10 years.

Even if a standard is determined, bias is just estimated. It is not determined accurately. Since bias is the difference between the average of mean-TFP for many replications, e.g. $\ddot{u}_f = \$185.50$ and the correct value, mean-TFP must be approximated by the mean-TFP for one replication (e.g. for the 2004 survey). If the standard is determined as \$155 within $\pm\$5$ for about 68/100 surveys. For 2004 data in which $\hat{u}_f$ is equal to \$200 within $\pm\$12$ for about 68/100 surveys, the bias is estimated as $\hat{B} = \$200 - \$155 = \$45$ within $\pm\$12$. Being within $\pm\$12$ is based on error propagation theory for two independent observations calculated as $(\$5^2 + \$12^2)^{1/2}$ (NIST/SEMATECH, 2003; Statistics Canada, 1997). Given that \$45 is taken to be the bias, estimates for 2004 until 2013 could be reduced by \$45 when they should just be reduced by \$30. This means that on average the estimated would be low by \$15. This is presumably better than on average being high by \$30 (i.e. being out by \$30 is twice the error). Being out on average by 10% is better than being out by 20% but it is not as desirable as variation around the correct value.

Considering Reliability When Bias is Not Known

When the amount of bias, if any, in an estimate is not known, the term reliability should be used in reference to the variability in an estimate. However, accepting *that the amount of bias in an estimate is not known* may seem to suggest that there is something wrong with the research being done. Should research be carried out when one will not know how accurate the results are? Well, finding out how close estimates of expenditures, amount of participation in activities, hunting/fishing harvest, etc. are to the correct value of what is being estimated may be extremely difficult and/or costly. An option is assuming that, e.g. survey estimates, even if biased, are affordable information that can be obtained. Therefore, realistically, survey research is unlikely to cease because concerns with knowing estimate accuracy are posed.

Reporting the reliability of estimates (by use of effect sizes) has recently received attention (Gliner et al., 2001). Providing information on variability of an "effect" rather than just giving a probability ($p > 0.01$) an effect is significant has become a requirement for scientific publications. The 4th edition of APA manual states "You are encouraged to provide effect-size information" (APA, 1994, p. 18). However, the 5th edition states that "For the reader to fully understand the importance of your findings, it is almost always necessary to include some index of effect size or strength of relationship in your Results section" (APA, 2001, p. 25).

The concerns that have been raised about knowing the reliability of estimates when reporting results in scientific journals translate to considerations in using estimates for planning and management. If someone is predicating a plan for a

Table 1. Simulated Results Concerning User Fee ($\ddot{u}_f = \$185.50$).

Year	Replication	Mean TFP	Observed Mean/ Overall Mean	% Growth from Year-to-Year	Growth for 10,000 Responses[a]
1990	01	176	0.948		
1991	02	201	1.082	14.3	7.15
1992	03	203	1.093	1.0	0.48
1993	04	168	0.904	−17.2	−8.62
1994	05	172	0.926	2.5	1.24
1995	06	179	0.964	3.7	1.84
1996	07	167	0.899	−6.5	−3.23
1997	08	193	1.039	15.7	7.83
1998	09	211	1.136	9.1	4.57
1999	10	189	1.017	−10.3	−5.16
2000	11	188	1.012	−0.4	−0.21
2001	12	182	0.980	−3.3	−1.67
Overall Mean		185.8	1.00	0.77	0.38

[a] This "growth" is based on the standard deviation being half as large for 10,000 responses as for 2500 $(1/2 = (2500/10,000)^{1/2})$.

facility on growth of 7%, when the actual growth is 3% instead, problems can be expected because of underutilization. Now, even if an estimate of growth of 7% was calculated using two surveys each with 2500 responses, simulation results (Table 1) show that the replications of the surveys could yield an estimate greater than 11% or less than 3%. Should the estimate be used? Knowing the reliability of the estimate provides critical information in assessing the risk of using the estimate. Retrospectively, reporting statistics by, e.g. publishing growth rates like 3.1% for 2001 and 6.4% the next year when the difference is probably occurring by chance invites problems. Even publishing 3% and 6% when these are only within ±2% for 68/100 replications is providing bad information. Where high variability in an estimate should be considered in using an estimate, its variability should be made apparent in some way such as by giving standard error in parentheses with the estimate [e.g. $3\%_{(2)}$, where 2 shows ± 2%]. To resolve the issue, the following sections present a practical approach to considering the reliability of estimates regardless of knowing their accuracy. Rationales for measures of reliability are provided.

MEASUREMENT OF RELIABILITY

Beaman et al. (2004) have recognized the need for reliability information even if accuracy is not known. They also recognized that how reliability is measured should relate to the use of an estimate. Therefore, they have presented three different reliability criteria: (1) J%P@K/100; (2) J%R@K/100; and (3) J%C@K/100. These expressions refer to an estimate $\hat{u}$ being close to its expected value ($\ddot{u} = E(\hat{u})$) within a certain percent (J), in about K/100 replications of a survey. The letters P, R, and C identify how %-closeness is to be measured. In general, these criteria determine what statisticians refer to as confidence intervals for estimates. The meanings of %P, %R, and %C are introduced sequentially below.

Pollsters often use a statement like J%P@K/100 in stating reliability for a poll (P). What they refer to is a particular percentage determined for a dichotomous response (e.g. yes and no) being within a certain range. However it is evident that misunderstandings about polls, sample size, and accuracy exist. Considering that a poll is conducted by selecting a sample large enough, the percent responding "yes" will be 2%P@95/100. To achieve this goal the total number of response is determined by $n = 10,000/J^2 = 10,000/2^2 = 2500$. Assuming that in a survey a sample of 4000 is drawn because it is known that the response rate will be about 62%. When about 2500 interviews are obtained and an estimate is made, what is obtained is actually an estimate for those who respond. The above discussions illustrate two limitations that may cause misconceptions about J%P@K/100 notation. First, the statement concerning poll results being J%@K/100 may not be about accuracy due to non-response bias. Secondly, J%P@K/100 can only be used in dichotomous responses.

Unfortunately, the number of responses meeting a criterion of 10%R@95/100 is much larger than for 10%P@95/100, because %R reliability depends on the square root of the number of responses (Scheaffer et al., 1996, pp. 83–100). For example, to achieve 5%R@95/100 it would require about 20,000 responses ($\approx 2500(14/5)^2$). Further, the %C criterion introduced by Beaman et al. (2004) is of importance because it is common to compute percentage change in an estimate between two surveys using Eq. (1). To compute a "per time rate" one would divide by the time difference resulting in (time)$^{-1}$. To arrive at values to use in a reliability criterion expressing *acceptable error* in a rate, one might think of 0.5%C being such that, e.g. estimates between 2.5% and 3.5% would round to 3%. On that basis the criterion 0.5%C@95/100 could be specified. Beaman et al. (2004) consider: (a) getting desirable rounding of estimates; and (b) requesting a reliability that can be achieved with a survey that is affordable.

Stating %C reliability for rates can imply determining how variability of the estimates for surveys of different sizes influences variability. Beaman et al. (2004) only deal with the relatively common situation of surveys repeated over time that are roughly the same size. In Beaman and Thomson (2004), there is a graph for determining the number of responses that two surveys of a roughly equal size should have to achieved a J%C@K/100 reliability criterion.

$$r = \frac{100(\hat{u}_t - \hat{u}_{t-1})}{(\hat{u}_{t-1})} \tag{1}$$

where $\hat{u}_t$ and $\hat{u}_{t-1}$ are estimates for time t and $t-1$

Table 1 was created by simulation data. Estimates in the table allow one to observe the potential problems that can arise in making decisions based on 2500 responses. When looking at column 4 as presenting results of replicating a survey, one sees that estimated mean-TFP ranges from 0.90 (replication 7) to 1.14 (replication 9) of the overall mean of 185.8 (last row, column 3). If replications are considered to be for different events, someone might compare two events (e.g. using replications 7 and 9). If they had been told that reliability was "2%" with dichotomous variables it is 2%P@95/100. The 20% difference between the events ($\approx$100 $\times$ (1.1–0.9)/0.9%) could suggest that one event was much more successful than the other. Therefore, it might suggest that these events could be further reviewed to find out why the differences exist. Such a comparison will not be influenced by bias since bias influences all replications equally.

Meeting Reliability Criteria: Some Practical Considerations

The previous discussions arguing that bias in estimate is rarely detected still researchers should specify the desired reliability. Researchers strive to develop the rules of thumb to make prudent managerial decisions when bias estimates are used. Bias is "factored in" when a rule of thumb is used. What really matters for researchers is (a) using the appropriate methodology and (b) that enough responses are obtained so that the estimate is adequately reliable. If the "traditional" methodology is not used and thus bias is different than it should be, then using the rule of thumb does not produce the results it should have. If the estimate is too variable, random variation will results in an estimate that is meaningless.

It is unarguable that the selection of reliability criteria is critical, especially, for large-scale surveys such as Canadian Travel Survey (CTS, see e.g. SC, 1997), National Fishing, Hunting, and Wildlife-Associated Recreation survey (USFWS, n.d.), and the Survey of Public Participation in the Arts (NEA, n.d.). Likely, making a conscious choice to accept a risk is very different than using estimates with no consideration of the risk.

CONCLUSIONS

Fourth and fifth edition publication manuals of American Psychology Association stipulates standards concerning reporting reliability. In spirit of the recent scholarly movement, this study attempted to shed light on measure problems in connection to trip estimates such as expenditures. It is recognized that leisure-related studies have rarely identified the amount of bias. However, getting reliability information for estimates is possible and, in general, is not costly compared to collecting and automating survey data.

With misconceptions on the use of reliability measurement, researchers may employ surveys that cannot yield results with the reliability desired. This study reiterates the usefulness of the %P, %R, and %C notations and renders the implications to the measurement issues. The central thesis of the study is to advocate a new direction for future leisure research "best practice" that entails the tasks of adding reliability information for estimates.

Finally, this paper has added a few new insights. It was mentioned that Eq. (1) involves algebraic computations. To perfect the calculation, it is necessary to consider the "the propagation of error" (NIST/SEMATECH, 2003; SC, 1997). To determine the "propagation" of variability, the variability in the estimates used in the computation, as embodied in reliability statements, must be available. This suggests that the users of estimates may need to exert pressure on the producers of the estimates. The producers ought to have the reliability information of every estimate.

REFERENCES

American Psychological Association (1994). *Publication manual of the American Psychological Association* (4th ed.). Washington, DC: Author.

American Psychological Association (2001). *Publication manual of the American Psychological Association* (5th ed.). Washington, DC: Author.

Beaman, J., Hill, A., & O'Leary, J. (2002). Recall salience: Concept, use, and estimation. *Tourism Analysis, 7*(2), 115–124.

Beaman, J. G., Beaman, J. P., O'Leary, J. T., & Smith, S. L. (2001). The impact of seemingly minor methodological changes on estimates of travel and correcting bias. In: J. A. Mazanec, G. I. Crouch, J. R. Brent Ritchie & A. G. Woodside (Eds), *Consumer Psychology and Leisure* (Vol. 2, pp. 91–96). New York: CABI Publishing. A short version appears in *Tourism Analysis, 5,* 91–96.

Beaman, J. G., Huan, T. C., & Beaman, J. P. (2004). Sample size and reliability in measuring relative change and magnitude. *Journal of Travel Research, 43*(1), 67–74.

Beaman, J. G., & Thomson, E. (2004). Market trends: Appropriateness of using a rates of change based on two independent samples and its reliability. *Proceedings of Travel Tourism Research Association of Canada.* Ottawa, Ontario.

Burton, S., & Blair, E. (1991). Task conditions, response formulation processes and response accuracy for behavioral frequency questions in surveys. *Public Opinion Quarterly, 55,* 50–79.

Chase, D. R., & Harada, M. (1984). Response error in self-reported recreation participation. *Journal of Leisure Research, 16*(4), 322–329.

Chu, A., Eisenhower, D., Hay, M., Morganstein, D., Neter, J., & Waksberg, J. (1992). Measuring the recall error in self-reported fishing and hunting activities. *Journal of Official Statistics*, 8(1), 19–39.

Crompton, J. L., & Tian-Cole, S. (2001). An analysis of 13 tourism surveys: Are there waves of data collection necessary? *Journal of Travel Research*, 39(4), 356–368.

Devore, J., & Peck, R. (1986). *Statistics, the exploration and analysis of data*. New York: West Publishing Co.

Dilman, D. A. (1978). *Mail and telephone survey: The total design method*. New York: Wiley.

FHWAR (United States Fish and Wildlife Service) (n.d.). National. *Survey of Fishing, Hunting, & Wildlife-Associated Recreation*. Retrieved May 18, 2004, http://www.fa.r9.fws. gov/surveys/surveys.html#surv_desc.

Gliner, J. A., Vaske, J. J., & Morgan, G. A. (2001). Null hypothesis significant testing: Effect size matters. *Human Dimensions of Wildlife*, 6, 291–301.

Hwang, Y. H., Wang, R. Y., Beaman, J., Fesenmaier, D. R., & O'Leary, J. T. (2002). Considerations in temporal aggregation: Applications to the U.S. in-flight survey data. *Tourism Analysis*, 6(3/4), 171–184.

Krosnick, J. A. (1999). Survey research. *Annual Review of Psychology*, 50, 537–567.

Lindblom, L., Roth, E., & Shifflet, D. K. (1992). Recall bias of the U.S. population in reporting travel behavior. In: *Travel Tourism Research Association 23rd Annual Conference Proceedings*. Westridge, CO: Travel Tourism Research Association.

National Endowment for the Arts (n.d.). 1997 survey of public participation in the arts: Summary report. Retrieved May 18, 2004, http://www.arts.endow.gov/pub/Survey/SurveyPDF.html.

National Institute of Standards and Technology/Semiconductor Manufacturing Technology (2003). Propagation of error considerations. In: *Engineering statistics handbook* (Section 2.5.5). Retrieved May 18, 2004, http://www.itl.nist.gov/div898/handbook/mpc/section5/mpc55.htm.

Scheaffer, R. L., Mendenhall, W., & Ott, L. (1996). *Elementary survey sampling* (5th ed.). Belmont, CA: Wadsworth.

Statistics Canada (1997). *Canadian travel survey microdata*. (Diskette; CD-ROM, Catalogue No. 87M0006XDB.) Ottawa: Statistics Canada.

Tarrant, M. A., & Manfredo, M. J. (1993). Digit preference, recall bias, and non-response bias in self reports of angling participation. *Journal of Leisure Research*, 15, 231–237.

THE EVALUATION OF NORWEGIANS' TRIP SATISFACTION TOWARD SOUTHERN EUROPEAN DESTINATIONS

Nina K. Prebensen

ABSTRACT

This research focuses on Norwegian tourists' destination satisfaction as influenced by the process of buying behaviour, which further affects tourists' behavioural intention by evaluating determinants and consequences of satisfaction. The data have been collected from Norwegian tourists travelling to European destinations. The findings show that the experience of the service/organisation of the journey explained about 50% of the variance in overall tourist satisfaction with the destination. Further, the results reveal that tourists are inclined to be rational while choosing activities that satisfy their inner motives. However, the relationships among tourist motivation, satisfaction, and behavioural intention are not as strong as expected.

INTRODUCTION

Recognizing tourist satisfaction is of utmost importance for the tourism industry (Petrick, 2003), satisfied tourists tend to communicate their positive experiences to others and use tourist products and services repeatedly (Barsky, 1992; Beeho &

Advances in Hospitality and Leisure
Advances in Hospitality and Leisure, Volume 1, 133–152
ISSN: 1745-3542/doi:10.1016/S1745-3542(04)01009-4

Prentice, 1997; Chen, 2003; Chen & Gursoy, 2001; Kozak & Rimmington, 2000; Pizam, 1994; Ross, 1993). Tourists' satisfaction with a trip or a destination could be a result of many aspects, such as the perceptions of products as well as their expectations before and during the trip. Consumer behavioural studies reveal that customer satisfaction is the result or the final step in a psychological process from need recognition to the evaluation of product experiences (Peter & Olson, 1996). Despite the recognition of the sequential relationship, consumer researchers tend to focus on the perceptions of the product when evaluating satisfaction issues.

Satisfaction is defined as "a judgement that a product or service feature, or the product or service itself, provides a pleasurable level of consumption-related fulfilment" Oliver (1997, p. 13) or as an overall evaluation of a purchase (Fornell, 1992). MacKay and Crompton (1990, p. 48) define satisfaction in a similar way by focusing on the "psychological outcome which emerges from experiencing the service" (MacKay & Crompton, 1990, p. 48). The overall satisfaction is seen as the result or the aggregate value of the relative importance in addition to the level of satisfaction experienced from all the single attributes (Ajzen & Fishbein, 1980).

Moreover, tourist satisfaction has been analysed within a variety of experience facets. Ross and Iso-Ahola (1991), for instance, observe the tourist satisfaction of cultural trips, while Hsieh et al. (1994) learn the perceptual differences in service quality among packaged and non-packaged tours. Other researchers focus on satisfaction with certain aspects of tourism offerings, such as accommodation (e.g. Saleh & Ryan, 1992; Heide et al., 1999). Toy et al. (2002) evaluate customer satisfaction of leisure activities. Several researchers (Chon & Olsen, 1991; Danaher & Arweiler, 1996; Joppe et al., 2001; Kozak & Rimmington, 2000) investigate tourists' satisfaction with destinations.

Following the tourist behavioural framework, this study attempts to take a holistic approach to examine the issues concerning tourist satisfaction i.e. to revaluate the causes (e.g. motivation) and consequences (e.g. behavioural intention) of satisfaction in the context of the international travel experiences of Norwegians. Specifically, this study aims to accomplish the following objectives: firstly, to understand Norwegian tourist satisfaction with a certain type of trip (e.g. charter trip); secondly, to determine the effects of trip motivations on the type of activities where tourists participated and achieved satisfaction; lastly, to assess the impact of tourist satisfaction on the intention to repurchase and recommend.

Tourist motivation has often been treated as identical to the purpose of travel, despite the general acceptance that motivation is only one of many variables (e.g. perceptions, cultural conditioning and learning) that contribute to tourist behaviour (e.g. Fodness, 1994). Numerous tourist motivation studies adopt the "push" – and "pull" doctrine, first presented by Dann (1977, p. 186). Push factors are regarded as dispositions within the traveller and pull factors as having evolved from the correspondingly appealing features of destinations.

The present study focuses on inner motives for travelling, which correspond to Dann's push factors. Pizam et al. (1979) define travel motivation as a "set of needs, which predispose a person to participate in a touristic activity." Further, according to Moutinho (1987, p. 16) motivation is linked to satisfaction by the following definition: "motivation is a state of need, a condition that exerts a 'push' on the individual towards certain types of action that are seen as likely to bring satisfaction." In other words, travellers seek particular needs that may be complemented by certain types of activity chosen in a decided destination. In this case, they choose places to visit and participate in activities that satisfy their psychological and physical needs. During- and after the trip travellers evaluate the varieties of trip experiences they encountered that subsequently effect their satisfaction of the destination as a whole.

It is unarguable that travel motivation will affect the choice of activities. Moscardo et al. (1995), in their analysis of Australian outbound travellers illustrates a clear linkage between the benefits travellers looked for and the activities that they pursue. Relationships between benefits sought at a destination and activities pursued are further presented in the research of Gitelson and Kerstetter (1990). They state that the type of activity is significantly associated with benefits sought. For example, individuals who fish, camp, or hike are likely to evaluate the relaxation dimension as more important than those visitors who do not enjoy these activities. Additionally, tourists playing golf during their vacation rate the "explorer" motivation dimension as less important than non-golfers, while respondents who visit a museum, camp, or go hiking during their stay rate the explorer dimension as more important than tourists who do not enjoy these activities.

In a similar vein, Chhetri et al. (2003) identify the underlying dimensions (motive related) influencing visitor behaviour (experiences) among hikers in a national park in Australia. The study recognises 11 factors based upon the hikers' feelings or emotions related to different experiences. It further reveals four key components related to the hiking experience: a desirable experience, an impelling experience, an apprehensive experience and a social interaction experience. In a study of inbound tourists in Norway, Kleiven (1998, 1999) reveals that tourist motives could be used as attributes to predict the tourists' choice of activity.

The study of Ross and Iso-Ahola (1991) finds similar results regarding the relationship between motivation and satisfaction. Their findings suggest that the high overall satisfaction (over 90%) of the respondents can be explained by the significant consistency between motivation dimensions and satisfaction.

Tourist choice of activities can thus be viewed as the link between motives for travelling and the perception of satisfaction. Certain activities are expected to fulfil certain needs. However, different types of activities might fulfil the same type of need. Further, the same type of activity might fulfil different needs. The fact that some destinations offer deficient products or even lack certain activities that tourists demand, and/or that the destinations might promote activities that tourists did not think of in the first place, make the picture of the relationship between the constructs challenging.

Tourists' satisfaction with a destination may reflect a type of tourist overall satisfaction with a journey, while satisfaction with transport, travelling party, accommodation, activities performed could impact on the total judgement of a trip to a particular destination. Tourist satisfaction is proven to be linked to the customer's intention to re-buy as well as the tendency to communicate via positive word of mouth (e.g. Kozak & Rimmington, 2000; Pizam, 1994; Ross, 1993). These consequences of experienced satisfaction are also discussed in relation to business profitability, as a way of reducing marketing costs (e.g. Peter & Olson, 1996). In conclusion, it is evident that the casual relationships among trip motivation, activities, tourist satisfaction and behavioural intention exist. Based on the above behavioural consequences, six hypotheses are proposed in the study.

H1. Certain tourist motives increase the likelihood of the tourist participating in certain touristic activities, while others reduce the likelihood of participating in these activities.

H2. Certain tourist motives increase the likelihood of future satisfaction with certain trip related attributes as well as with the destination visited.

H3. Certain tourist activities undertaken during a vacation, increase the likelihood of being satisfied with certain trip related attributes as well as the destination visited.

H4. Tourist satisfaction with various aspects of a trip will effect overall satisfaction with the destination dependent on the tourist motive-activity structure.

H5. Tourist satisfaction with different aspects of a trip and overall satisfaction with a destination drives the tourist's intention to re-purchase a package tour, dependent on the motive-activity structure.

H6. Tourist satisfaction with different aspects of a trip and overall satisfaction with a destination drives the tourist's intention to communicate via positive word of mouth, dependent on the tourist motive-activity structure.

METHODS

Study Population

A group of Norwegian tourists purchasing charter products to countries having a reputation for a warm climate were interviewed. Experiencing a warmer weather is often an unconcealed demand among Norwegian tourists. Thus, many tours cater to such a plea. Witt (1980) reports that countries with a good climate and coastline, e.g. Mediterranean countries, appear to be very attractive for both the British and German markets, as well as for many northern countries in the world (e.g. Northern part of USA, Canada, other Scandinavian countries etc.). In general, a charter product consists of a number of different aspects of single-products such as transport, accommodation, restaurants, attractions etc. and is often described in the context of a package tour.

Middleton (1994, p. 292) defines a package tour as "Standardised, quality controlled, repeatable offers comprising two or more elements of transport, accommodation, food, destination attractions, other facilities, and services (such as insurance)." Tour operators in Norway offer their clients diverse package tours to international destinations. However, most of the charter tours provided to Norwegians centre on the vacation destinations of Spain, Greece, Turkey, Portugal, and Italy. Other warm southern European countries as well as some Asian destinations such as Thailand are recently experiencing a surging demand among Norwegian tourists.

Data Collection

A survey was selected as the data collection method using structured questionnaires that measure tourist motivation, activities, satisfaction (overall and single component), intention to repurchase and recommend the journey taken by the respondents. Subjects who had taken a charter-flight within the last 12 months were asked to answer the questionnaire. In total 5000 questionnaires were mailed to Norwegian respondents based on a list acquired from one of the largest tour-operators in Norway. The study questionnaires were mailed out during August 2002.

Twelve hundred and twenty-two (1222) charter-flight tourists travelling from Norway to different destinations responded by mail questionnaire after they had returned from their trips. Seventy-eight questionnaires were returned unanswered for a variety of reasons ranging from wrong address to death. As a result, the response-rate was 24.8% (1222/4922). The number of outbound tourists from

Norway, travelling by charter-flight was estimated in 2002 to be 905,000 passengers (Startour, 2004). No systematic differences in responses across demographic variables were observed.

Measurements

The variation of overall satisfaction was measured by "how satisfied are you with the destination?" with a five-point Likert-type scale (1 = Not Important; 5 = Very Important). The item-specific satisfaction measurements assess the perceptions of various aspects of the journey with a five-point scale, ranging from Very Dissatisfied (=1) to Very Satisfied (=5). With a factor analysis, those satisfaction items were grouped into four components (Appendix A).

Activity items were mainly based upon products offered by Norwegian tour-operators. Before determining the activity items, several interviews were held with the representatives from the tourism industry regarding the most common activities offered by outbound charter tours. Consequently, 24 activities were included in the survey that include sunbathing, swimming in the sea, swimming in the pool, playing on the beach, sailing at sea, boat trips, fishing, playing football/handball, golf/tennis/squash, surfing/water-skiing, going for a slow walk, going for a hard walk, reading about the culture and history of the destination, reading about attractions, reading other types of literature (books, magazines etc.), learning about the culture of the destination, family trips by car, playing/being together with children in the family, shopping, sightseeing tours, sightseeing alone, attending the theatre/opera/ballet, attending concerts/festivals, visiting restaurants, visiting theatre/opera/ballet. The respondents were asked to state their involvement in these activities on a six-point scale from not at all (=1) to more than 6 hours per day (=6). These items were further reduced into six components via a factor analysis (Appendix B).

Trip motivation was measured with a five-point scale ranging from Not Important (= 1) to Very Important (= 5). The motivation questions were mostly adapted from Kleiven (1998, 1999) and adjusted to outbound charter tours from Norway after discussing the items with representatives from the industry. In total, 35 motivation items were selected for the questionnaires. Kleiven (1998, 1999) adopted his motivational attributors from both qualitative and quantitative investigations (Beard & Ragheb, 1983; Jamrozy & Uysal, 1994). The factor analysis of the motive items is presented in Appendix C.

Tourists behavioural intention (intention to re-purchase and recommend the product) were adapted from Oliver (1997) and revised to fit the trip characteristics of Norwegian outbound charter trips: "Will you take a charter tour for your next holiday?" and "Will you recommend the trip to other people?" These two "consequences of tourist satisfaction" variables, were measured on a 3 point scale from 1 (= I will) to 3 (=I will not). A category for "don't know" was also available for the respondents.

FINDINGS

This section reports on the research results. First, the results of factor analysis of satisfaction items, activity items, and motive items are presented. Then it reports on the findings from the regression analysis of motivation on the choice of activity, the effects of activities on satisfaction, and the impact of motivations on satisfaction. Finally, the regression analysis of tourist satisfaction on the intention to repurchase and recommend are presented.

Tourist Satisfaction, Activity, and Motivation

Since the three psychological constructs including satisfaction, activities, and motives are new and are specifically designed to assess the opinions of Norwegian outbound travellers, it is good practice to further evaluate the underlying dimensions of the proposed scales. As a result, factor analysis was conducted. First, unrotated factor analysis was performed for all constructs in order to decide the number of factors. Varimax rotated analysis was conducted for all three sets of scale that resulted in four satisfaction factors, six activity factors and four motivation factors.

Further, an advantage of using factor scores was to avoid the muliticollinearity effect of the model due to the possibilities of high inter-correlations among variables, given the fact the study revaluates the causal relationship among the constructs. In sum, the first factor analysis conducted on 22 satisfaction items shows four factors explaining a 51.43% of the variance. The second factor analysis of 24 activity items derives six factors consisting of a 51.25% variance. The third factor analysis on 35 motivational items extracts four factors entailing a 51% variance.

Table 1 shows the number of items, mean, standard deviation and Cronbach's alpha for each component of the three scales of the test. Carmines and Zeller (1979) suggest that Cronbach's alpha should not be lower than 0.80 for widely used scales. In this study, the alpha values of satisfaction subscales ranged from 0.72 to 0.84. Additionally, activity subscales for the values of the coefficient ranged from 0.52 to 0.77 while motivation subscales had higher coefficients from 0.82 to 0.87.

Table 1 also reveals the inter-correlations among the resulting factors. The relatively high correlation scores for the satisfaction scale might be explained by the fact that tourists' satisfaction (negative or positive) might be transferred from

Table 1.   Consistency and Inter-Correlation of Scales.

The Name of Scale and its Components					Inter-Correlation Among the Components				
	# of Terms	Mean	S.D.	Alpha	2	3	4	5	6
Satisfaction[a]									
Service/organising	9	3.91	0.479	0.75	0.507	0.447	0.389		
Activities (in general)	3	3.87	0.517	0.84	–	0.442	0.440		
Activities (specific)	7	3.67	0.728	0.72	–	–	0.446		
Culture	3	3.37	0.52	0.78	–	–	–		
Activities[b]									
Learning about destination	4	2.19	0.801	0.77	0.161	0.162	0.094	0.253	0.261
Traditional charter-sun activities	6	2.79	0.634	0.64	–	0.119	0.456	0.050	0.006
Water activities	4	1.18	0.383	0.53	–	–	0.132	0.065	0.042
Play	3	1.35	0.562	0.52	–	–	–	0.014	0.078
Trips	4	2.13	0.755	0.53	–	–	–	–	0.138
Culture	2	1.10	1.110	0.65	–	–	–	–	–
Motives[c]									
Relax/sun	12	3.66	0.787	0.87	−0.47	0.294	0.199		
Learning/culture	9	3.46	0.768	0.86	–	0.455	0.310		
Lifestyle/social	10	2.72	0.745	0.83	–	–	0.479		
Fitness	4	3.09	0.996	0.88	–	–	–		

Note: In the present study, the activity variable are considered to reflect a disposition within the tourist.
[a] The measurement scale ranges from 1 to 5, where 1 = very dissatisfied, 3 = neutral and 5 = very satisfied.
[b] The measurement scale ranges from 1 to 6, where 1 = did not perform, 6 = more than 6 hours per day.
[c] The measurement scale ranges from 1 to 5, where 1 = not important at all, 3 = neutral and 5 = very important.

one experience to the next. For the activity scale the correlations score seemed low, which might be explained by the fact that the time spent on one activity reduced the time available to perform another. Personal interests could also explain the low correlation. Further, in the motivation scale the inter-correlations between relaxation/sun and fitness seemed low. Apparently, other motivation factors were more inter-correlated. It suggests that the subscales should be treated with caution.

Motives and Activities

Table 2 illustrates how motives, such as relaxation/sun affected positively on traditional charter/sun activities; and how motives such as learning and

Table 2. The Impact of Tourist Motives on Choice of Activities.

Variables	Beta	*t*-Statistic	Sig.
Dependent variable: Traditional charter/sun			
Independent variables			
Relax/sun	0.703	28.363	0.000
Learning/culture	−0.079	−2.949	0.003
Lifestyle/social	−0.003	−0.086	0.931
Fitness	−0.115	−4.274	0.000
$R^2 = 0.495 \ (=49.5\%)$			
Dependent variable: Learning about destination			
Independent variables			
Relax/sun	−0.249	−9.500	0.000
Learning/culture	0.640	22.572	0.000
Lifestyle/social	−0.125	−3.993	0.000
Fitness	−0.081	−2.868	0.004
$R^2 = 0.440 \ (=44.0\%)$			
Dependent variable: Play			
Independent variables			
Relax/sun	0.305	9.256	0.000
Learning/culture	−0.096	−2.708	0.007
Lifestyle/social	0.062	1.570	0.117
Fitness	0.014	0.396	0.693
$R^2 = 0.116 \ (=11.6\%)$			
Dependent variable: Water activities			
Independent variables			
Relax/sun	0.031	0.884	0.377
Learning/culture	0.103	2.746	0.006
Lifestyle/social	0.069	1.657	0.098
Fitness	−0.056	−1.488	0.137
$R^2 = 0.019 \ (=1.9\%)$			
Dependent variable: Trips			
Independent variables			
Relax/sun	−0.048	−1.467	0.143
Learning/culture	0.134	3.749	0.000
Lifestyle/social	−0.020	−0.504	0.614
Fitness	0.276	7.724	0.000
$R^2 = 0.109 \ (=10.9\%)$			
Dependent variable: Culture			
Independent variables			
Relax/sun	−0.178	−5.191	0.000
Learning/culture	0.077	2.085	0.037
Lifestyle/social	0.076	1.856	0.064
Fitness	0.006	0.157	0.875
$R^2 = 0.043 \ (=4.3\%)$			

fitness, negatively affected these activities ($F = 231.360, R^2 = 0.50, p < 0.001$). Relaxation/sun had a positive effect on play activities while learning/culture showed a negative relationship ($F = 30.980, R^2 = 0.116, p < 0.001$). The learning motive had a positive effect on water activities; however, the explained variance was rather low ($F = 4.465, R^2 = 0.019, p < 0.005$). Learning/culture, as well as the fitness motive had a positive effect on trips ($F = 28.830, R^2 = 0.109, p < 0.001$). As for cultural activities, relaxation/sun had a negative relationship with it. The explained variance, however, was rather low ($F = 10.538, R^2 = 0.043, p < 0.001$).

Motives and Satisfaction

Table 3 presents the causal relationship between motives and satisfactions. The leaning/culture affected positively on the satisfaction of service/organising side of the journey ($F = 7.962, R^2 = 0.032, p < 0.000$). Relaxation/sun influenced satisfaction with activities in general ($F = 2.087, R^2 = 0.009, p < 0.05$). Further, the motives of relaxation/sun posed a negative impact on special activities while learning/culture yielded a positive relationship with special activities ($F = 19.895, R^2 = 0.088, p < 0.001$). In reference to tourist satisfaction with culture, both relaxation /sun and fitness reflected a negative linkage however, learning/culture showed a positive path ($F = 33.562, R^2 = 0.146, p < 0.001$). Lastly, overall satisfaction with the destination was affected positively by the learning/culture motive ($F = 2.644, R^2 = 0.011, p < 0.05$).

Activities and Satisfaction

Table 4 presents the causal relationship between activities and satisfactions. The activities concerning learning about the destination positively related to the satisfaction with the service/organising side of the trip ($F = 5.431, R^2 = 0.027, p < 0.000$). Traditional charter/sun activities created a negative impact on satisfaction with specific activities and learning about destination activities; play activities imposed a positive strength on satisfaction with specific activities ($F = 20.76, R^2 = 0.11, p < 0.05$). Regarding tourists' satisfaction with culture, traditional charter/sun and trips revealed a negative influence while learning about the destination and performing cultural activities a positive one ($F = 27.55, R^2 = 0.15, p < 0.01$). Traditional sun/charter activities and learning about destination activities affect positively on overall satisfaction with the destination ($F = 2.439, R^2 = 0.013, p < 0.05$).

Table 3. The Impact of Tourists' Motives on Satisfaction by Linear Regression Analysis.

Variables	Beta	*t*-Statistic	Sig.
Dependent variable: Satisfaction with service/organising			
Independent variables			
Relax/sun	0.017	0.493	0.622
Learning/culture	0.172	4.647	0.000
Lifestyle/social	0.017	0.426	0.671
Fitness	−0.003	−0.069	0.945
$R^2 = 0.032$ (=3.2%)			
Dependent variable: Satisfaction with activities in general			
Independent variables			
Relax/sun	0.076	2.214	0.027
Learning/culture	0.005	0.141	0.888
Lifestyle/social	0.013	0.327	0.744
Fitness	0.029	0.781	0.435
$R^2 = 0.009$ (=0.9%)			
Dependent variable: Satisfaction with specific activities			
Independent variables			
Relax/sun	−0.104	−2.876	0.004
Learning/culture	0.278	7.097	0.000
Lifestyle/social	−0.037	−0.863	0.388
Fitness	−0.036	−0.930	0.352
$R^2 = 0.088$ (=8.8%)			
Dependent variable: Satisfaction with the culture			
Independent variables			
Relax/sun	−0.263	−7.328	0.000
Learning/culture	0.223	5.959	0.000
Lifestyle/social	0.065	1.566	0.118
Fitness	−0.149	−3.871	0.000
$R^2 = 0.146$ (=14.6%)			
Dependent variable: Overall destination satisfaction			
Independent variables			
Relax/sun	0.027	0.765	0.444
Learning/culture	0.080	2.103	0.036
Lifestyle/social	0.029	0.699	0.484
Fitness	0.008	0.218	0.828
$R^2 = 0.011$ (=1.1%)			

Tourist Satisfaction and Intention Behaviour

A regression analysis was deployed to assess the behavioural consequences of tourist satisfaction (intention to repurchase and recommend). The first model

Table 4.   The Impact of Tourists' Choice of Activities on Satisfaction.

Variables	Beta	t-Statistic	Sig.
Dependent variable: Service/org.			
Independent variables			
Traditional sun/charter	0.060	1.798	0.072
Learning about destination	0.118	3.753	0.000
Play	−0.105	−3.188	0.001
Water	−0.024	−0.809	0.419
Trips	0.042	1.408	0.159
Culture	0.022	0.731	0.465
$R^2 = 0.027\ (=2.7\%)$			
Dependent variable: Activities (in general) satisfaction			
Independent variables			
Traditional sun/charter	0.053	1.565	0.118
Learning about destination	0.040	1.261	0.208
Play	0.038	1.144	0.253
Water	−0.016	−0.519	0.604
Trips	0.079	2.619	0.009
Culture	0.013	0.436	0.663
$R^2 = 0.014\ (=1.4\%)$			
Dependent variable: Specific activity satisfaction			
Independent variables			
Traditional sun/charter	−0.101	−2.933	0.003
Learning about destination	0.309	9.469	0.000
Play	0.071	2.102	0.036
Water	0.016	0.508	0.612
Trips	−0.043	−1.410	0.159
Culture	−0.005	−0.175	0.861
$R^2 = 0.110\ (=11.0\%)$			
Dependent variable: Culture			
Independent variables: Traditional sun/charter			
Learning about destination	−0.214	−6.082	0.000
Play	0.234	7.154	0.000
Water	−0.101	−0.290	0.772
Trips	0.021	0.666	0.506
Culture	−0.28	−0.906	0.365
$R^2 = 0.148\ (=14.8\%)$	0.097	3.122	0.002
Dependent variable: Overall destination satisfaction			
Independent variables: Traditional sun/charter			
Learning about destination	0.079	2.309	0.021
Play	0.071	2.239	0.025
Water	−0.056	−1.659	0.097
Trips	−0.047	−1.542	0.123
Culture	0.035	1.168	0.243
$R^2 = 0.013\ (=1.3\%)$	0.024	0.785	0.433

Table 5. Factors Affecting Overall Destination Satisfaction, Word of Mouth, and Intention to Repurchase.

Variables	Beta Coefficient
Dependent variable: Overall satisfaction	
Independent variables	
Factor 1 (service/organising)	−0.663
Factor 2 (specific activities)	−0.008
Factor 3 (activities in general)	−0.095
Factor 4 (culture)	0.024
$R^2 = 0.5016 (=50.3\%)$	
Dependent variable: Repurchase the charter product	
Independent variable	
Factor 1 (service/organising)	0.152
Factor 3 (specific activities)	−0.060
Factor 2 (activities in general)	0.042
Factor 4 (culture)	0.049
Sat. with Destination	0.037
$R^2 = 0.041 (=4.1\%)$	
Dependent variable: Word of mouth	
Independent variable	
Factor 1 (service/organising)	0.245
Factor 2 (specific activities)	0.060
Factor 3 (activities in general)	0.050
Factor 4 (culture)	0.025
Satisfaction with destination	0.286
$R^2 = 0.3075 (=30.75\%)$	

(Table 5) examined overall satisfaction in relation to the four satisfaction factors (based on single attributes). It was observed that only two independent variables, Factor 1 (service/organising) and Factor 3 (specific activities) had beta coefficients that were statistically significant ($p < 0.001$) while $R^2 = 0.503$. The more satisfied the tourists were with the service/organising side of the journey and with activities in general, the more satisfied they were with the destination visited. The total variance explained was 50.3% in the model. Items loaded on Factor Two (activities in general) and Factor Four (culture) did not have any impact on the level of overall satisfaction of the destination visited.

The results also show that Factor One (service/organising) mediated a positive intention to repurchase a charter tour "the more positive they evaluate the service/organising side of the trip the more they intend to re-buy the trip" ($F = 106.891$, $R^2 = 0.041$, $p < 0.01$). The explained variance was however low. Interestingly, the total destination satisfaction did not alter the intention to repurchase. The results further provide information on the tourists' intention to recommend the destination to family and friends (Table 5) ($F = 55.58$, $R^2 = 0.3075$, $p < 0.001$). Factor One (service/organising) and "the satisfaction with destination" impact positively upon the "intention to recommend."

CONCLUSION

This study divulges that Norwegian charter tourists have been satisfied with travel destinations in southern European countries. Consequently, they intend to purchase the products again and make positive recommendations to others. This reaction is analogous to the behavioural consequences found in most satisfaction studies, such as the research of Fornell et al. (1996). Further, the study validates the assumption that activities performed at a destination could be explained by different motives for travelling.

It is interesting to find that charter/sun activities had a negative effect on satisfaction with specific activities and culture experiences. The result implies that those tourists engaged in charter/sun activities did not heavily take part in other types of activity. The findings seem to suggest a viable research topic for a future study to further investigate the characteristics of underlying travel segments that could be distinguished by activities undertaken. For example, Norwegians traditionally travelling to Southern Europe are often labelled as sun-birds and have a variety of activity preference. This research shows that the respondents could be grouped into two main segments; "beach-bums" and "learners" based on motive-activity structures. However, in addition to the above-suggested method, post-hoc segmentation approaches could also be an alternative method for segmentation evaluation.

Regarding the predictive models derived from the study, it is speculated that the low explained variance tied to activities and tourist satisfaction is attributed to the fact that the provision of leisure activities familiar to Norwegians is utterly insufficient among those European destinations. An improvement on tourists' satisfaction with the activities of interest would help augment tourists' overall satisfaction and their intention to communicate via a positive word of mouth.

The findings in the present study might be of interest for Norwegian tour operators from the aspects of product development and marketing communication. For product development, popular activities should be identified, such as visiting quality restaurants, while the supporting services to tourists such as pre-trip planning could be delivered by the internet that ensures a timely assistance. As for marketing communication, the travel industry might concentrate on the development of persuasive communication strategies addressing the needs (e.g. relax/sun) of travel consumers at an individual level and on a group base.

ACKNOWLEDGMENT

The author would like to thank Professor Kjell Grønhaug from Norwegian School of Economics for his helpful feedback on early versions of the manuscript.

REFERENCES

Ajzen, I., & Fishbein, M. (1980). *Understanding attitudes and predicting social behavior*. Englewood Cliffs, NJ: Prentice-Hall.

Barsky, J. D. (1992). Customer satisfaction in the hotel industry: Meaning and measurement. *Hospitality Research Journal, 16*(1), 51–73.

Beard, J. G., & Ragheb, M. G. (1983). Measuring leisure motivation. *Journal of Leisure Research, 15*(3), 219–228.

Beeho, A. J., & Prentice, R. C. (1997). Conceptualizing the experiences of heritage tourists: A case study of New Lanark world heritage village. *Tourism Management, 18*(2), 75–87.

Carmines, E. G., & Zeller, R. A. (1979) *Reliability and validity assessments*. Beverly Hills, CA: Sage.

Chen, J. S. (2003). Market segmentation by travelers' sentiments. *Annals of Tourism Research, 30*(1), 178–193.

Chen, J. S., & Gursoy, D. (2001). An investigation of tourists' destination loyalty and preferences. *International Journal of Contemporary Hospitality Management, 13*(2), 79–85.

Chhetri, P., Arrowsmith, C., & Jackson, M. (2003). Determining hiking experience in nature-based tourist destinations. *Tourism Management, 25*(1), 31–43.

Chon, K. S., & Olsen, M. D. (1991). Functional and symbolic approaches to consumer satisfaction/dissatisfaction in tourism. *Journal of International Academy of Hospitality Research, 28*, 1–20.

Danaher, P. J., & Arweiler, N. (1996). Customer satisfaction in the tourist industry: A case study of visitors to New Zealand. *Journal of Travel Research, 34*, 89–93.

Dann, G. (1977). Anomie, ego-enhancement and tourism. *Annals of Tourism Research, 4*(2), 184–194.

Fodness, D. (1994). Measuring tourist motivation. *Annals of Tourism Research, 21*(3), 555–581.

Fornell, C. (1992). A national customer satisfaction barometer: The Swedish experience. *Journal of Marketing, 56*, 6–21.

Gitelson, R. J., & Kerstetter, D. L. (1990). The relationship between sociodemographic variables. *Journal of Travel Research, 28*(Winter), 24–29.

Heide, M., Grønhaug, K., & Engset, M. G. (1999). Industry specific measurement of consumer satisfaction: Experiences from the business traveling industry. *International Journal of Hospitality Management, 18*, 201–213.

Hsieh, S., O'Leary, J. T., & Morrison, A. M. (1994) A comparison of packaged and non packaged travelers from the United Kingdom. In: M. Uysal (Ed.), *Global Tourist Behaviour* (pp. 79–100). New York: International Business Press.

Jamrozy, U., & Uysal, M. (1994). Travel motivation variations of overseas visitors. *Journal of International Consumer Marketing, 6*(3/4), 135–160.

Joppe, M., Martin, D. W., & Waalen, J. (2001). Toronto's image as a destination: A comparative importance-satisfaction analysis by origin of visitor. *Journal of Travel Research, 39*(February), 252–260.

Kleiven, J. (1998) Skalaer for måling av aktivitets- og motivmønstre i en norsk lokalbefolknings ferie og fritid. [Scales for measuring activity and motive patterns in a Norwegian local population's leisure and vacations.] Working Paper No. 77/1998. Lillehammer: Lillehammer College.

Kleiven, J. (1999) *Leisure motives as predictors of activities: The Lillehammer scales in a national survey*. Report No. 49. Lillehammer: Lillehammer College.

Kozak, M., & Rimmington, M. (2000). Tourist satisfaction with Mallorca, Spain, as of season holiday destination. *Journal of Travel Research, 38*(February), 260–269.

MacKay, K., & Crompton, J. (1990). Measuring the quality of recreation services. *Journal of Park and Recreation Administration, 8*(3), 47–56.

Middleton, V. T. C. (1994) *Marketing in travel & tourism*. Oxford: Butterworth-Heinemann.

Moscardo, G., Morrison, A. M., Pearce, P. L., Lang, C. T., & O'Leary, J. T. (1995). Understanding vacation destination choice through travel motivation and activities. *Journal of Vacation Marketing, 2*(2), 109–122.

Moutinho, L. (1987). Consumer behaviour in tourism. *European Journal of Marketing, 21*(10), 1–44.

Oliver, R. L. (1997) *Satisfaction. A behavioral perspective on the consumer*. Boston: Irwin/McGraw-Hill.

Peter, P. J., & Olson, J. C. (1996). *Consumer behavior* (4th ed.). Chicago: Irwin.

Petrick, J. F. (in press). Are loyal visitors desired visitors. *Tourism Management*. Available online 23 October 2003.

Pizam, A. (1994). Monitoring customer satisfaction. In: B. David & A. Lockwood (Eds), *Food and Beverage Management: A Selection of Readings* (pp. 231–247). Oxford, UK: Butterworth-Heinemann.

Pizam, A., Neuman, Y., & Reichel, A. (1979). Tourist satisfaction: Uses and misuses. *Annals of Tourism Research, 6*, 96–107.

Ross, G. (1993). Destination evaluation and vacation preferences. *Annals of Tourism Research, 20*, 477–489.

Ross, E. I. D., & Iso-Ahola, S. E. (1991). Sightseeing tourists' motivation and satisfaction. *Annals of Tourism Research, 18*, 430–448.

Saleh, F., & Ryan, C. (1992). Client perceptions of hotels. *Tourism Management, 13*(June), 163–168.

Startour (2004). http://www.corporate.startour.no/. Oslo.

Toy, D., Kerstetter, D., & Ragheb, R. (2002). Evaluating customer satisfaction. *Tourism Analysis, 6*, 99–108.

Witt, S. F. (1980). An econometric comparison of UK and German foreign holiday behavior. *Managerial and Decision Economics, 1*(3), 123–131.

APPENDIX A: FACTOR ANALYSIS OF SATISFACTION ITEMS

	h^2	Service/ Organising	Activities (in General)	Activities (Specific)	Culture
1. Service	0.58	0.70			
2. Restaurants	0.49	0.62			
3. Tour operator	0.39	0.61			
4. Food	0.39	0.59			
5. Hotel	0.45	0.57			
6. Flight (transportation)	0.32	0.57			
7. Nature/environment	0.50	0.49			
8. Shopping facilities	0.37	0.48			
9. Your own planning	0.22	0.42			
10. Type of activities	0.89		0.87		
11. Number of activities	0.81		0.86		
12. Sightseeing	0.53		0.57		
13. Active play/training	0.66			0.67	
14. Beach/swim	0.41			0.60	
15. Travelling party	0.43			0.58	
16. Meet new people	0.47			0.49	
17. Boating/sailing	0.32			0.50	
18. Walking facilities	0.39			0.43	
19. Play	0.66			0.70	
20. Theatre	0.78				0.87
21. Concerts/festivals	0.83				0.90
22. Culture amenities	0.53				0.51
Percentage of common variance	11.35	3.48	2.89	2.55	2.43
Percentage of trace	100.00	30.7	25.5	22.5	21.40
Eigen value		6.07	2.08	1.67	1.49
Alpha		0.7459	0.8414	0.7161	0.7806

APPENDIX B: FACTOR ANALYSIS OF ACTIVITIES

	h^2	Learning About the Destination	Traditional Charter – Sun Act.	Water Activities	Play	Trips	Culture Activities
1. Read about attractions	0.83	0.89					
2. Read about the culture and history of the destination	0.82	0.89					
3. Learned about the culture of the destination	0.78	0.87					
4. Went on organised sightseeing	0.43	0.44					
5. Sunbathing	0.68		0.75				
6. Bathing in the sea	0.58		0.68				
7. Visited restaurants	0.18		0.40				
8. Bathing in the pool	0.36		0.46				
9. Shopping	0.16		0.35				
10. Read newspapers, magazines, books etc.	0.32		0.46				
11. Sailing at sea	0.67			0.81			
12. Boat trip	0.57			0.71			
13. Fishing	0.25			0.42			
14. Waterskiing etc.	0.38			0.56			
15. Playing football/handball etc.	0.56				0.73		
16. Golf/tennis/Squash	0.44				0.65		
17. Played/was together with children in the family	0.53				0.65		
18. Played at road/beach	0.59				0.54		
19. Sightseeing alone	0.57					0.70	
20. Went for a slow walk	0.47					0.66	
21. Went for a hard walk	0.45					0.65	
22. Trip with family by car	0.36					0.45	
23. Theatre/opera/ballet	0.67						0.82
24. Concerts/festivals	0.68						0.80
Percentage of common variance	51.26	14.94	12.09	7.51	6.28	5.65	4.79
Percentage of trace	100.00	29.2	23.6	14.7	12.3	11.0	9.3
Eigenvalue		3.584	2.902	1.802	1.506	1.355	1.149
Alpha		0.7650	0.6408	0.5344	0.5183	0.5307	0.6490

APPENDIX C: FACTOR ANALYSIS OF MOTIVATION

	h^2	Relax/ Sun	Learning/ Culture	Lifestyle/ Social	Fitness
1. Get away from stress	0.61	0.76			
2. Enjoy beach and sea	0.61	0.74			
3. Get new strength	0.58	0.72			
4. Enjoying the sun	0.58	0.69			
5. To have time to do what you please	0.50	0.68			
6. Swim in the sea	0.50	0.67			
7. Time for the family	0.44	0.65			
8. Avoid stress concerning the transfer	0.51	0.61			
9. Let the kids have a good time	0.44	0.59			
10. Get away from noise and pollution	0.45	0.55			
11. Be romantic	0.34	0.50			
12. Swim in the pool	0.30	0.45			
13. Learning about another – country and culture	0.74		0.86		
14. Visiting known places and attractions	0.67		0.79		
15. Experiencing the nature and the surroundings	0.74		0.78		
16. Cultural experiences	0.60		0.75		
17. To learn something new	0.54		0.64		
18. Travel around	0.40		0.60		
19. Experience the atmosphere	0.45		0.58		
20. Go on organised sight-seeing trips	0.38		0.55		

APPENDIX C *(Continued)*

	h^2	Relax/ Sun	Learning/ Culture	Lifestyle/ Social	Fitness
21. Practicing language skills	0.41		0.51		
22. To keep in touch with friends	0.53		0.40		
23. Get to know new people	0.52			0.71	
24. To demonstrate what you can do	0.53			0.70	
25. Keep in contact with the family	0.39			0.65	
26. To use your capabilities	0.53			0.58	
27. To develop your personality/hobby	0.53			0.57	
28. Not being lonely at holiday	0.36			0.54	
29. Change your lifestyle	0.39			0.53	
30. Eat and drink in good company	0.36			0.50	
31. Have fun	0.32			0.44	
32. To get exercise	0.71				0.81
33. Get new energy	0.58				0.81
34. Take care of your health	0.65				0.75
35. To work out hard – get tired	0.60				0.70
Percentage of common variance	51.02	22.28	15.97	7.21	5.62
Percentage of trace	100.0	43.67	31.30	14.13	11.01
Eigenvalue		7.780	5.590	2.522	1.967
Alpha		0.8702	0.8592	0.8256	0.8786

MARKET DEVELOPMENTS IN THE HOTEL SECTOR IN EASTERN CENTRAL EUROPE

Colin Johnson and Maurizio Vanetti

ABSTRACT

This paper analyses expansion strategies of international hotel operators in Eastern Central Europe (ECE) in relation to the changes in tourism supply and demand in ECE. Potential market sectors for the ECE region are explored, with the most promising for Eastern Central Europe being an emphasis on green or nature tourism, cultural tourism, the tourist business market and, finally the rejuvenation of the traditional spas and medicinal tourism of the region. Two groups of International hotel companies are identified. The majority group who are pursuing a follow-the-customer approach for the international business client in Prague, Budapest or Warsaw, and the smaller group who have expressed interest in supplying the budget and mid markets in secondary and tertiary locations.

INTRODUCTION

This paper derives from desk and field research undertaken on expansion strategies of international hotel operators in Eastern Central Europe (ECE). Because of the growing importance of services in economic development, there is an impressive body of knowledge on the process of internationalization and service industries

Advances in Hospitality and Leisure
Advances in Hospitality and Leisure, Volume 1, 153–175

ISSN: 1745-3542/doi:10.1016/S1745-3542(04)01010-0

that may be traced back to Carmen and Langeard (1980), and has since been added to *inter alia* by Dunning (1989), Segal-Horn (1994, 1998), Lovelock and Yip (1996), Vandermerwe and Chadwick (1992), McLaughlin and Fitzsimmons (1996), Edvardsson et al. (1993).

The last comprehensive academic study on internationalization and the hotel industry was undertaken at the beginning of the 1990s, however (Kundu, 1994) and it is believed that with the major changes impacting upon the industry, especially the effects of technology and globalization, it would be useful to establish the important key factors in the internationalization process, in the context of Eastern Central Europe. Although there are many different geographical groupings of "Eastern Central Europe," for the purpose of this thesis, Kostecki's (1994) definition of the region as including Hungary, Poland and the Czech and Slovak Republics is used, together with another country in the region that had a border with the West, Slovenia. These five countries are at a comparable stage of economic transformation, and constitute the study region.

In determining an appropriate methodology, it was decided to use the cut-off method. This methodology is widely used in applied research on business sectors, and consists of ranking companies from the largest to the smallest (Kuhn & Fankhauser, 1996), starting with the former; further companies are added until the sample represents at least 75% of the total market. In the present study, 88% of the hotel rooms controlled by international hotel operators were included in the sample. It was believed that the cut-off method would allow for an appropriate range of descriptive statistical applications, thus providing a powerful tool.

It has been estimated that by the end of 1998 there were approximately 15.4 million hotel rooms worldwide (WTO, 1998). Growth in rooms has been estimated at 3% per year, resulting in 16.24 million rooms by the end of 2000. This figure includes both domestically controlled hotel rooms, and those controlled by international chains. It has been estimated that chain control of hotel rooms amounts to approximately 33.1% of the total rooms worldwide.

The population for the study consisted of 86 of the largest international companies identified from the directory of the American Hotel and Lodging Association, from the annual hotel ranking of the International Hotel and Restaurant Association, and from the Hotel Report of Travel and Tourism International (2001). The total number of rooms controlled by these 86 companies is 3,987,595, i.e. some 24% of total rooms worldwide. All major international hotel chains have been included. The many large chains that operate solely within national borders, notably in the U.S., account for the discrepancy with the overall world total supply by chains.

A comprehensive questionnaire in four sections was developed and tested. The first section sought general historical information and was designed to give a general picture of the dynamics of the industry in terms of growth, concentration and internationalization. The second section dealt with the structural and behavioral variables considered important to an international hotel operator when it decides to "go international" and also the perceived competitive strengths of international hotel companies compared to other major competitors in the arena, and also compared to indigenous hotel operators from the study region.

The third section was concerned with the critical locational considerations for hotel operators when deciding on international expansion. The final section's aim was to provide an overview of the market in terms of years of operation and form of involvement, foreign direct investment (FDI) management contract or franchising.

Respondents were asked to rate on an 11-point Likert scale (from –5 "significant disadvantage" to +5 "significant advantage") covering the issues of the perceptions of the competitive advantages, the ownership, "O" advantages of their company and perceived sources of specific locational "L" advantages within the region. The resulting rankings for the major variables were then averaged and the results displayed in graphical and tabular form.

Owing to the complexity of the questionnaire it was necessary to solicit correspondents repeatedly and encourage them to complete it. This was undertaken throughout June and July 2001. The response rate from the overall population, especially from the major players, was extremely high at 47.7%. Each of the ten major companies by number of rooms and 15 out of the top 20 hotel operators were included in the sample.

The momentous events of the late 1980s, which culminated in the collapse of communism in the former centrally planned economies of Eastern Central Europe, are common knowledge. One of the major consequences for the international hotel industry was the re-evaluation of tourism and the hotel industry within the economies of the nations in the region. Governments became more aware of the value of travel and tourism in generating hard currency earnings and creating employment and investment opportunities. In the immediate aftermath of the transition from planned to market economies, international hotel operators eagerly anticipated the possibilities of entering a large, potentially very lucrative market that had been hidden by the iron curtain for more than half a century.

It appeared that almost every major international hotel operator wanted to have a property in the region (Hunt, 1993). This euphoria quickly evaporated, however, to be replaced by scepticism and cynicism on the part of international hotel companies, who had become impatient with the legal framework, administrative bureaucracy and inherent corruption in many of the countries concerned. It is clear that the massive challenges involved in changing from totally planned economies to free market economies could not be dealt with in the short- or medium-term, but rather within a timeframe of ten to fifteen years. Specific problems that affected the hotel industry were the shortage of external funding, uncertainties on the part of international hotel operators over long-term political stability in the region, economic performance and property title (Trew, 1993). In addition, there was a lack of local capital to fund development projects, and per capita income was insufficient to generate domestic demand.

TOURISM IN FORMER COMMUNIST COUNTRIES

The key difference between tourism in Western Europe and in Eastern Central Europe may be attributed to the importance of the Marxist ideological legacy, which considered the service sector as "non productive." As a service industry, tourism was therefore of low significance among the priorities of national governments in the region (Hall, 1992; Williams & Balaz, 2000). The main role of tourism was in rejuvenating the workforce and in providing collective holiday and recreation facilities. This peculiar state form of tourism provided domestic provision in the form of resorts for trade union members, and other sectors of society including, for example, mothers with infants, offering those holidays at reduced cost, or sometimes even free (Baum, 1995). This development of networks of tourist resorts has had a major impact on the distribution and nature of hotel and para-hotel stock in the region. The vacation centres, often in large numbers and of considerable size, tended to be of low quality.

In addition, the socialist model also took the form of cumbersome visa regulations, strict levels of security, regimented tours and restrictive currency regulations (Business Central Europe, July/August 1993). Kerpal (1990) gives a clear account of the workings of the tourism "system" as practiced towards both local populations and foreign visitors. As a result of such policies, in 1987, only 3% of international arrivals to Eastern Central Europe came from outside the continent and over 60% from within that region (Hall, 1999). There were also severe limitations on the local population within Eastern Central Europe wishing to travel outside the Comecon states, while Western visitors were often regarded with deep suspicion. With the exception of business trips or visiting friends and relatives (VFR), western visitors were "welcomed" only as part of an organised group (Kerpal, 1990). An additional factor was the effect of the policy on attitudes to service and client orientation, considered so important by marketing writers (Lovelock, 1992; Zeithaml & Bitner, 1996). Owing to the communist system, in which everybody had guaranteed employment, it was not considered necessary, or even useful, to take into account the needs of the clients. There was a form of "studied indifference" (Hall, 1999) on the part of the service staff towards guests, which was prevalent throughout communist states.

It was not surprising, therefore, that this model of tourism organization was not perceived as attractive to Western Europeans and tourists from outside Europe. As a result, the region missed the opportunity of mass holidays in the 1970s (Hall, 1991), which were subsequently exploited by Mediterranean destinations such as Spain and Greece. Towards the late 1970s and early 1980s, there was a reassessment of the role of tourism, however, and governments began to realize its potential, especially in the creation of foreign exchange.

Increasing Importance of Tourism

Despite the role that tourism has played in restructuring the economies of Eastern Central Europe, there are few explanatory models for tourism development in the region (Hall, 1998b; Williams & Balaz, 2002). Many Western European and U.S. tourism experts responded quickly to mandates from the European Union and other agencies to draw up tourism development plans and strategies at regional and national levels. The U.S. consultancy company Arthur D. Little, for example, assessed the intrinsic value of Polish tourism and estimated that if Poland developed 170 tourist sites there was a potential for tripling tourism levels by 2004. The company believed that even through natural development tourism would grow by 70% between 1994 and 2004, increasing tourism revenues from US$1.6 billion to US$2.8 billion (Tour and Travel News, 1994).

The journey to a market economy was evidently not going to be easy for tourism and hotel enterprises, however. On the one hand there were still frequent examples of extreme bureaucracy, backward technology, obsolete equipment and under-utilized maintenance and service departments, and on the other there was an urgent need to develop a more effective framework for market regulation (Williams & Balaz, 2000). As a major service industry, it has had an economic and social impact by exposing domestic enterprises to national and international market forces, encouraging foreign direct investment (FDI) in tourist-related facilities, by stimulating comparative market advantage and niche specialization and finally by encouraging greater and closer interaction between formerly restricted host populations and the outside world (Hall, 1999).

Changes in Supply and Demand

Tourism now plays an increasingly important role in the economies of the countries in Eastern Central Europe. Six countries receive over $1 billion per annum from tourist revenues (Hall, 1999). In 1985 there were 36 million tourist arrivals, which doubled within a decade, and which are forecast to grow six-fold from the original figure by 2020 (Paci, 1995; WTO, 2000). By 2020, it is estimated that one tourist in every three coming to Europe will choose a Central or Eastern European destination, and average annual growth in the region will be 4.4%, which is 1.3% above that of Europe as a whole (TTI, 2000a).

The reasons for these optimistic forecasts include both internal developments, such as the easing of entry, exit and currency restrictions, and the growth of GDP in the region, together with increased disposable income and the mobility of many Eastern Europeans themselves, thereby stimulating domestic demand for tourism products. Externally, there was a change in the image of the region and more substantial Western media attention to it, as well as increasing Western involvement in aspects of tourism development, including improvements to infrastructure; financial support, especially from the European Union (EU), through both EU development funds and supportive trade policies and investments, as countries in the region have applied and been successful in applying for full membership of the EU. The net result has been substantial increases, especially in terms of arrivals and receipts.

International Arrivals

Often industry analysts focus upon the level of tourist arrivals to a country as an indicator of tourism success. Figure 1 shows the evolution and projections of tourist arrivals in Eastern Central European countries from 1988. As shown in

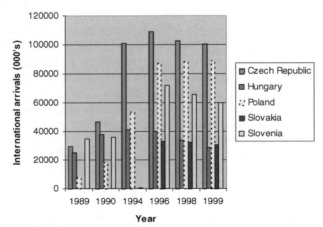

Fig. 1. Tourist Arrivals in Eastern Central Europe 1988–1998 (Thousands). *Source:* Euromonitor (1995), WTO (2001).

Fig. 1, while there is strong growth in Poland, the Czech Republic and Hungary, international tourism in the region started from an extremely low base; additionally, the figures should be regarded with some caution, as arrivals contain a significant number of low-spending day trippers/excursionists, especially from other Eastern Central European countries, as well as cross-border traders and local cross-border customers for many services ranging from medicinal to prostitution, reflecting differences (and availability) of goods and services across borders (Hall, 1995). Despite these caveats, however, the progress is impressive. By 1994, Hungary, Poland and the Czech Republic were in the top 10 rankings of the WTO, in 4th, 7th and 8th positions respectively. The change was the most dramatic for Poland, which had been ranked 16th in 1984. Unfortunately for the countries concerned, these huge increases were not sustainable over the longer-term, and by 1999 Poland had slipped to 10th place, with the Czech Republic and Hungary 13th and 14th respectively.

Tourist Receipts

As seen in Fig. 2, the three major tourism markets of Hungary, the Czech Republic and Poland record the most impressive growth in tourism receipts during this period. The first two both increased their receipts during the period by a factor of seven, while in comparison with 1988 Poland does so by a factor of 42. Again at a much lower overall level, Slovakia and Slovenia have 9 times and 3.6 times more revenues respectively. Also of note is that despite relative stagnation in terms of

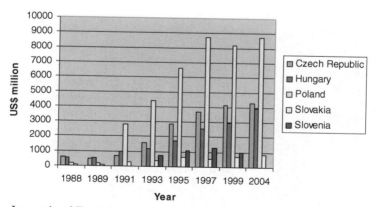

Fig. 2. International Tourism Receipts in Eastern Central Europe 1980–2004 (Excluding Transport U.S.$ Million). *Source:* Euromonitor (1995, 2001), Hall (1992), WTO (2000).

tourist arrivals, within the last five years Slovakia and Slovenia have both managed to increase their receipts.

However, as with Figure 1 and Figure 2 should be interpreted with some caution. Although it shows significant, even spectacular, growth in receipts, one should remember that the base was extremely low, when 61% of the international arrivals were from within Comecon countries, with extremely limited spending power. Central Eastern Europe still lags behind the rest of Europe in terms of per capita levels of tourism income generated. Although the region takes 25% of all European arrivals, it receives only one-eighth of the revenues (WTO, 1999). These trends need to be taken into account by international hotel operators considering expansion into the area. Another equally important trend is the potential of the domestic market, as discussed in the next section.

The Importance of Domestic Tourism in Eastern Central Europe

For many years it has been a criticism of Eastern Central Europe that there is no domestic demand. However, on closer examination of the data, it is clear that there are considerably inter-country differences (Fig. 3). Evident from Fig. 3 is the large share of Hungary's participation in domestic tourism, more than five times greater than that of the Czech Republic, which has a slightly larger population. Also clear from the chart is the major increase in Polish domestic tourism, with over 2.5 times the number of overnight stays in hotels in five years. Given the potential size of the Polish market, this should be of interest to international hotel operators, especially

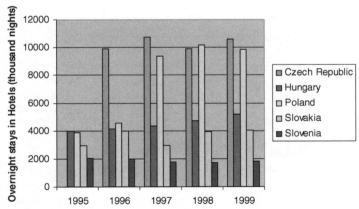

Fig. 3.   Trends in Domestic Tourism 1995–1999, by Country. *Source:* WTO (2001).

those such as Accor who have "hard-budget" products like "Formule 1," targeted at the domestic market.

Current and Future Tourism Markets

The diversity of physical and cultural environments within Eastern Central Europe offers significant possibilities for market segmentation. Tourism to the area has traditionally focused on particular attractions. *Coastal tourism* is well developed in the study countries, including the Polish Baltic littoral and Slovenia. *Winter upland tourism*, for both the domestic and international markets, has long been a feature of the region in Poland, Slovakia, e.g. in the Tatra Mountains, and Slovenia, but the general quality of facilities and the winter sports product available is low in comparison with major western markets. The demand has therefore often come from package-tour companies, specialising in the less advanced, younger markets, and selling predominantly on low price (Hall, 1995). As in many Western European ski resorts, the lack of snow in recent years has also affected operators, which if prolonged may eventually have far-reaching results.

There is recent evidence, however, of new market niches being opened up, which may provide a higher value-added. As may be gathered from the preceding sections, tourist supply in Eastern Central European countries has until recently been more angled towards quantity rather than quality and has not been overly concerned with sustainability. This is now changing, as it has been recognized that one of the major trends in tourism development is towards sustainability, owing to the importance for the environment and providing for the future (World Travel and Tourism Council, 1995). In addition, it can be shown that, provided resources are properly managed, the economic return for the provider and so for the national economy can be higher than otherwise. Research is therefore focusing on targeting high-spending groups such as adherents of "eco-tourism," including nature and rural or farm tourism; the meetings, incentive conference and events markets (MICE) (Hall, 1995); and cultural tourism, all of which attempt to alleviate seasonality.

Green, Rural, and Ecotourism

There are many definitions of "eco" or "green" tourism. To be judged "truly eco," a tourism product should involve travel to a natural area, be supportive of the conservation of the biosphere, bring benefit to local communities and lead to a greater understanding of the natural or cultural environment visited. For our present purposes, the general concept of "green tourism" is more important than compliance with each and every possible criterion; green tourism is therefore taken to include nature and rural or farm tourism. Paradoxically, when the image of Eastern Central Europe is often one of widespread pollution, and when large areas, such as the summer holiday camps around Lake Balaton Hungary, were transformed under unimaginative socialist schemes, the region as a whole was in reality under-urbanized by Western European standards. There are indeed wide tracts of unspoilt countryside. In some countries, e.g. Poland, a large proportion of the population still live and work in rural areas, where farm tourism has been identified as a major possibility. Rural tourism is also an integral part of the tourism planning for Slovenia (Sirse & Mihalic, 1999) and has been identified as having potential in Slovakia (Clarke et al., 2001) and Hungary (Suli-Zakar, 1993).

Other eco-tourism projects include the large, wooded, mountain region in Czech Bohemia, marketed as "Europe's green roof," the Biospher reserves in Aggtelek (Hungary)and Trebonsko (the Czech Republic) (Johnson, 2004) and monitoring the effects of wolves in the Carpathian areas in Southeast Poland. In the winter, cross-country skiing also has potential, in contrast to its more destructive and energy- and capital-intensive Alpine cousin, classified as "hard tourism." The "softer" cross-country form is far less damaging, and makes good use of environmental assets (Hall, 1995). Such developments can complement and diversify rural enterprises, transforming them into tourism and leisure SMEs offering accommodation, food, local crafts, and other services (Hall, 1998a), bringing improved incomes and standards of living, and the lessening of urban attractiveness and rural decline (Hall, 1995).

Eco-tourism is potentially a very lucrative market, when eco-tourists typically spend more per capita than the package tour "mass tourist." It is estimated that at present, however, the eco-tourist market represents only some 2–4% of all travel expenditure (Travelmole 29.01.02).

Meetings, Incentive, Conference and Events Market (MICE)

The development of the meetings, incentive, conference and events markets (MICE) sector is directly linked to the development of business travel in both continents and individual countries. Meetings and conferences are relatively underdeveloped in Eastern Europe, and the sector has been identified as having potential (Hall, 1995). The size of the market is estimated at 1–4% of business tourism, but the latter is difficult to estimate in certain countries, e.g. in a wide range between 6 and 35%. For example, the WTO estimated 6.5% of travel to India was business travel, compared to 33.9% for Taiwan (TTI, 2000b, p. 159). The potential in Eastern Central Europe may be seen by reference to Poland, which, despite having 36% of arrivals as business travelers, has less than 2% of the meetings market (TTI, 2000b, pp. 30–31).

Cultural Tourism

Although defining "culture" is even more problematic than defining "tourism," the conceptual definition used by Richards (1997) is adequate for this relatively brief section. Cultural tourism is "The movement of persons to cultural attractions away from their normal place of residence, with the intention to gather new information and experiences to satisfy their cultural needs" It is the learning factor that is the most important constituent of cultural tourism. Within Europe the importance of culture and the possibilities for cultural tourism have been compared economically to that of the major motor vehicle producers of the USA, and recognized as deserving priority by political decision makers such as the European Union (Richards, 1997).

In Eastern Central Europe there are examples that fit into every category of the typolology, which will add to the already abundant European *richessse*. Examples of cultural tourism already evident in the region include examples of cultural tourism centered around monuments (which is also sometimes referred to as Heritage tourism), include the cities of Prague, Budapest and Krakow, which have been well publicised. Additionally there are, especially in the Czech Republic, many smaller historic towns that are richly endowed in cultural monuments.

Art events are also widely held with "high culture" being represented by Poland's "Warsaw Autumn" contemporary music festival, the Czech Republic's "Prague Spring" music festival and the Hungarian Budapest summer opera and ballet festival. There is also a range of national, regional and local dance groups, choirs and folklore music events (Hall, 1998a) In addition there are a wide range of theatres, art galleries and open-air village museums. The latter were constructed to give a sense of national pride and identification, rather than for foreign tourists (Hall, 1998a). One such example of a village museum is to be found near Luhochiviche in the Czech Republic, and there are over 30 in Poland.

On the accommodation side, there are a number of guide books and listings offering stays in historic palaces and country houses "Indeed Poland" describes over 20 historic properties throughout Poland including the 13th Century Cistercian monastery at Podklasztorze. Other segments being developed include wine tourism in Slovakia (centered around Pizinok, Modra and Valtice) Hungary and Slovenia. Much of the tourism development is in the development of wine routes that are included in tourist maps and in specialist viticultural maps of the countries. For example in Hungary there is detailed information on the 22 wine producing regions (Hungary is the eleventh largest wine producer in the world), published by the Hungarian Agricultural Marketing Centre (Hall et al., 2000). Due to the region's diverse religious background, there are numerous churches, monasteries, synagogues and shrines that lend themselves to religious tourism.

Rejuvenation of Spa and Health Tourism

Owing to the presence of mineralized water in many of the countries in Eastern Central Europe, there is a tradition of spa and medicinal tourism going back several centuries. Under the *ancien régime*, some of the resorts became fashionable through patronage from the aristocracy. Unfortunately, however, many of the establishments over time were managed along institutional lines for a largely domestic population, and so suffered from a lack of investment. The Danubius chain in Hungary has specialized in this niche, and are now also internationalizing into neighboring countries. Spa tourism is excellently placed both to tap into the senior or "grey market" that is increasingly health-conscious and to diversify into sports or activity tourism (Hall, 1998). In contrast to regular tourism in the region, spa tourism has longer stays (often 1–2 weeks) and can be high value-added.

EMERGING INTERNATIONAL HOTEL INDUSTRY STRUCTURE IN EASTERN CENTRAL EUROPE

Many of these factors relating to supply and demand in Eastern Central Europe have had a major impact upon the structure of its hotel industry. The supply of hotel accommodation before 1989 was met almost exclusively through national hotel chains, despite the fact that some international chains, such as Accor, Intercontinental and Hilton had been present since the 1970s and 1980s.

Changes in Capacity by Country

While statistics available for the region can be misleading and are not always comparable (Hall, 1992; Trew, 1997), certain conclusions can nonetheless be drawn. There have clearly been major changes in the supply of hotel rooms since the fall of communism. Figure 4 shows the dynamics of hotel room supply. As seen in Fig. 4 the most dramatic change has been in the Czech Republic, especially from 1995 to 1997, when room supply almost doubled, although it has since stabilized. This may be due to the fact that tourism in the Czech Republic was heavily centered on Prague, and initially there was a chronic shortage of rooms in the capital. Growth, albeit at a reduced rate, is also apparent in Hungary and Poland. The two smaller hotel markets in the study, Slovakia and Slovenia, have experienced fluctuations in their hotel room supply over the period. This is likely to be the result of the closure of certain state hotels, as subsidies became harder to find.

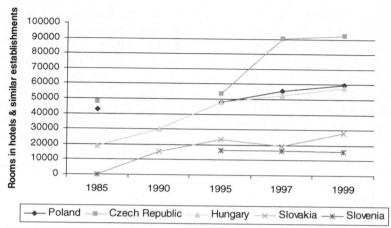

Fig. 4. Room Supply by Country, 1985–1999. *Source:* WTO (2000, 2001), Trew (1997).

After the fall of communism the lack of appropriate hotel accommodation was identified as a major problem in the region. The European Bank for Reconstruction and Development (EBRD) stated, "the lack of modern hotels and commercial facilities is constraining the development of the private sector" (EBRD, 1994, p. 27). Before this, tourism academics and hotel analysts (Bartl, 1997; Hall, 1991, 1995; Kerpal, 1993; Trew, 1997) had also been highlighting the need for mid-market and budget accommodation in the region.

Figure 5 appears to belie the experts at first glance, as the vast majority of existing rooms are in the mid-market sector. The problem, however is not the supply, but

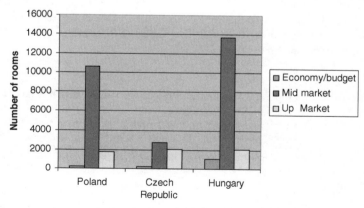

Fig. 5. Room Supply by Sector and Country, June 1999. *Source:* Mather and Todd (1999).

the quality of the hotel stock: the head of development strategy for Kosice City Council (Slovakia), Mrs Rozila Mundra, was reported to say "our problem is not lack of capacity, but the quality of what we have" (HICEE, July-August 1994, p. 13). There are two main problems with hotel supply in the region: (1) the design itself of many of the hotels, which are of post-war, Soviet, concrete-block style; and (2) the serious lack of investment for renovation and refurbishment throughout the working lives of the hotels (Roh & Andrew, 1994). Hence the need for a massive injection of funds to bring the hotels up to international standards in areas such as heating and ventilation, bathrooms and information technology. It has been estimated, for example, that to bring properties in the Orbis chain in Poland up to international standards would require between U.S.$3 and U.S.$15 million per property (HICEE, 1994).

Hotel Industry Concentration

As mentioned previously, before 1989 hotels – as components of travel and tourism enterprises – were owned entirely by the State. In contrast to the rest of the European hotel industry, which in this period displayed signs of classic service fragmentation and SME dominance, the hotel markets in Eastern Central Europe were heavily concentrated.

Different governments pursued varying methods of dealing with this concentration, either adopting "short sharp shock therapy" or adopting a more evolutionary approach. Some governments (e.g. in Hungary and Poland) wished to privatize the hotel stock by finding buyers who would purchase the chains' entire portfolio of hotels. Other governments (e.g. in the Czech Republic and Slovakia) sold individual properties, so that by 1999 over 90% of the hotel stock in these two countries was privately owned and run. This had an obvious effect on concentration in the industry, as shown by Table 1.

Table 1. Hotel Operator Concentration Ratios, 1999 (Market Share % of Turnover).

	Leading Company	Leading 2 Companies	Leading 3 Companies
Poland	37.0	65.0	90.0
Hungary	28.6	46.5	49.1
Czech Republic	3.2	6.2	8.2
Slovakia	4.6	8.1	9.4

Source: Euromonitor (2000).

There is a wide variation in levels of concentration, especially between Poland and the Czech Republic. The high level of concentration in the former is due mainly to the influence of the semi-privatized national company Orbis on the national market. In Hungary, the indigenous chain Danubius acquired individual properties and a smaller chain, which largely determined the level of concentration in the national market. This came in parallel to the Accor joint venture with the other indigenous chain, Pannonia, which accounts for almost 18% of the market. The German-based hotel company Kempinski controls 2.6% of the value. The situation in the Czech and Slovak republics is therefore the reverse of that in Hungary and Poland, with no real leaders controlling the markets.

International Hotel Operators' Locations and Choice of Entry Mode

International hotel chains appear to be pursuing a classic "hub and spoke" development strategy, searching for gateway city locations and adopting a very cautious approach. Despite academic and industry experts stating for almost ten years that the need in the region is for mid-market and budget accommodation, the properties developed have almost exclusively (with the exception of Accor) been at the upper and luxury end of the market. There are several chains with over half a dozen properties in the region (Marriott, Intercontinental, Accor, and Vienna International). The latter is one of the large numbers of Austrian companies serving the business community in the region. Choice of location is again of note, with Holiday Inn and Intercontinental having a spread of properties in four of the five countries, while Vienna International heavily focuses on the Czech (and principally Prague), market.

Accor has adopted the most ambitious strategy, with its joint venture with the Pannonia chain in Hungary: with its major presence, the company has begun the distribution of its main Ibis, Mercure and Novotel brands. Holiday Inn has also been adventurous, signing a franchise agreement with Global Hotels Development Group (GHDG) to develop 20 hotels within Poland over 20 years. The agreement gives Holiday Inn approximately 4% of revenues in return for its expertise and brand name. Total investment is approximately U.S.$116 million, with construction of four Crowne Plaza Hotels (five star), 4 Holiday Inns (mid range), and ten Holiday Inn Express (budget).

GHDG also intends to modernize existing properties and include them in the chain. Best Western has also developed its marketing consortium in the area, with independent hoteliers subscribing in Prague, Brno and Ljubljana.

It is useful at this stage to have an overall view of hotel chain activity in the region, and per country. Table 2 gives an overview of the major hotel chains presence.

Table 2. Profile of Hotel Chain Operations in Eastern Central Europe, September 2001.

	Poland	Czech Republic	Hungary	Slovakia	Slovenia
Total Rooms	59,704	92,138	57,674	27,983	15,753
Hotel group rooms	17,048	8,543	17,548	346	306
No. Hotel operators	11	14	16	1	1
No. Hotel brands	15	18	23	2	2
No. Hotels operated by publicly quoted companies	75	14	64	2	2
No. Hotels operated by domestic groups	79	24	100	N.K	N.K

Source: International Hotel database, 04.09.01; WTO (2001).

As may be seen in Table 2, the Czech and, in particular, Hungarian hotel markets have the highest chain penetration. At first glance the Polish and Hungarian markets appear to be very similar. The major difference, however, is in potential, for Poland has 15–20 secondary cities which would support mid-market and budget hotels; Hungary, less than a third of the size of Poland in population and area, is much more limited. Details from our questionnaire survey yielded additional information on the companies present in the region.

As may be seen from Fig. 6, the bulk of the hotel properties in the study are in Poland and Hungary, accounting for 82% of all hotel developments. This is mainly due to Accor's long-term strategy of investment in the region, particularly in those two countries (the company has 19 properties in Hungary and 62 in Poland). With 84 properties in the region, Accor's development represents 65% of all international developments. Bass (now re-named Intercontinental) second in worldwide ranking

Fig. 6. International Hotel Distribution in Eastern Central Europe. *Source:* Our questionnaire.

scale, is far behind with just 14% of hotel developments, but is the only company with properties in all five countries in the region.

Marriott with six hotels (4.6%) and Choice with four (3%) are next in line, followed by Cendant, Carlson, and Hilton International who all have three hotels (2.3%) each.

The actual number of internationally operated hotels included in the study is considered to be quite representative, covering in the order of 83% of all international hotels in the region. A search of secondary sources in September 2001 found that there were a total of 157 internationally operated properties in Eastern Central Europe (The European Hotel Groups Database, International Hospitality Research-Industry Intelligence and Pricewaterhousecooopers).

It is of note that Poland has increased in importance fairly recently, due mainly to its progress in economic and financial reforms and the obvious potential of the market compared with its much smaller neighbors. The Czech Republic, with 15% of the total hotel developments in the region is evidently important, but most of the developments have tended to focus solely on Prague, resulting in congestion and concentration in the capital, at the expense of investment in the provinces. In relation to Eastern Central Europe, there has been frequent reference to the problems encountered by hotel developers in seeking suitable locations and developing properties. Table 3 gives information on types of market entry mode used by the hotel companies in the study.

Table 3. Forms of Involvement by Company.

Company	Fully Owned	Partly Owned	Mgt. Contract	Franchise	Total
Accor		25	3	56	84
Intercontinental	1	1	3	13	18
Marriott	2			4	6
Choice Hotels				4	4
Cendant				3	3
Carlson			3		3
Hilton International			3		3
Forte		2			2
Dorint Hotels & Resorts			2		2
Starwood Hotels			1		1
Hyatt			1		1
Barcelo Hotels			1		1
Four Seasons			1		1
Kempinski AG			1		1
Total	3	28	19	80	130

Source: Our questionnaire: Various media.

As may be seen, only 2.3% of the hotels are fully owned. A relatively high proportion (22%) are partly owned, owing mainly to Accor's ownership agreements with Pannonia in Hungary and Orbis in Poland, with 15% of the involvement relating to management contracts, and the overwhelming majority, 62%, in the form of franchising. This reflects the companies' perception of instability in the region, with the lower risk option of non-equity being preferred. There has also been evidence recently that owing to the economies of scale and scope the returns from non-equity modes may at least equal those of FDI (Contractor & Kundu, 1998).

Previously, there were two major brakes on tourism development – a lack of capital and no or extremely limited domestic demand. There are now signs, however, that local and regional entrepreneurs are appearing who have the capital and the inclination to invest in hospitality enterprises (Trew, 1997). In Poland, for instance, Electrum SA, a holding of several Polish companies has created Elector a chain with the potential for 100 hotels across the country. The company is seeking to franchise the Elektor brand name, with partners taking a 49% share in individual properties. An additional issue considered crucial for development by international hotel operators is that of potential sales in the region. Table 4 provides data on projected sales by country.

As this shows, the growth in hotel sales after 1999 has been extremely varied, with reduced but substantial growth still continuing in the Hungarian, and to a lesser degree the Slovak markets. Growth in the Czech market is much reduced, however, and in the Polish market is in the decline. This figure should be treated with some caution, however, as it is based on the assumption that domestic tourism will decline. International tourists are forecast to increase slightly in this period, however, and whilst it is evident that tourism infrastructure will have to be improved considerably, an actual decline seems unlikely, and there may well be rather a modest growth.

Table 4. Hotel Sales by Country, 1999–2004.

	1999 U.S.$ (Million)	% Growth 1995–1999	2004 U.S.$ (Million)	% Growth 1999–2004
Czech Republic	1585	101.3	1637	3.2
Hungary	264	63.8	387	46.5
Poland	2379	88.1	2172	−8.7
Slovakia	79	71.5	93	17.7

Note: 2004 figures are estimates.
Source: Euromonitor (2000).

CONCLUSIONS

Tourism within the region is in many respects at a crossroads. On one hand, there is the temptation of providing the older model of mass tourism that took off in Western Europe during the late 1960s and 1970s. There is clear demand from the domestic markets expressed in large numbers of charter holidaymakers flying to the Mediterranean. This model of tourism, however, is increasingly viewed by tourist experts (Poon, 1993) as unsustainable in the long term, and not appropriate for modern business practices. Alternatively, there is the better, far more sustainable model of seeking to exploit higher value-added niches, e.g. nature and rural tourism, which would use the rich rural heritage of the region to its best advantage, both in the summer and by promoting cross-country skiing in the winter (Hall, 1998a). Other highly viable niches include the various forms of cultural tourism described, as well as health tourism and the lucrative business tourism.

Turning specifically to the locational strategies of the international hotel operators, it is useful to consider their strategies from the aspect of: (1) which locations were considered the most attractive and why; (2) which mode of market entry was used; and (3) which markets the operators were targeting. It is apparent that of the 14 hotel operators included in the study, two main groups may be discerned. The majority group belongs to those operators who operate a small number (1–3) of properties in the region. These are located in the main cities of Prague, Budapest, Warsaw and latterly, Krakow. Marriott is something of an exception with six properties in the region, due to determined efforts by Marriott to expand in Europe, along with a strong brand name. This strategy is wholly consistent with expansion strategies of hotel companies entering new markets in other parts of Europe.

The second group consists of just two companies, Accor and Bass, who together control almost 80% of the properties in the study. These two companies are the largest, most international hotel operators and both have held a long-term presence in the region. Accor has by far pursued the most adventurous and long-term strategy in the region, having completed two major mergers and acquisition activity with chains in Hungary (Pannonia) and in Poland (Obis). This strategy is the result of Accor's innovativeness and ability to live with a certain degree of ambiguity within one of its major brand names. An important factor in this development is the particular structure of the hotel industry due to the legacy of communism. As mentioned earlier, the structure of the hotel industry in Eastern Central Europe was the inverse of Western Europe. The hotel industry was heavily concentrated, often with either monopolistic or oligopolistic structures. Accor saw long-term market opportunities by marrying one or more of its brands to sizeable domestic chains.

Historically, there is evidence of a clear preference for non-equity expansion methods by the hotel industry. This is due mainly to the applicability of franchising and management contracts modalities, and the benefits of marginal costing. The study showed that the majority of international hotel companies have adopted this form of market-entry strategy for the region. Over 76% of the properties in the study are either management contracts or franchised, with the latter dominating with a 62% market share. This shows a higher non-equity rate for the region of nearly 10% compared to the 54.4% reported by Kundu in his worldwide study in 1994. Only 2.3% of the properties are fully owned by the hotel corporations.

One of the findings relating to perceptions of the region was that, in the view of hotel executives, Eastern Central Europe is still somewhat volatile politically and suffers from problems of endemic corruption and limited international demand. The majority group operators have, therefore, deliberately decided to expand cautiously with flagship properties in key cities for high value-added international business tourists before considering locating in secondary and tertiary sites with lower-market properties.

Our study shows that this strategy does not exploit the full potential of the region, for two main reasons. Firstly, there is evidence that the deluxe end of the market is reaching saturation point in Budapest and Prague. Secondly, and more importantly, there has been evidence for a number of years of the need in the market to bridge the polarization between the extremely expensive five-star international markets and the very cheap, but far from internationally acceptable domestic provision. This presents market opportunities ideal for the standardized one, two and three-star branded accommodation that could operate at internationally recognized standards for both domestic and international leisure tourists.

The survey showed that for European chains, leisure tourism was regarded as important. These properties would also be appealing to the increasing domestic markets. Rather than slowly establishing a lone bridgehead, a network of budget and mid-sector properties could be created, gaining valuable brand recognition and customer loyalty by being first in the market. Western hotel brands, relatively unknown outside of the major metropolis, could enjoy great advantages and differentiation from the largely domestic supply.

Eastern Central Europe has a total population of more than 65.5 million people, greater than the population of the U.K. or France. It would seem that, due to both the geographical origin of the chains and the current market segments that they serve, the possibilities of successfully operating in Eastern Central Europe have not been fully appreciated by hotel executives (especially in relation to companies from Asia and the United States). It would appear from the research that Eastern Europe is physically and culturally alien to many hotel operators. It is of note that two-thirds of the companies had no properties in the region (including Hilton hotel

Corporation, based in Beverly Hills, CA, the fifth largest in the world), and of these 27 companies, 50% were not considering opening properties in the region in the short or medium term.

It would be naïve to assume that there will not be major obstacles to future developments in the region, especially a lack of investment, high seasonality and the absence of comprehensive tourism strategies being implemented. Nor should one underestimate the magnitude of the problems in areas such as administration and bureaucracy, continuing confusion over property rights and widespread corruption and crime. Removing bureaucracy does not create entrepreneurs (Paliwoda, 1997). Problems still to be resolved include high taxes on imports, finding partners who have the experience necessary in negotiating contracts and the ongoing lack of sophisticated business skills. Fortunately, among the companies that have pursued new opportunities in the region, some have adopted far-sighted strategies, and foregoing immediate profits so as to build long-term partnerships that will ultimately benefit both parties. Their readiness to take risks is a tacit recognition of the relative stability of the business environment and the adaptation of local society to enormous social, political, economic and financial changes, as economies "in transition" move to "normal" business environments.

ACKNOWLEDGMENT

The authors would like to express their sincere apprecition to Dr. Kundu for his advice in the development of the questionnaire.

REFERENCES

Bartl, H. (1997). The hotel market in the former Eastern Bloc-An overview. *Journal of Vacation Marketing, 3*(4), 343–353.

Baum, T. (1995). *Managing human resources in the European tourism and hospitality industry.* London: Chapman and Hall.

Carmen, J. M., & Langeard, E. (1980). Growth strategies for services firms. *Strategic Management Journal, 1*, 7–22.

Clarke, J., Denman, R., Hickman, G., & Slovak, J. (2001). Rural tourism in Ronava Okres: A Slovak case study. *Tourism Management, 22*, 193–202.

Dunning, J. H. (1989). Multinational enterprises and the growth of services: Some conceptual and theoretical issues. *Services Industries Journal, 9*(1), 5–39.

Edvardsson, B., Edvinsson, L., & Nystrom, H. (1993). Internationalisation in service companies. *The Service Industry Journal, 13*(1), 80–97.

European Bank for Reconstruction and Development (1994). *Annual report.*

Hall, C. M., Sharples, L., Cambourne, B., & Macionis, N. (2000) *Wine tourism around the world.*
Oxford: Butterworth-Heinemann.

Hall, D. R. (1991). *Tourism and economic development in Eastern Europe and the Soviet Union.*
London: Belhaven,

Hall, D. R. (1992). The challenges of international tourism in Eastern Europe. *Tourism Management,*
March, 41–44.

Hall, D. R. (1995). Tourism change in central and Eastern Europe. In: A. Montanari & A. M. Williams
(Eds), *European Tourism: Regions, Spaces and Restructuring.* Chichester, UK: Wiley.

Hall, D. R. (1998a). Central and Eastern Europe: Tourism, development and transformation. In: A. M.
Williams & G. Shaw (Eds), *Tourism and Economic Development: European Experiences* (pp.
345–375). Chichester, UK: Wiley.

Hall, D. R. (1998b). Tourism development and sustainability issues in central and Southeastern Europe.
Tourism Management, 19(5), 423–431.

Hall, D. R. (1999). Destination branding, niche marketing and national image projection in central and
Eastern Europe. *Journal of Vacation Marketing, 5*(3), 227–237.

Hotels in Central and Eastern Europe (1994). *Development Journal Limited* (July-August). London,
UK.

Hunt, J. (1993). Foreign investment in Eastern Europe's travel industry. *EIU Travel and Tourism Analyst,
3*, 65–85.

Johnson, C. (2004). Ecotourism planning considerations in Central and Eastern Europe. In:
D. Diamantis & S. Geldenhuys (Eds), *Ecotourism.* London: Continuum Books.

Kerpal, E. (1990). Tourism potential in Eastern Europe. *EIU Travel and Tourism Analyst,* 68–86.

Kostecki, M. M. (Ed.) (1994) Strategies for global service markets. In: *Marketing Strategies for Services.*
Oxford: Pergamon Press.

Kuhn, R., & Fankhauser, K. (1996). *Marktforscung, ein arbeitbuch fur das marketing-management.*
Bern: Verlag Paul Haupt.

Kundu, S. (1994). *Explaining the globalisation of service industries: The case of multinational hotels.*
Ph.D. Thesis, Rutgers, The State University of New Jersey, USA.

Lovelock, C. H. (Ed.) (1992) *Managing services.* Upper Saddle River, NJ: Prentice-Hall.

Lovelock, C. H., & Yip., G. S. (1996, Winter). Developing global strategies for service businesses.
California Management Review, Berkeley.

McLaughlin, C. P., & Fitzsimmons, J. A. (1996). Strategies for globalizing service operations.
International Journal of Service Industry Management [on-line], *7*(4), Available:
www.emerald-library.com/brev/08507dcl.htm.

Paliwoda, S. J. (1997). *Investing in Eastern Europe: Capitalizing on emerging markets.* Workingham,
UK: Addison Wesley.

Poon, A. (1993). *Tourism, technology and competitive strategies.* Oxon: CAB International.

Richards, G. (Ed.) (1997). *Cultural tourism in Europe.* Oxon: CAB International.

Roh, Y. S., & Andrew, W. (1994). U.S. hospitality investment in six potential eastern European markets.
The Council on Hotel Restaurant and Institutional Education, 17(3), 41–50.

Segal-Horn, S. (1998). The internationalization of services. *The strategy reader.* Oxford: Blackwell
Business/The Open University.

Sirse, J., & Mihalic, T. (1999). Slovenian tourism and tourism Policy – a case study. *The Tourist Review,
3*, 34–47. Association of Scientific Experts in Tourism (AIEST), St. Gallen, Switzerland.

Suli-Zakar, I. (1993). A socio-geographical study of agricultural enterprises in villages of eastern
Hungary. In: *Communications from the Geographical Institute of the Kossuth University of
Debrecen, 181*, Debrecen, Hungary.

Travelmole – Statement and Briefing on Year of Ecotourism. Available: www.travelmole.com/cgi-bin/item.cgi.

Travel and Tourism Intelligence (2000a). *Tourism in central and eastern Europe*. London: Author.

Travel and Tourism Intellligence (2000b). *Meetings, incentives, conferences and events (MICE)*, London: Author.

Travel and Tourism Intelligence (2001). *The International Hotel Industry: Special industry sector report*. London: Author.

Trew, J. (1997). Hotels in eastern Europe. *Travel and Tourism Analyst, 4,*

Williams, A. M., & Balaz, V. (2000). *Tourism in transition*. London: I. B. Tauris.

Williams, A. M., & Balaz, V. (2002). The Czech and Slovak Republics: Conceptual issues in the economic analysis of tourism in transition. *Tourism Management, 23*(1), 37–45.

World Tourism Organisation (1998). *Tourism market trends: Europe*. Madrid: Author.

World Tourism Organisation (2000). *Tourism market trends: Europe*. Madrid: Author.

World Travel and Tourism Council (1995). *Agenda 21 for the travel and tourism industry*. London.

Zeithaml, V. A., & Bitner, M. J. (1996). *Services marketing*. Singapore: McGraw-Hill.

RESEARCH NOTES

FACTORS INFLUENCING GERMAN HOTELIERS' ATTITUDES TOWARD ENVIRONMENTAL MANAGEMENT

Philip Sloan, Willy Legrand and Joseph S. Chen

ABSTRACT

This research initiates an exploratory research assessing the general attitudes of hoteliers from independently owned properties toward environmental management issues and determines the facilitators motivating them to introduce environmental management policies as well as the inhibitors hindering the adoption. This study distributes the questionnaires via email to 250 medium-sized hotels, from the rating of three to five stars, in Germany. As a result, 41 useful questionnaires are obtained and analysed. The findings suggest that the communication of new environmental initiatives between hoteliers and environmental organizations is not so effective. In general, the respondents agree that environmental policy is necessary and they view that sound environmental management systems would have a positive effect on customers' perception of the hotel.

INTRODUCTION

Since the Rio Earth Summit in 1992 and the much-publicised debate on climate change and global warming, the green movement has gained more recognition in the Hotel Industry worldwide although progress towards sustainability is slow to

Advances in Hospitality and Leisure
Advances in Hospitality and Leisure, Volume 1, 179–188
Copyright © 2004 Elsevier Ltd.
All rights of reproduction in any form reserved
ISSN: 1745-3542/doi:10.1016/S1745-3542(04)01011-2

say the least. Many larger hotel chains produce yearly environmental reports such as Accor and examples exist of eco-hotels producing low environmental impacts e.g. the Bloomfield House Hotel, Bath, U.K. and the Victoria Hotel, Freiburg, Germany (www.sustdev.org, 2004). However the majority of hotels seem not to catch up with the environmental standards promoting sustainable living.

During the past decade there has been a flurry of information made available by governmental organisations, hotel groups and scholars for hoteliers wishing to improve their environmental performance (Green Globe, 1994; Green Seal, 2002; International Hotels Environment Initiative, 1993; Marriot International, 1998; Reynolds, 1995; Webster, 2000). Although these publications prescribe different approaches to address the problem, one of their shortcomings is the lack of information on how to quantify environmental impacts resulting from hotel operations.

Environmental degradation has been high on the political agenda for the past decade following substantial press coverage of the many recent natural catastrophes. The ecological footprint (Hart, 2001) of nations, describing the use of non-renewable natural resources in terms of land acreage required to supply the average person's basic needs, can also be adapted to tourist destinations. The consumption of resource needs by tourists is creating an enormous ecological, social, and cultural legacy in many destinations around the world. Thus, the hotel business must carry a large part of the responsibility. Hotels are generally considered to be major energy end users and are involved in activities that have adverse environmental effects. Through their intensive consumption of fossil fuels directly for heating systems and indirectly in the form of electricity they are responsible for high emissions of toxic chemicals such as sulphur dioxide and nitrogen oxide that have environmental implications such as acid rain and global warming (Chan & Lam, 2002). By following what is known in the industry as "standard practices" such as daily linen cleaning, hotels consume substantial quantities of natural resources, chemical detergents, and energy. A typical hotel guest creates 1 kg of waste per night (Greenhotelier, October, 2000) and consumes large amounts of water. By introducing environmental management systems hotels can reduce their dependence on natural resources and lower operating costs at the same time as maintaining the same high quality standards.

In a recent survey conducted in both France and Norway, 70% of the study population replied that they have a preference for buying environmentally friendly products whenever possible. However, in the purchase of luxury products, like five-star accommodations, consumers are often likely to demonstrate a different buying behaviour. In some three-and four-star accommodations there are opportunities to introduce towel and sheet changing programmes on a departure only basis. However, in five-star hotels, guests pay high rates, spend more time in their rooms and like to be pampered and regard such programmes negatively (Bass Hotels & Resorts, 2001). Guests in luxury class hotels appreciate environmental systems that enhance the efficiency of the hotel infrastructure but are often not willing to accept a drop in service quality.

For many hotels promoting a greener image is undoubtedly seen as a means of increasing market segment. According to Polonsky and Rosenberg (2001), for strategic or tactical "green" marketing, to be effective, it must extensively coordinate many functional areas with the ultimate goal of creating value. In recent years the IHEI (International Hotels Environment Initiative), originally set up by eleven of the world's leading chains, has been promoting environmental progress across the industry worldwide and has worked with hotel groups such as Accor, Inter-Continental, Hilton International, and Marriott International to name a few. Marriott International's "spirit to serve" philosophy, Accor's "Hotels Environment Charter," Marco Polo Hotels' "Hotel Group Eco-Tournament" are various schemes aimed at addressing critical environmental issues (Green Hotelier, 2002). Yu (1999) states that the IHEI exemplified the concept of "environmental sponsorship" by the fact that individual hotel corporations take the initiative to involve the global industry. Other chains took the initiative into their own hands. Fairmont Hotels and Resorts (former Canadian Pacific Hotels & Resorts) undertook the development of an environmental programme for all its hotels (Go & Pine, 1995). Fairmont Hotels & Resorts' "Green Partnership Program," covering issues of waste management, water conservation, food redistribution, industrial composting to name a few, is considered one of the most comprehensive environmental schemes in the North American industry (Green Hotelier, 2002).

Webster (2000) analyses hotel corporations' environmental policy statements outlining the general principles and argues that this is the first step of many toward increase awareness and action. Brown (1996) warns of organisations giving the appearance of treating environmental concerns strategically without changing the control system of the business. This marketing-oriented concept is often referred to as "green washing." However, the publication and dissemination of policy statements is a primary stage, which a company must undertake to increase awareness among stakeholders of the principles governing the business. Increasing awareness means training and education as well as involving guests in a hotel's green initiatives. In many cases, this will be the first level of partnership. As formulated in Agenda 21, partnerships are an indispensable element in optimising sustainability strategies for business. Ryan (2003) writes that businesses may simply need to take a leading position in what is called "enviropreneurialism."

Ayala (2000) provides a clear example of a working partnership between hospitality, science and conservation in Panama. By supporting various conservation schemes and providing financial contribution to educational tourism research, hotels enhance their image and take a leadership role in advancing knowledge, conservation and sustainable development (Ayala, 2000). Ayala predicted, in an earlier article, that in order for hotels and hotel corporations to achieve a greater level of sustainable development, there is a need to revise not only the hardware of hotels, but rather to acquire a helicopter view of their business and their interaction with partners (Ayala, 1995). The International Tourism Partnership (ITP) brings together organisations including airlines, car rental companies, tour operators, various non-governmental organisations and hotel chains with the purpose of working on special projects and promoting responsible and sustainable actions (ITP, 2004). The ITP model exemplifies the concept of partnerships for the benefit of the whole.

Even though international legislation concerning pollution has been strengthened and accreditation for improved environmental performance such as Viabono (DEHOGA – Hotel-und Gaststättenverband) in Germany has been introduced, few examples can readily be found of hotels using significant environmental management systems. Certification is an important promotional tool for sustainable tourism and hospitality. However, the Green Hotelier (2003) reports that with around 40 regional, national and international ecolabels for tourism operating in Europe, there is potential for confusion. Font (2002) analyses the many accreditation schemes already available to tourism and hospitality businesses and also argues that the proliferation of labelling may result in more confused consumers. In addition, ecolabels are claimed to be expensive and time consuming. They also tend to attract customers interested in eco-tourism and have limited marketing power. Local and regional certification programmes should be linked to an international accreditation system (Font, 2002).

The Voluntary Initiatives for Sustainability in Tourism (VISIT) is an example of such a scheme whereby various eco-labels can be promoted via VISIT only if they meet a particular requirement level. An advisory board including the United Nations Environemental Programme (UNEP), the World Tourism Organisation (WTO) and the European Hotel and Restaurant Association (HOTREC) to name a few support VISIT (Green Hotelier, 2003). Certification, reports the Green Hotelier (2002) tends to fall into two categories. The "process" led approach, such as ISO 14001, is a certification type, which identifies the elements in setting up and implementing an environmental management system. The "performance" based method is another type where certification is then only attained by meeting certain performance criteria. Certification schemes, which involve a combination of minimum performance benchmark requirements and the implementation of management systems are amongst the strongest labels (Green Hotelier, 2002). Hotels around the world have made the first steps and have implemented environmental management systems in accordance with ISO 14001 (Green Hotelier, 2002). Starkey (1999) provides details on the conception of environmental standards and the processes by which companies can implement ISO 14001, ISO 14004 and EMAS. Fretz (1997) describes the procedures required in the successful implementation of an environmental system following ISO 14001 using a four star property located in Bonn, Germany. The case study portrays in detail the steps taken along the path to certification and also paints the potential financial benefits using environmental management accounting techniques. Bennet and James (2001) argue that environment-related management accounting practices directly affect not only the bottom line, but help businesses prioritise environmental actions, guide product pricing and enhance customer value.

Hotel managers face constant pressure to provide value to customers, ensure that their practices are not destroying their resource base, and juggle financial needs. Cater and Goodall (1997) argue that tourism enterprises are in business for the profits and "if a hotel can minimize costs by discharging untreated sewage directly into the sea, because building regulations permit, it will do so" (p. 88). Government and stakeholders constantly pressure businesses to adopt a proactive and transparent stance on environmental practices. The first environmental reports published by hotels were by Inter-Continental Hotels and Resorts and Grecotel in 1996 (Green Hotelier, 1999). Webster (2000) states that, as a core tool, the environmental audit is critical in assessing and improving performance. Environmental audits should cover a number of issues regarding a hotel's environmental policy, performance targets, measurement structure, training and education, public relations, community involvement, investment and finances. Naturally, a fundamental constituent is the examination of the operational performance comprising ecological activities of suppliers, landscaping and site management, energy-water-waste management as well as packaging and recycling (Webster, 2000). Noting that these activities are essential for businesses to "walk the talk," there is still a perception that many hoteliers simply aren't aware or are not interested in the impacts of their operations on the environment, let alone constituting an environmental audit.

Leslie (2001) conducted a project to examine the attitudes of guesthouse owners towards adopting environmentally friendly management systems. In a similar study, Kirk (1995) examined the balance of international environmental initiatives and local actions in a study of hotels in Edinburgh, Scotland in 1995. Small and medium size hospitality businesses often find the set up of environmental programmes to be the major hurdle. However, one conclusion by Kirk is that once a sound environmental management system is established many hotels see significant benefits, particularly from a public relations point-of-view, whether customers are ready to pay for some of cost incurred or not.

In general, privately owned and operated hotels do not benefit from the planning of head offices, as in hotel chains. The set up of environmental management systems, the various control systems needed, the performance reviews and reports are in the hands of owners and managers of these small and medium sized enterprises. Environmental issues often become a priority once it is already too late instead of being part of the overall business strategy. Given the current deficiencies of environmental research in the field of hospitality management, this study attempts to initiate an exploratory research assessing the general attitudes of hoteliers from independently owned properties toward environmental management issues and to determine the facilitators motivating them to adopting environmental management policies as well as the inhibitors hindering the adoption.

METHOD

A survey was deployed as the mechanism for collecting necessary data while a structured questionnaire was the instrument for measuring the opinions of the respondents. To develop the survey questionnaire, a two-stage approach using both qualitative and quantitative techniques was adopted. The qualitative method was used to determine the appropriate attributes to be included in the study questionnaire while a quantitative approach was to test if those study questions based on a continuous scale could be considered as a reliable measurement.

At the onset of the questionnaire development, several structured interviews were first conducted on hotel managers from mid-size properties. Researchers summarized the interview results and developed appropriate questions measuring the major facilitators and inhibitors pertaining to the implementation of environmental management schemes. To enhance the reliability and validity of the study questions, a pilot test was conducted on convenient samples embodying a group of hoteliers from the cities of Bonn and Cologne.

Regarding the data collection, the study distributed the questionnaires via email to two hundred and fifty medium-sized hotels, from the rating of three to five stars, in Germany. Follow-up telephone calls on those who did not reply to the survey were made a week after the first email survey was distributed. Subsequently, the second wave of follow-up calls on non-response hoteliers were given two weeks after the initial email. As a result, this study gathered 41 (response rate = 16.4%) useful questionnaires. Since hospitality and leisure researchers have just started delivering questionnaires via the Internet, this study attempts to find out if the email survey is a useful method to collect data. Regarding the response rate, 5% of questionnaires were completed and returned to the researcher team one day after the email. Within a week after distributing the questionnaires, the response rate was about 13%. Within two weeks the response was about 15%.

The major research variables analysed in this study are: (1) the factors motivating managers to adopt environmental management; and (2) the factors hindering environmental practices. For the first type of variables, this study operationally defined it as a facilitator and the second as an inhibitor. Accordingly, the facilitators comprise eight attributes and the inhibitors consist of six indicators. All attributes are based on a five-point, Likert-type scale.

RESULTS AND SUGGESTIONS

This study finds that most hoteliers are not aware of the Agenda 21 Rio Declaration on the Environment and Development while only a small proportion of respondents belong to a number of environmental organisations. The correlation (= 0.20) between the awareness of an environmental-related issue (Agenda 21) and the membership in environmental organizations is low. It implies that joining environmental organisations is not likely to enhance hoteliers' awareness towards new initiatives and environmental stewardship. The findings seem to suggest that the communication of new environmental initiatives between hoteliers and environmental organisations is not so effective.

Table 1 reports the hoteliers' awareness toward environmental management. The results show that hoteliers view the support for local conservation schemes as critical in enhancing the awareness of environmental issues. However, they do not think that hotels create much negative impact on the environment. The study also reveals that hoteliers demonstrate a positive attitude to the incorporation of environmental policies into company management philosophy. Most hoteliers agree that concern for the environment is more important than improving profitability. Additionally, the results indicate that the Industry has some

Table 1. Hoteliers' Environmental Awareness and Attitude.

Items	Mean
Hotel should support local conservation scheme	4.05
Environmental impact should be considered when deciding company policy	4.05
Environmental report is as important as the concern for environment	3.10
Improving profitability is more important than concern for environment	2.51
Hotel activities have a negative effect on the environment	2.02

Table 2.   The Facilitators Promoting Sound Environmental Practice.

Items	Mean
Producing cost saving through energy consumption	4.22
Producing cost saving through water consumption	4.17
Producing cost saving through waste management	4.12
Improving community relationship	3.56
Attracting additional market segment	3.34
Improving hotel revenue due to a better image	3.29
Improving hotel revenue due to guest satisfaction	3.15
Improving staff moral	3.00

reservations concerning improved profitability resulting from the implementation of environmental management systems.

The above findings show that hoteliers have a positive attitude towards environmental protection, regardless of their level of awareness of environmental initiatives. This is certainly welcome news to environmental organisations; however, hoteliers often need assistance in implementing environmental management systems that are not being effectively applied. Future research might further identify the particular areas of hotel operations that require assistance with regard to environmental management.

Regarding the environmental facilitators, the cost savings in energy consumption, water consumption, and waste management are considered as the major incentive that could prompt hoteliers to consider a new environmental management scheme (see Table 2). Table 3 shows that that the respondents viewed the necessity of obtaining training on environmental management as the most significant burden in implementing such a policy. Furthermore, hoteliers regard the potential cost of introducing new environmental management schemes

Table 3.   The Inhibitors Hindering Sound Environmental Practice.

Items	Mean
Requiring too much training	2.83
Being too costly	2.59
Being too complicated	2.51
Frightening away customers	1.80
Being unnecessary	1.46

as well as their perceived complication as other critical inhibitors that hinder progress towards sustainable management. Retrospectively, the respondents agree that environmental policy is necessary and they consider that environmental management systems would have a positive effect on customers' perception of hotels.

CONCLUSIONS

Incorporating the concept of sustainable development as advocated by the United Nations, this research attempts to delineate the problems and issues hindering sustainable development in the context of hotel management. This study illustrates that the problem in part lies in ineffective communication of environmental concern by governments and NGO's. The sheer amount of various eco-labels, certification and accreditation programmes works as a counter-informative instrument. Hotel managers and owners find themselves confronted with many different alternatives, without effectively being able to distinguish the differentiating benefits. A regrouping of eco-labels would certainly facilitate communication and ease the process of choosing the appropriate certification scheme by decision-makers.

Additionally, hotel profitability might later be found to be a critical consideration in determining the adoption of new environmental practices. Hotels which are privately owned and operated enterprises do not benefit from headquarter planning and support in setting up environmental schemes, usually involving auditing, analysis, corrective action and that finally lead to certification. Hence, private hoteliers must utilise their own resources to obtain eco-labelling, which appears to be too costly in terms of the investment needed. Further investigation into the costs associated with the adoption of environmental policy would shed light on the level of initial investment required.

However, it is rather enlightening to discover that most hoteliers in the sample have positive attitudes towards environmental stewardship, regardless of whether they have one form or another of certification or are members of an environmental organisation. It appears that the German hotel industry is making efforts towards gradually moving in line with other sections of its society. In conclusion, the dissemination of updated information and the development of environmental benchmarks will be vital tasks to address in the years to come.

REFERENCES

Ayala, H. (1995). Ecoresort: A 'green' masterplan for the international resort industry. *International Journal of Hospitality Management, 14*(3/4), 351–374.

Ayala, H. (2000). Surprising partners: Hotel firms and scientists working together to enhance tourism. *Cornell Hotel and Restaurant Administration Quarterly, 41*, 42–57.

Bennet, M., & James, P. (2001). The green bottom line. In: R. Welford & R. Starkey (Eds), *The Earthscan Reader in Business & Sustainable Development* (pp. 126–153). London: Earthscan Publications Ltd.

Brown, M. (1996). Environmental policy in the hotel sector: "Green" strategy or stratagem? *International Journal of Contemporary Hospitality Management, 8*(3), 18–23.

Cater, E., & Goodall, B. (1997). Must tourism destroy its resource base? In: L. France (Ed.), *Sustainable Tourism* (pp. 85–89). London: Earthscan Publications Ltd.

Chan, W., & Lam, J. (2002). Prediction of polluant emission through electricity consumption by the hotel industry in Hong Kong. *International Journal of Hospitality Management, 21*, 381–391.

DEHOGA – Hotel-und Gaststättenverband. Viabonno – Ein Weg aus dem Öko-Dickicht: Neue Dachmarke für umweltgerechten Tourismus in Deutschland (Press Release).

Font, X. (2002). Environmental certification in tourism and hospitality: Progress, process and prospects. *Tourism Management, 23*, 197–205.

Go, F., & Pine, R. (1995). *Globalization strategy in the hotel industry* (pp. 327–359). London: Routledge.

Green Hotelier (1999). Measuring, benchmarking and environmental reporting. October (16), 12–16.

Green Hotelier (2000). *Managing and reducing waste.* October (1).

Green Hotelier (2002). *Environmental labels and certification schemes.* May (25–26), 12–19.

Green Hotelier (2003). *Common standards for ecolabels.* October (29), 6.

Hart, S. (2001). Beyond greening: Strategies for sustainable world. In: R. Welford & R. Starkey (Eds), *The Earthscan Reader in Business & Sustainable Development* (pp. 7–19). London: Earthscan Publications Ltd.

Kirk, D. (1995). Environmental management in hotels. *International Journal of Contemporary Hospitality Management, 7*(6), 3–8.

Leslie, D. (2001) *Benchmarks in hospitality and tourism.* Sungsoo Pyo (Ed.) (p. 144). Binghamton: Hayworth Hospitality Press.

Polonsky, M., & Rosenberg, P., III (2001). Reevaluating green marketing: A strategic approach. *Business Horizon* (September–October), 21–30.

Ryan, P. (2003). Sustainability partnerships: Eco-strategy theory in practice? *Management of Environmental Quality: An International Journal, 142*(2), 256–278.

Starkey, R. (1999). The standardization of environmental management systems: ISO 14001, ISO 14004 and EMAS. In: R. Welford (Ed.), *Corporate Environmental Management* (pp. 61–89). London: Earthscan Publications Ltd.

Webster, K. (2000). *Environmental management in the hospitality industry: A guide for students and managers* (pp. 203–253). London: Cassell.

Yu, L. (1999). *The international hospitality business: Management and operations* (pp. 178–181). Binghamton: Hayworth Hospitality Press.

AN EXAMINATION OF THE BRAND RELATIONSHIP QUALITY SCALE IN THE EVALUATION OF RESTAURANT BRANDS

Yuksel Ekinci, Tae-Hwan Yoon and Harmen Oppewal

ABSTRACT

The relationship between brands and consumers is seen as an important element of strategic brand management. Past studies have examined different aspects of branding (e.g. brand equity, brand personality, brand image, brand loyalty), but there has been limited research investigating the quality of the relationship between consumers and brands. The present study aimed to examine various dimensions of the brand relationship quality from the European consumer's point of view in the context of restaurant brands using Fournier's (1994) short version of the brand relationship quality (BRQ) scale. The findings provided strong support for the validity of the brand relationship concept. Of the seven dimensions tested, four were found to be valid and reliable. The study produced a scale to measure the relationship between consumers and restaurant brands.

Advances in Hospitality and Leisure
Advances in Hospitality and Leisure, Volume 1, 189–197
Copyright © 2004 Elsevier Ltd.
All rights of reproduction in any form reserved
ISSN: 1745-3542/doi:10.1016/S1745-3542(04)01012-4

INTRODUCTION

In consumer behaviour research, considerable attention has been paid to branding; indeed branding has been one of the most important marketing strategies in recent years. Some would say that successful branding has the potential to increase gross profit by up to 50% (Blumenthal, 1995). Past studies have examined different aspects of branding (e.g. brand equity, brand personality, brand image, brand loyalty), but there has been little research concerning the quality of the relationship between consumers and brands.

Fournier (1998) suggests that the quality of the brand relationship is an important element of strategic brand management. She developed a scale to measure brand relationship quality. Although the study supported validity of the brand relationship quality construct, her study investigated only the U.S. consumers' perceptions of brand relationship using mainly product oriented brands (Fournier, 1994). The purpose of the present study is to examine European consumers' perceptions of the brand relationship quality using the restaurant brands which is more service oriented.

A person's relationship with different people can be classified as being functional or emotional (e.g. a functional relationship with an accountant or an emotional relationship with a friend). This relationship may eventually develop a favourable attitude towards the person in general, his work or his personality in particular. Aaker (1996) argues that, in a similar way, consumers interact with brands and can develop an active relationship with brands like people would with a friend. Supporting this premise, Fournier (1998) states that consumers can have emotional attachments to brands (involving love, affection, passion etc.). According to the act frequency theory the perception of human personality is mainly dependent upon observation of repeating behaviour (Buss & Craik, 1983). Fournier argues that everyday execution of marketing plans and tactics is perceived as "behaviour" of a brand. Hence, consumers draw conclusions about the characteristics of a brand and establish a relationship. As a result, the brand moves from being a passive object to an active partner in our mind. When a strong relationship is established, consumers often look on that brand as an irreplaceable and inseparable part of their life.

Blackstone (1993) argues that a brand becomes an active partner of a consumer on the basis the brand-consumer relationship. His study suggested that card users' perceptions were different from those of non-users, although two groups were virtually identical in terms of their demographic and socioeconomic profiles. Those customers who used a branded credit card describe the card as worthy, powerful, sophisticated or distinguished, while the non-users described it as intimidating, snobbish and condescending. The card users think that the card might say something like: "I can help you to be a classy person" or "My job is to help you get accepted." In contrast, the non-users think that the card might say: "Are you ready for me? I'm only saying it to protect you from spending more than you can afford" or "You know what the conditions are, if you don't like them, go and get a different card" (Blackstone, 1993, pp. 119–120).

Belk (1988) explains the notion of attachment between consumers and brands by the self-concept theory. He suggests that consumers evaluate brands by referring to their self-concept. If a brand image and self-concept share a degree of communality, there will be a degree of congruence between the two (de Chernatony & Riley, 1997; Phau & Lau, 2000, 2001). This notion eventually motivates to establish a relationship between consumers and brands. Solomon (1999) states that self-concept is one of the essential components of brand evaluation. He (1999, p. 172) notes that "consumers appear to have little trouble assigning personality qualities to all sort of inanimate products, from personal care products to more mundane, functional ones." Brand personality is seen as key to understanding the symbolic importance of consumption, contrary to the traditional view of function-oriented consumption (see, for e.g. Heylen et al., 1995). Indeed, Phau and Lau (2001) show that consumers project their own personality characteristics onto the brands when describing them. His study also indicates that the customers who project their self on brands display strong attachment with the same brand.

The aforementioned arguments suggest that people can form active relationships with inanimate objects, such as brands. Fournier (1994) tested the validity of this notion and identified seven facets of the quality of the brand relationship, as shown in Fig. 1.

As can be seen from Fig. 1, BRQ (brand relationship quality) consists of the following aspects: partner quality, love, intimacy, self-concept connection, nostalgic connection, personal commitment and passionate attachment. These facets are the determinants of a strong relationship between consumers and brands. In the confirmatory factor analysis, the two facets – passionate attachment

Fig. 1. Facets of Brand Relationship Quality (BRQ). *Source:* Fournier (1994, p. 167).

and personal commitment – were found to be highly correlated and therefore they were merged into one factor. The revised scale found to be successful in predicting a number of theoretically related variables such as consumers' willingness to support the brand via recommendation, relationship depth, stability, brand loyalty, customer's resistance to competitive action. The following four facets were found to be statistically significant in predicting consumer's intention to purchase behaviour: partner quality, love, self-concept connection and passionate attachment/personal commitment. The study suggests that the relationship between consumers and brands can be managed using these facets.

METHODS

The BRQ scale was adopted to measure the relationship between restaurant brands and consumers (Fournier, 1994). The original scale consisted of 39 items split into seven sub-scales. We selected 3 items from each scale (a total of 21 items) using the selection criterion that chosen items must have yielded higher factor loading.

The pool of restaurant brands used in this study split into 9 different categories on the basis of menu types (e.g. fast food, ethnic food restaurant, pizza restaurant, beef restaurant) and service category (Key Note, 2000). Respondents were asked to make two types of choice from 28 reasonably known restaurant brands in the U.K. (e.g. McDonalds, Burger King, KFC, T.G.I Friday's, Bella Pasta, Pizza Express, Harvester, Wetherspoon, Café Uno, Little Chef, Angus Steak House, etc.). First, respondents were asked to select a restaurant from the list where they would be "most likely to eat" and then rate the BRQ statements on a 5-point scale with (1) being strongly disagree and (5) being strongly agree. Then, the same respondents were asked to select a restaurant where they would "least likely to eat" and rate the same BRQ statements. One of the predetermined conditions was that participants should be familiar with the chosen restaurants. In order to test concurrent validity of the scale, respondents were also asked to rate their overall relationship with the selected restaurant brand on a 7-point scale ranging from (1) (extremely poor) to (7) (extremely good).

A total of 800 self-administered questionnaires were distributed to British nationals at the Heathrow Airport in England. They were asked to return their completed questionnaire with an attached pre-paid envelope. A total of 225 usable questionnaires were returned within the 4-week period. Each respondent rated their most and least likely to eat restaurant and therefore the total sample size was 450. Of these, 64% were female and 36% male. The median age group was 34–44.

FINDINGS

The 21-item relationship scale was analysed using exploratory factor analysis with oblique rotations. The initial analysis failed to produce the seven brand relationship facets recommended by Fournier (1994). The obtained scree plot suggested a four-factor solution but some of the items loaded more than two factors and were, therefore, deleted from the scale. Table 1 summarises the findings of the factor analysis.

Table 1. The Restaurant Brand Relationship Quality Scale: Exploratory Factor Analysis with Oblique Rotation.

Scales	Factor Loadings			
	Factor 1	Factor 2	Factor 3	Factor 4
Partner quality				
This restaurant treats me like an important and valuable customer.	0.86			
This restaurant takes good care of me.	0.85			
I feel very loyal to this restaurant.	0.74			
I really love this restaurant.	0.70			
This restaurant shows a continuing interest in me.	0.66			
Nostalgic connection				
This restaurant will always remind me of a particular phase of my life.		0.90		
The restaurant reminds me of things I've done or places I've been.		0.85		
The restaurant reminds me of what I was like at a previous stage of my life.		0.80		
Self-concept connection				
The restaurant reminds me of who I am.			0.90	
The restaurant says a lot about the kind of person I am or I want to be.			0.79	
This restaurant plays an important role in my life.			0.72	
Something would be missing from my life if this restaurant wasn't around any longer.			0.66	
I have made a pledge of sorts to stick with this restaurant.	0.35		0.60	
Intimacy				
I know a lot about this restaurant.				0.89
I feel as though I really understand this restaurant.				0.75
I feel as though I have know this restaurant forever.				0.73
Eigen value	7.62	1.94	1.06	1.02
Percentage of variance explained	47.63	12.01	6.52	6.40

Note: Item loadings less than 0.35 omitted. Total percentage of variance explained = 72.79%.

The four-factor solution explained almost 73% of the total variance. Although the findings of the present study did not produce the seven facets suggested by Fournier (1994), the factors termed "nostalgic connection" and "intimacy" were the same as in her study. The first and third factors were labelled "partner quality" and "self-concept connection" as they were closely related to Fournier's findings.

The scale's construct validity was re-examined by confirmatory factor analysis using the Maximum Likelihood estimator of LISREL-VIII causal modelling procedure (Jöreskog & Sörbom, 1996). The two items of each scale having the highest loading in the exploratory factor analysis were selected for the confirmatory factor analysis. The model fit statistics produced acceptable goodness-of-fit

Table 2. Reliability of the Restaurant Brand Quality Relationship Scale.

Scales	Cronbach's Alpha (α)	Mean	Item to Total Correlation
Partner quality	0.86	2.38	
This restaurant treats me like an important and valuable customer.			0.79
This restaurant takes good care of me.			0.76
I feel very loyal to this restaurant.			0.79
I really love this restaurant.			0.77
This restaurant shows a continuing interest in me.			0.67
Nostalgic connection	0.85	2.86	
This restaurant will always remind me of a particular phase of my life.			0.75
The restaurant reminds me of things I've done or places I've been.			0.75
The restaurant reminds me of what I was like at a previous stage of my life.			0.69
Self-concept connection	0.88	1.71	
The restaurant reminds me of who I am.			0.72
The restaurant says a lot about the kind of person I am or I want to be.			0.66
This restaurant plays an important role in my life.			0.71
Something would be missing from my life if this restaurant wasn't around any longer.			0.71
I have made a pledge of sorts to stick with this restaurant.			0.75
Intimacy	0.78	2.99	
I know a lot about this restaurant.			0.66
I feel as though I really understand this restaurant.			0.63
I feel as though I have know this restaurant forever.			0.58

$\chi^2 = 18.92$ (df $= 12, p = 0.09$, not sig., GFI $= 0.99$, CFI $= 0.98$, AGFI $= 0.97$, NFI $= 0.99$, RMSEA $= 0.03$). In addition, the factor loadings were all statistically significant at the $p < 0.05$ level. As the factor loadings were high and significant ($p < 0.05$) this satisfied the criteria for convergent validity of the scale.

In order to test the criterion (concurrent and predictive validity) related validity of the scale, the summated scales were regressed according to the respondents' global evaluation of the relationship and choice. The scale successfully estimated the respondents' global evaluation of the relationship with brands [OLS regression statistics: $R^2 = 0.67$, df $= 4$, $F = 219.5$, $p = 0.000$, partner quality ($p = 0.000$), nostalgic connection ($p = 0.006$), self-concept connection ($p = 0.01$), intimacy ($p = 0.53$)] and choice behaviour [logistic regression statistics: Nagelkerke $R^2 = 0.73$, 2, Log likelihood $= 254.76$, Cox and Snell $R^2 = 0.55$, $p = 0.000$, overall correct classification rate $= 89\%$, partner quality ($p = 0.000$), nostalgic connection ($p = 0.06$), self-concept connection ($p = 0.01$), intimacy ($p = 0.000$)].

The internal consistency of the restaurant brand quality relationship scale was estimated using the Cronbach's alpha statistic (Churchill, 1979). Table 2 shows the reliability of the four sub-scales, mean scores and item to total correlations.

The results of the present study suggested that alpha reliabilities of the sub-scales were equal to or above 0.70 and (partnerquality $= 0.86$, nostalgic connection $= 0.85$, self-concept connection $= 88$, intimacy $= 0.78$) were therefore deemed to be reliable (Churchill, 1979).

CONCLUSION

Overall, the findings provide strong support for the validity of the brand relationship quality concept from the European consumer's point of view in the context of restaurant brands. This study suggests that the brand relationship scale is multidimensional. The four dimensions identified by this study were partner quality, nostalgic connection, self-concept connection and intimacy. Confirmatory factor analysis supported construct validity of the four dimensions. The revised scale was also found to be successful in estimating the respondents' global evaluation of relationship with brands and restaurant choice behaviour. Although the current findings are slightly different from Fournier's (1994) seven dimensions, she reported that the scale may contain less than seven dimensions as intercorrelation between some of the dimensions were high and therefore were not distinct.

This study makes contribution by stimulating thinking on the concept of relationship beyond interpersonal relationships (Sheth & Parvatiyar, 2000) as the present scale development study provides evidence for the existence of relationship between consumers and brands. The outcome of the research may assist restaurant managers in at least two ways. First, the scale could be used to measure the degree of relationship between consumers and brands. Managers can identify the stages of relationship between consumers and brands. This could lead to the development of appropriate marketing strategies and tactics for developing a long term (and therefore profitable) relationship between consumers and brands. Second, managers should pay attention the four brand relationship concepts as identified by this study in order to establish a successful relationship with their customers and improve brand loyalty.

Although the study makes important contributions to our understanding of the relationship between consumers and restaurant brands, it has certain limitations that need to be taken into account when interpreting the findings. A key limitation of this study is the use of non-probability sampling (a convenience sample) in high to medium service experience involvement organisations (restaurants only). The study did not cover the full scale of possible options. Furthermore, the sample included only British nationals. Accordingly, future research using a more sophisticated sampling design and different service organisations (e.g. the insurance sector) would establish the external validity of our findings. Also future studies could include variables such as customer satisfaction, brand personality and perceived value. The inclusion of complaining behaviour would also expand the scope of the present findings.

REFERENCES

Aaker, D. A. (1996). *Building strong brand*. New York: Free Press.
Belk, R. W. (1988). Possessions and the extended self. *Journal of Consumer Research, 15,* 139–168.
Blackstone, M. (1993). Beyond brand personality: Building brand relationships. In: D. A. Aaker & A. Biel (Eds), *Brand Equity and Advertising* (pp. 113–124). Hillsdale, NJ: Lawrence Erlbaum.
Blumenthal, I. (1995). What's in a name? *Hospitality Industry International, 5,* 30.
Buss, D. M., & Craik, K. H. (1983). The act frequency approach to personality. *Psychological Review, 90*(2), 105–126.
Churchill, G. A. (1979). A paradigm for developing better measures of marketing construct. *Journal of Marketing Research, 16,* 64–73.
de Chernatony, L., & Riley, F. D. (1997). An assessment of the atomic brand model. In: *Academy of Marketing Conference Proceedings* (pp. 289–300). Manchester: Academy of Marketing.
Fournier, S. (1994). *A consumer-brand relationship framework for strategic brand management.* Unpublished doctoral dissertation, University of Florida, Florida.
Fournier, S. (1998). Consumer and their brands: Developing relationship theory in consumer research. *Journal of Consumer Research, 24,* 343–373.

Heylen, J. P., Dawson, B., & Sampson, P. (1995). An implicit model of consumer behaviour. *Journal of Market Research Society, 37*(1), 51–67.

Jöreskog, K. G., & Sörbom, D. (1996). *LISREL 8 user's reference guide*. Chicago: Scientific Software International.

Key Note (2000). *Restaurant market report plus* (15th ed.). London: Key Note Ltd.

Phau, I., & Lau, K. C. (2000). Conceptualising brand personality: A review and research propositions. *Journal of Targeting, Measurement and Analysis for Marketing, 9*(1), 52–69.

Phau, I., & Lau, K. C. (2001). Brand personality and consumer self-expression: Single or dual carriageway? *Brand Management, 8*(6), 428–444.

Sheth, J. N., & Parvatiyar, A. (2000). *Handbook of relationship marketing*. London: Sage.

Solomon, M. R. (1999). *Consumer behaviour* (4th ed.). Upper Saddle River, NJ: Prentice-Hall.

DEVELOPMENTS IN EMPLOYEE PRIVACY RIGHTS AMONG HOSPITALITY ORGANIZATIONS: A PROGRESSION TO A DICHOTOMY OF ETHICAL INTERPRETATIONS

Dana V. Tesone and Peter Ricci

ABSTRACT

Relative to other industries, hospitality organizations tend to be labor intensive, employing large numbers of individuals in hotels, resorts, restaurants, and other related enterprises. There has been long-standing debate between the rights of worker personal privacy and the need for employers to know information concerning prospective and current employees. This article presents an evolution of employment relationships in the hospitality industry to demonstrate the complex nature of employment from legal, moral, and ethical perspectives that exists at the current time. It provides discussion of the balance between the rights of individuals and employers' "need to know" private information to draw conclusions and suggestions for practicing hospitality human resource managers.

Advances in Hospitality and Leisure
Advances in Hospitality and Leisure, Volume 1, 199–209
Copyright © 2004 Elsevier Ltd.
All rights of reproduction in any form reserved
ISSN: 1745-3542/doi:10.1016/S1745-3542(04)01013-6

INTRODUCTION

Certain individuals contend that a right is an entitlement owed to a person by law or nature (DeGeorge, 1999). There is common discussion on a global level concerning human rights, which provides a focus on the general treatment of individuals as human beings who are worthy of basic respect and dignity. Constitutions and other statutes as legislated in the United States and other countries protect human rights from government intrusion to privacy. However, this base of legal protection does not extend to employment relationships within private sector enterprises such as those that comprise the hospitality industry.

The hospitality industry is considered to be "labor intensive" relative to other service-based enterprises (Blum, 1996). In addition to large payroll expenditures, hotels, resorts, restaurants, and other hospitality sectors are reported to employ wide ranges of workers in positions that might be categorized as unskilled, semi-skilled, skilled, professional and managerial (Kelliher & Perrett, 2001). These factors contribute to a set of challenges that are unique to hospitality human resource practitioners when compared with counterparts in industries such as retail, financial, and other services.

While specific challenges are inherent within certain industries, human resource practitioners in all organizations do participate in recruitment, selection, employee retention, and legal compliance functions. It is commonly known that employee recruitment is intended to attract a pool of qualified job candidates, while selection practices are designed to choose the most suitable individuals from that pool for employment (Tesone, 2004). Human resource practitioners also implement solid employee relations practices in efforts to retain the most productive workers in the organization. And, of course, all of these functions fall within the domain of legal compliance guidelines to ensure the protection of the organization's assets. As might be expected of any long-term interpersonal interaction, the employment relationship begins at the point of introduction (application) and continues beyond employee separation.

This article discusses employment relationships between individuals and hospitality organizations from the viewpoint of employee rights to privacy. It begins with a discussion of the evolution of employment relationships. Next, the article presents employee privacy issues within the context of legal, moral, and ethical considerations from the viewpoints of the worker, as well as employment agents of the hospitality organization. It then establishes that employment relationships commence before the time of hire and continue beyond the point of employee separation. Over time, employee privacy rights among hospitality businesses seem to be continually balanced with concerns for organizational assets, guest security, and overall hospitality operation success. Finally, conclusions are drawn and suggestions are rendered concerning the balance of employee privacy and employers' "need to know" information concerning prospective and current workers.

AN EVOLUTION OF EMPLOYMENT RELATIONSHIPS

The issue of employee privacy from the past through the present appears to represent a micro indicator of an overall social evolutionary macrocosm. Emergent relationship patterns demonstrate a shift from interpersonal familiarity among workers to one of individual anonymity, separating personal and professional roles within all industries (Kelly, 2003). This is certainly true concerning the hiring practices for hotels and restaurants in the years prior to the 1970s, when reference letters from well-known restaurateurs and hoteliers served as the sole criterion for hiring decisions. It was also common practice during those years to base managers' salaries on marital status and numbers of dependents, with married males with children earning more than single or married men with no children (Greenwood, 2004). This practice continued despite the enactment of federal statutes to include the Equal Pay Act (1963) and Civil Rights Act (1964).

During that time a common law tort borrowed from Great Britain known as the Employment-At-Will (EAW) doctrine provided the prevalent outline of relationships between workers and their employers. The EAW doctrine arose during the 1600s in England through chancery accounts of resolutions concerning employee and employer disputes (Stokes, 1985). This tort doctrine was carried over to the U.S. and became part of what is known today as Common Law. Under EAW, both employee and employer are free to engage in employment relationships "at will," and hence possess the right to terminate any arrangement at any time, for any reason, or no reason at all by unilateral decision (Sharder-Frechette, 2003). With few exceptions, employers perceived the need to focus solely on daily employee performance issues during the days when the Employment-At-Will (EAW) doctrine was in vogue (Van Marrewijk & Timmers, 2003). However, certain hiring organizations did thorough investigations of current and prospective employees during those times to include interviewing family members and neighbors about the living habits of candidates for employment and existing workers who were demonstrating poor job performance (Greenwood, 2004). A shift began to occur concerning employment relationships during the 1970s, when organizations chose to make investments in human capital. This human resource movement caused the relationships between employers and employees to become more complex over time through voluntary and involuntary benefit programs (Tesone, 2004).

THE RIGHTS OF EMPLOYERS AND EMPLOYEES

The focus of governmental agencies upon employment relationships has enhanced the burden of employer legal responsibility and hence, financial liability based upon statutory regulations and tort law doctrines. At the present time, hospitality employers are held to be liable for the actions of their management agents, as well as those of other employees in cases of third party negligence claims (Schultz, 2003). Additionally, organizations are charged with safeguarding their employees against actions on the part of co-workers that are deemed to create hostile environments. Finally, an incentive exists to reduce the costs of health insurance and workers' compensation by using employee information to reduce potential risk from frivolous or catastrophic claims. For these reasons, employers are becoming increasingly convinced in their perception of the "need to know" information concerning the propensity for a variety of behaviors on the part of current and prospective employees (Blackwell, 2004).

On the other hand there is a perception among individuals of an inherent right to privacy regarding personal information and behaviors away from the workplace. This philosophy is consistent with the human rights doctrine mentioned earlier. Additionally, individuals may feel that security practices within a hospitality organization constitute invasions of personal privacy.

THE LEGAL ENVIRONMENT

Interestingly, the federal and state governments within the United States appear to adopt a neutral posture concerning the rights of individuals versus the "need to know" investigative practices of private sector organizations. This is evident in the longstanding tort law doctrine that permits employers to establish their own rights to employee investigation, search, and seizure practices via written company policies (Parnell, 1998). Most states uphold practices to include biometric testing, background investigations, desk, locker, parcel, and vehicle searches, as well as workplace activity surveillance (Schultz, 2003). Hospitality organizations may subject employees to all of these practices providing they state their right to do so within the terms and conditions of employment at the time of hire (Stokes, 1985).

A body of civil rights statutes exists at the federal and state levels for the purpose of preventing employers from discriminating against individuals who are members of identified protected classes. The four definitions of employer discrimination include disparate treatment, disparate impact, perpetuation of past practices, and accommodations theory as defined by the precedent setting case of Griggs vs. Duke Power Co. (1971). On one hand, civil rights laws preclude employers from knowing certain categories of information during pre-employment activities. On the other hand, the laws require employers to maintain and disclose protected class status statistics for each member of employment populations. Employers are additionally required to document efforts made to reasonably accommodate those individuals within those protected classes that warrant legal accommodation (religion and disability, for example). When it comes to privacy protection for individuals, the body of civil rights law appears to be a double-edged sword. The laws prevent the disclosure of information during pre-employment on one hand, while on the other; they require the disclosure of the same information while employed. This privacy dichotomy may also be true within the context of common law torts as applied to employment relationships.

It is within the rights of an individual to seek legal remedy for invasion of privacy arising from information collection activities during employment and pre-employment investigations. However, the burden is placed on that litigant to demonstrate that harmful information was disclosed to a third party whom did not have a "need to know" for such information. Most employment inquiries meet the "need to know" criterion, as long as there is a job related connection to the information that is shared between parties. However, individuals who are in possession of information concerning job applicants and existing employees become the "custodians of record," which implies a duty to secure that information. A breach of such duty could constitute legal action within the jurisdiction of another tort law doctrine known as "negligent maintenance and disclosure" of records. For instance, an agent for an employer may possess files that contain background information concerning an individual. Another employee may gain unauthorized access to the files and use the information to spread rumors about that employee (litigant) among other workers. In such a case, there is legal standing to establish invasion of privacy, in which the custodian of record and the unauthorized person with the information would be potentially held liable. Additional allegations of defamation could result if the unauthorized party falsifies the information with the intent to cast the character of the litigant in "poor light." For these reasons, agents with authorized access to private information concerning applicants and employees take precautionary measures to secure that information. It is, however, commonly held that the access of job related information concerning job applicants and employees of a private sector company by authorized agents does not constitute an invasion of privacy (Stokes, 1985).

At this point the issue of "job relatedness" becomes a matter for discussion. From a narrow perspective it could be deemed that job related factors are those that provide an indication of the ability to perform within an employment position. However, it could be argued that complex employment relationships extend beyond the simple matter of job performance. It has already been established that employers incur responsibility for the actions of its agents concerning co-workers and other third parties (Schultz, 2003). Additionally, the employer bears at least a portion of the cost of health care for each full-time worker. The employer is also required to provided mandatory benefits, such as workers' compensation insurance for each employee. So, in a broader perspective, the behaviors of every employee pose potential legal and financial liabilities upon the assets of the organization. Hence, it becomes the duty of that organization to determine the propensity for employee behaviors on the part of each individual that could jeopardize the assets of the company. These factors present a basis for expanding the definition of job relatedness beyond work performance to include any behavior that may cause potential harm to the organization.

Currently, there is a movement within the lodging sector of the hospitality industry specifically in response to the brutal murder of a guest by a maintenance manager at a franchise location of a major national chain. The victim, Nan Toder, was "bound, slashed, and strangled" (DeVise, 2003, p. B5) by the maintenance manager whose employer did not know of his criminal past which included arrests for auto theft, criminal trespass, and unlawful use of a weapon. Reference checks would have revealed these incidents as well as the stalking of a female colleague (DeVise, 2003).

> In 1996, Nan Toder was murdered at age 33 in a suburban Chicago hotel by the facility's maintenance manager. Investigators said Christopher Richee used his master key to enter an unoccupied room next to hers, rig the door between her room and the empty one, and then slip in and bludgeon her to death (Silver, 2003).

In an attempt to improve protection of guests who secure paid lodging accommodations, the victim's parents have initiated a grass-roots-level crusade to nationalize the standard of care innkeepers must take when hiring employees. The murder of their daughter has spurred a national movement with the goal of improving guest safety and security (Silver, 2003).

At the present time, the American Hotel and Lodging Association (AHLA) does not track incidents where a hospitality operations' assets or reputation have been negatively impacted by an employee who did not have his or her background checked in advance. AHLA is not a regulatory body. The largest regional association similar in function and format to the AHLA is the Central Florida Hotel and Lodging Association (CFHLA). CFHLA, additionally, does not provide regulatory oversight to its members in the southeast. According to DeVise (2003), "anecdotal evidence suggests rapes or murders of hotel guests by employees are extremely rare" (p. B5). In the particular incident involving Nan Toder, a civil lawsuit against the hotel's owners resulted in a $4.6 million settlement and a conviction of murder by jury in 2002 for the assailant without possibility of parole. The "web of companies that owned and operated the Hampton Inn admitted no wrongdoing in the settlement" (DeVise, 2003, p. B5). The parents of Nan Toder, who are proposing the "Nan's Law" movement around the country, did not name the Hampton Inn chain or its parent company and present owner, Hilton, in the lawsuit.

The differences of job relatedness definitions between government agencies and the courts provide yet another example of the privacy "catch-22" regarding rights of employees and those of employers. It would seem that governmental agencies within the legal environment are in conflict concerning privacy rights and responsibilities of employees, as well as employers. And, as witnessed in the two above examples, guest safety and security issues in a post-9/11 environment may cause the general public to expect more from hospitality operators in the way of employee background checks. With current security attention in the United States at high levels, exposure of insufficient background checks resulting in negative incidents may cause hospitality operators to receive substantial amounts of negative publicity and reputation degradation.

MORAL AND ETHICAL ARGUMENTS

Proactive hospitality organizations usually subscribe to employment standards that are above the legal law. Evidence of this philosophy exists within codes of ethics and mission statements that highlight the importance of an organization's workforce. Morality and ethics comprise a branch of thinking referred to as "normative philosophy," with the purpose of determining, monitoring, and evaluating correct behaviors among individuals (Kelly, 2003).

It has already been established that employment relationships have evolved over time from historically simple agreements into relatively complex interactions that exist in the present. This is evident in the transition of the purest form of the Employment-At-Will (EAW) doctrine into the current state of complicated bodies of statutory and judge-made (common) law. From an ethical perspective, there are two established arguments in existence that support the viewpoints of individuals as well as employers.

Proponents of the employer position regarding the need to know information would argue that the ends justify the means. In other words, the employer may pry into the privacy of its prospective and current employees, because that action benefits the constituents of the organization as a whole. Hence, the majority benefits from a burden that is incurred by a few individuals. This is an example of the Utilitarian or consequential argument of least harm – most good, an apparently dominant argument among government regulators and the courts.

The Formalist school of ethical thought provides an argument that is in favor of the preservation of personal privacy rights for all individuals, regardless of employment status. Formalist arguments disregard the consequences of an action, with focus on the action in and of itself. Prominent formalist ethical tests include the Categorical Imperative (Kant, 1997) and the Theory of Justice (Rawls, 1971). Proponents of this ethical approach place the rights of individuals in higher order than those of the collective society and organizations within that society.

It is evident that a litigious society, such as the United States, would consider utilitarianism to be a pragmatic argument when compared with the idealism associated with the formalist school of ethical thought. However, a reasonable person must conclude from the application of both tests that the infringement on an individual's privacy is clearly a "wrong" action from a moral and ethical perspective. It is only in light of the legal doctrines of protectionism and negligence that the utilitarian argument would appeal to common sense and dignity. An experienced hospitality human resource practitioner who is exposed to this knowledge must admit that it is immoral to infringe on a person's right to privacy under any circumstance. The follow-up comment would conclude that the practice of privacy infringement is a necessary evil used to protect an organization from its own social environment.

THE EXTENT OF THE EMPLOYMENT RELATIONSHIP

The employment relationship begins before the time of hire during the recruitment and selection processing of employment candidates. The employer begins the prescreening process when a candidate completes an employment application blank. The prospective employer seeks to acquire information about the applicant from outside sources in order to make a hiring decision during that pre-employment process. In most cases this is the most active phase of personal data collection that often includes credit checks, background investigations, job references, and pre-employment tests. A job offer is usually contingent upon biometric screening for substances, job related health, and in some cases physical accommodation requirements.

At the time of hire, the new employee will agree to submit to a number of potential investigative procedures as a term and condition of employment. These processes may include random and "for cause" biometric testing for health and substances, interrogation interviews, various forms of searches for contraband, surveillance procedures, and exit processing. These conditions will remain in force for the duration of active employment through the completion of that person's exit from the organization. At this point, the organization becomes a source of information for new employers, which is a continuation of the employment relationship. This "post employment" relationship will exist for as long as there are active records of past employment with the organization. Hence, the employment relationship does not come to an end when the employee exits the organization.

CONCLUSION

Hiring decisions in the hospitality industry were historically based on the reputations of an applicant's references, a process that is the equivalent of a word-of-mouth referral system. This system seemed to work well during a time when virtually all positions consisted of "casual labor" agreements, in which a person would provide a day's labor for a day's pay.

Over time the employment relationship has become more complex due to worker mobility, the development of corporate entities, the advancement of human capital strategies, and the development of legal doctrines aimed at regulating and litigating employment scenarios. The result of this advancement and evolution is the current situation in which employing organizations continue to delve deeper into the private lives of prospective and current employees based on the need to know such information as a means to protect the assets of the hiring organization. This creates resentment among some people who feel that the investigative practices of employers constitute invasions of individual privacy. Yet, with such proposals as Nan's Law (DeVise, 2003), the general public often seems to expect thorough background checks for those who work in hospitality operations as an added gesture of comfort, security, and good business practice.

The current legal environment appears to adopt a neutral posture between the rights of individuals and employers, which results in legal dichotomies that influence the employment practices of human resource managers. The legal environment has expanded the responsibilities of employers to include pre-employment through post employment levels of responsibility concerning worker privacy and information. Finally, there are established moral and ethical arguments that directly support the practices of employers to a lesser degree than the inherent rights to privacy for individuals.

IMPLICATIONS FOR HOSPITALITY HUMAN RESOURCE PRACTITIONERS

It has been established that legal compliance issues surround the functions of recruitment, selection and employee retention. It has also been established that the hospitality human resource practitioner must be adept in the practice of complying with contradicting legal doctrines. For these reasons, the author poses the following five suggestions for practicing human resource managers:

(1) Practitioners should continually monitor the decisions of the courts in the areas of both statutory and tort law findings.
(2) Practitioners should divide the "chain of custody" for biometric testing, background investigations, and other pre-employment tests among expert third party entities (health care providers, professional investigation firms, and social psychologists, for example).
(3) Practitioners should subscribe to a code of ethics and apply established ethical tests to management policy decisions in all human resource related matters.
(4) Practitioners should take steps to ensure that all informational documents (to include personnel files) are secured and available exclusively to a limited number of authorized individuals (H. R. managers and specific executives) who possess a thorough understanding of the "need to know" mandates (as demonstrated through corporate and legal training) and policies for specific areas of information regarding employees.
(5) Practitioners should maintain a level of sensitivity to the desire of individuals to safeguard personal privacy by carefully limiting inquiries to areas of information that are absolutely necessary for the protection of the organization.

In the final analysis, there would be no controversy surrounding the issue of privacy matters in employment relationships in an ideal society. Unfortunately, human resource practitioners currently operate in a litigious and regulated environment. It is the responsibility of the hospitality human resource manager to access information concerning prospective and current employees of an organization in an effort to protect the business interests of the corporation. It is the further duty of the human resource practitioner to temper these activities when feasible to preserve the privacy concerns of all individuals.

REFERENCES

Blackwell, C. W. (2004). Current employee privacy issues. *Journal of Applied Management and Entrepreneurship*, 6(1), 113–118.
Blum, S. C. (1996). Organizational trend analysis of the hospitality industry: Preparing for change. *International Journal of Contemporary Hospitality Management*, 8(7), 20–27.
DeGeorge, R. (1999). *Business ethics*. Upper Saddle River, NJ: Prentice-Hall.
DeVise, D. (2003, December 26). Slaying prompts parents to seek better hotel security. *Orlando Sentinel* (p. B5).

Greenwood, R. A. (2004). Employee privacy issues of the early 20th Century: 1900 through Hawthorne studies. *Journal of Applied Management and Entrepreneurship, 9*(1), 94–99.

Griggs v. Duke Power Co. (1971). 401 U.S. 424.

Kant, I. (1997). In: G. Hatfield (Ed.), *Prolegomena to any future metaphysics*. New York: Cambridge University Press.

Kelliher, C., & Perrett, G. (2001). Business strategy and approaches to HRM: A case study of new developments in the United Kingdom restaurant industry. *Personnel Review, 30*(4), 421–438.

Kelly, E. (2003). Ethical perspectives on layoffs of highly compensated workers and age discrimination in employment. *Journal of Applied Management and Entrepreneurship, 9*(3), 84–97.

Parnell, J. A. (1998). *S. A. M. Advanced Management Journal, 63*(1), 35–42.

Rawls, J. (1971). *A theory of justice*. Cambridge, MA: Harvard University Press.

Schultz, V. (2003). The sanitized workplace. *The Yale Law Journal, 112*(8), 2061–2092.

Sharder-Frechette, K. (2003, August). Sound science? *America, 189*(3), 28–35.

Silver, J. D. (2003). *Mt. Lebanon couple settle lawsuit in daughter's murder*. PG Publishing Co. Retrieved February 20, 2004, from http://pittsburghfirst.com/neigh_south/20030416toder4.asp.

Stokes, A. (1985). *How do I sue thee? Let me count the ways*. Atlanta, GA: Stokes, Lazarus, and Carmichael, Attorneys at Law.

Tesone, D. V. (2004). *Human resource management for the hospitality industry: A practitioners' perspective*. Upper Saddle River, NJ: Prentice-Hall.

Van Marrewijk, M., & Timmers, J. (2003). Human capital management: New possibilities in people management. *Journal of Business Ethics, 44*(2/3), 171–182.

THE EFFECTS OF WEBPAGES ON CUSTOMER SATISFACTION: A RESTAURANT CASE STUDY

Kuo-Ching Wang, Shao-Cheng Cheng
and Chu-Min Huang

ABSTRACT

Numerous studies have investigated the customer's expectations and satisfaction. Due to the prevalence of e-commerce, this study attempts to take a further look at how the design of webpages could influence consumers' expectations and satisfaction. Both qualitative and quantitative methods are utilized. The customers of TGI Friday's are selected for empirical validation. The findings show that there was a gap between what consumers actually perceived in the restaurant and the information presented on the website. Marketing implications for restaurateurs along with suggestions for future research are provided in the conclusion section.

INTRODUCTION

Customer satisfaction has been an important issue of study for both practitioners and researchers. In recent years, due to the powerful effect of webpages on restaurant goers' purchasing desire, marketers are teeming to develop persuasive webpages to attract more customers. Retrospectively, from the customers'

Advances in Hospitality and Leisure
Advances in Hospitality and Leisure, Volume 1, 211–222
Copyright © 2004 Elsevier Ltd.
All rights of reproduction in any form reserved
ISSN: 1745-3542/doi:10.1016/S1745-3542(04)01014-8

perspective, surfing on the Internet to search for a desired restaurant could become a necessary information inquiry procedure before choosing a restaurant. Thus, it is important to know what types of web attributes could bring awareness to restaurants as well as enhance customer satisfaction for services.

However, as indicated by Murphy (1999), the details of how to design a website so that visitors will "stay and play" are elusive and there is a lack of scientific research regarding website design. Consequently, this study attempts to take a further look at how the design of webpages could influence consumers' expectations and satisfaction.

Earlier expectation and satisfaction studies like Oliver (1980) once argued that satisfaction can be seen as a function of the expectation level and perception of disconfirmation. By contrast, the study also found a direct effect of expectation on consumer satisfaction. In Yi's (1993) moderating study on ambiguity and consumer satisfaction, he clearly noted that when the product is ambiguous, consumer expectations have direct effects on consumer satisfaction as well as indirect effects through disconfirmation.

The preceding discussions suggest that if a potential customer perceives the restaurant as an ambiguous product (difficult to evaluate the quality), after surfing on the restaurant's website, consumer expectation is likely to have direct effects on consumer satisfaction as he/she visits the restaurant. From restaurateur's viewpoint, whether the above relationship exists is a very important issue for their restaurant's website design. However, as far as the researchers have been aware, there has been no study focused on the relationship between the actual restaurant dining experiences and relevant website design inducing customers.

Accordingly, the aims of this study were to: (1) discover if there is a gap between the restaurant dining experience and the relevant website design; and (2) to further find out if such a gap affects customer satisfaction.

RESTAURANT SELECTION

Since this research focuses on the dis/satisfaction attributes between restaurant and its website, a criterion in selecting study restaurants is that the study website must be freestanding, not part of some local network website. At present, there are many restaurant websites in Taiwan, to employ all of them for the research is not possible. Therefore, in the first stage, only two styles of restaurants were taken into consideration: Chinese and Western style restaurants.

However, fast food restaurants, such as McDonalds, were excluded from the Western style restaurant. The consideration rests on the fact that once a restaurant is selected for research, in the second stage of the research design, only individuals who have not been to such a restaurant will be asked to browse on the selected restaurant's website. It would be very difficult to find study subjects who have never been to a fast-food restaurant, such as McDonalds.

During the first stage study, 77 respondents, based on a convenience sampling procedure, were asked to write down the name of restaurants they can think about (each of the styles should comprise at least three restaurants). The results indicated that TGI Friday's (45/77, Western style) and Hai Pa Wang (56/77, Chinese style) were most frequently mentioned by the respondents. Subsequently, the websites of TGI Friday's and Hai Pa Wang were further evaluated by the researchers and it was found the two restaurants' websites were quite fit for the experiment in this research.

Finally, as was noted in the previous section, consumer expectations have direct effects on consumer satisfaction when the product is ambiguous (Yi, 1993). Therefore, in order to test the ambiguity (defined as difficult to evaluate quality) of these two restaurants: TGI Friday's and the Hai Pa Wang, Yi's (1993) concept, high ambiguity products (insurance, microwave oven, computer, aspirin, camera, laundry detergent) and low ambiguity products (e.g. soft drinks, bread, jeans, ball-point pen) were tested. In the last part of the data collection, 74 undergraduate students were invited to evaluate product ambiguity on a seven-point scale. The results were shown in Table 1.

As displayed in Table 1, the website of Hai Pa Wang differs significantly from the high ambiguous products (e.g. insurance, laundry detergent, microwave oven, computer, aspirin, and camera). Except ball-point pens, the website of Hai Pa Wang does not set itself apart from low ambiguous products. On the other hand, with the exception of soft drinks, the website of TGI Friday's was significant different from all low ambiguous products (e.g. jeans, ball-point pens, and bread) and no significant difference was found from most of the high ambiguous products (laundry detergent, computers, and cameras). Accordingly, TGI Friday's was selected as the target restaurant for the second stage study.

After the restaurant was chosen, critical incident technique (hereafter abbreviated to CIT) was further used to collect the attributes of consumers' dis/satisfaction of the selected restaurant. An on-site intercept interview procedure was utilized at each of the TGI Friday's branches (front door) in Taipei over a one-month period. The questionnaire asked for actual personal experiences. In general, respondents answered the following questions:

Q1: Of the TGI Friday's you have eaten in during the last six months, please think about if there was any service that you were dis/satisfied with?

Q2: Please tell us exactly what happened? How you felt?

Table 1. The Mean Difference Between Each Product.[a]

	Insurance	Hai Pa Wang	Laundry Detergent	Jeans	Microwave Oven	Computer	Ball-Point Pen	Aspirin	Camera	Soft Drink	TGI Friday's	Bread
Insurance	–											
Hai Pa Wang	1.77*											
Laundry detergent	0.93*	0.83*										
Jeans	1.72*	4.0E-02	0.79*									
Microwave oven	0.70*	1.06*	0.22	1.02*								
Computer	1.20*	0.56*	0.27	0.52*	0.50*							
Ball-point pen	2.37	0.60*	1.44*	0.64*	1.67*	1.17*						
Aspirin	0.29	1.47*	0.63	1.43*	0.40*	0.90*	2.08*					
Camera	0.95*	0.81*	2.7E-02	0.77*	0.25	0.24	1.41*	0.66*				
Soft drink	0.56*	0.20	0.63*	0.16	0.86*	0.36	0.81*	1.27*	0.60*			
TGI Friday's	1.24*	0.52*	0.31	0.48*	0.54*	4.0E-02	1.13*	0.94*	0.28	0.32		
Bread[b]	1.78*	1.3E-02	0.85*	5.4E-02	1.08*	0.58*	0.59*	1.48*	0.82*	0.21	0.54*	–

[a] Each score represents the mean difference between two products' ambiguity score, as measured on a scale where 1 = very easy to evaluate product's quality and 7 = very difficult to evaluate product's quality.

[b] In Yi's study cereal was used for ambiguity evaluation, since the cereal is not so popular to the undergraduate students; the study used bread instead of cereal.

* Represents t significant at 0.05 level.

Furthermore, the respondents were also asked to provide information on their socio-demographic data including gender, marital status, age, education level, occupation, and monthly income. In total, 270 respondents were interviewed. Four samples were excluded because of an incomplete answer. Finally, 266 usable samples remained. 59.4% of respondents were female. 81.2% were single. Most respondents ranged in age from 18 to 27, which was 63.9%. The study group was well educated, with 82.3% holding at least a bachelor's degree. Students and business people accounted for 35.7 and 34.2%, respectively. Since the average income per month was influenced by occupation, most respondents were below NT\$ 60,000 (about U.S.\$ 1765), 35.3% were between NT\$ 0–20,000, 34.2% were between NT\$ 20,001–40,000, and NT\$ 40,001–60,000 were 15.0%.

Subsequently, according to the respondents' critical incidents regarding their meal experiences at TGI Friday's, this study further categorizes the incidents into dis/satisfaction attributes. The procedures were mainly based on Keaveney (1995), Bitner et al. (1994), and Bitner et al.'s (1990) suggestion to complete the CIT classification. The entire procedures were shown in Fig. 1. The first step in data analysis is to determine the appropriate unit of analysis. Therefore, two judges independently coded the 266 samples into 945 separate critical behaviors (including 586 satisfaction behaviors and 359 dissatisfaction behaviors). Upon completing the unit of analysis coding task, the two judges compared their decisions regarding discrete behaviors and resolved disagreements by discussion.

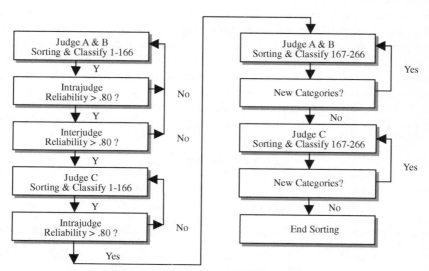

Fig. 1. Critical Incident Sorting and Classification Process.

The next step was to sort the critical behaviors into categories. Two judges (A and B) independently developed categories for samples 1–166 (675 behaviors composed of 427 satisfaction and 248 dissatisfaction). For the following post hoc method of evaluating sample size, the remaining samples 167–266 (as confirmation samples) were not incorporated in this stage.

Next, the intra-judge reliability was examined to determine whether the same judges classified the same phenomena into the same categories over time. The period of test-retest was two weeks (Davis & Cosenza, 1993) and the 0.8 was the threshold. Judges A and B compared their categorization methods and resolved disagreements by discussion. Inter-judge reliability was also conducted in this study, which is a measure of whether different judges classify the same phenomena into the same categories. When the inter-judge agreement between judge A and B exceeded 0.8, their results became the benchmarks (Latham & Saari, 1984).

Subsequently, new judge C sorted the 675 behaviors into the categories provided by judges A and B. Judge C was instructed to create new categories if appropriate. When intra-judge reliability (two weeks period) of judge C exceeded 0.8, the classification decisions were then compared against the benchmarks. The results of all the reliability were shown in Table 2.

A sample is of sufficient size for critical incident analysis when the addition of 100 new incidents (here this study used sample instead) does not create any new categories (Keaveney, 1995). The confirmation of 167–266 sample responses collected in this research yielded 270 behaviors (159 satisfaction behaviors and 111 dissatisfaction behaviors). Judges A and B sorted responses 167–266 into the classification system explained previously with an eye to developing new categories. No new categories emerged in this process, indicating that no further analysis was necessary. Finally, judge C sorted responses 167–266, again, no new categories emerged, and the sorting and classification process was completed. The final classification results are shown in Fig. 2.

As Fig. 2 shows, 12 categories satisfaction attributes emerged: service attitude, flavor, dining environment, atmosphere, quantity of meal, service speed, restaurant

Table 2. Judges' Reliability.

| | Judges' Reliability | | |
	Satisfaction	Dissatisfaction	Total
Judge A (Intrajudge)	0.9532 (407/427)	0.8952 (222/248)	0.9319 (629/675)
Judge B (Intrajudge)	0.9087 (388/427)	0.9597 (238/248)	0.9274 (626/675)
Interjudge (A and B)	0.9180 (392/427)	0.8790 (218/248)	0.9037 (610/675)
Judge C (Intrajudge)	0.9461 (404/427)	0.8952 (222/248)	0.9274 (626/675)

Satisfaction   Dissatisfaction

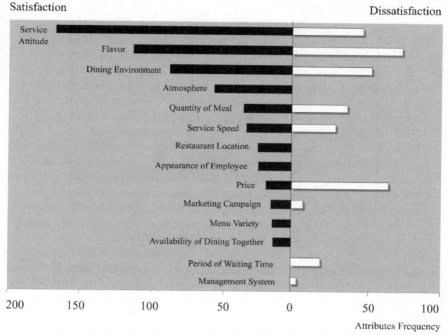

Fig. 2. Attributes/Frequency of Dis/satisfaction.

location, appearance of employee, price, marketing campaign, menu variety, and availability of dining together. On the other hand, 9 categories emerged as dissatisfaction attributes: service attitude, flavor, dining environment, quantity of meal, service speed, price, marketing campaign, period of waiting time, and management system. In total, 14 different categories were emerged either in satisfaction or dissatisfaction attributes.

MEASUREMENT OF THE GAP

Once the attribute classification of the dis/satisfaction of the physical restaurant was completed, the results were further utilized to develop the questionnaire for the dis/satisfaction (gap) testing between the physical restaurant and its website.

In this stage, the investigation was conducted in the computer classrooms at one university that was located in Taipei, Taiwan. Initially, 461 undergraduate students were invited to participate in this investigation. Since the participants

Fig. 3. Homepage of TGI Friday's.

in this stage were required to those potential consumers who had never visited TGI Friday's before. The requirement is designed to prevent the respondents' prior physical restaurant experience of TGI Friday's influencing the respondents' judgement. Therefore, only 208 samples were retained for valid analysis. Of all the respondents, most were from the Department of Computer Science, amounting to 62.6%, seconded by International Trade of 13.5%. Males amounted to 62.5%, while females were 37.5%. The disparity between the sexes was due to the students mainly from the Department of Computer Science. Most respondents ranged in age from 20 to 22, accounting for 68.8%, followed by those under 19, accounting for 18.8%.

During the investigation, first the researchers asked the respondents to browse carefully over each page of the TGI Friday's website. The homepage of TGI Friday's is shown in Fig. 3.

The respondents were instructed to ignore those functional problems of the website such as the downloading speed, format of web page . . . etc., they only had to concentrate on the website's content problems, that is, to the 14 dis/satisfaction attribute questions (e.g. How much information could be perceived about the *Dining Environment* on the website. How much information could be perceived about the *Service Speed* on the website) in the questionnaire. Furthermore, were the dis/satisfied with the amount of information they could perceive of the 14 dis/satisfaction attributes were also measured.

The gap between the physical restaurant and its website. The result is shown in Table 3. From the 208 potential customers' perspectives, among the 14

Table 3. The Gap Between the Restaurant and its Website.

Attributes	Information Perceived[a]	Dis/satisfaction[b]	R
Dining environment	2.7644	3.0529	0.61[*]
Service speed	2.7067	2.9567	0.67[*]
Quantity of meal	2.9087	3.0817	0.57[*]
Atmosphere	2.9087	3.1538	0.63[*]
Period of waiting time	2.6683	2.8462	0.65[*]
Service attitude	2.6779	3.0000	0.66[*]
Flavor	3.4808	3.4904	0.71[*]
Management system	2.8365	3.0192	0.59[*]
Price	3.6154	3.3029	0.45[*]
Marketing campaign	3.1346	3.1538	0.69[*]
Restaurant location	3.6731	3.6010	0.69[*]
Appearance of employee	2.6923	2.8942	0.65[*]
Menu variety	3.4663	3.4183	0.73[*]
Availability of dining together	2.9471	3.0240	0.70[*]

[a] Each score represents the mean of each of the attributes that can be perceived by the respondents on TGI Friday's website and it was measured on a five-point Likert-type scale where $1 = $ *very few* and $5 = $ *very much*.
[b] Each score represents the level of dis/satisfaction regarding to the 14 attributes that were browsed by the respondents. It was measured on a five-point Likert-type scale where $1 = $ *very dissatisfied* and $5 = $ *very satisfied*.
[*] Represents significant at 0.01 level.

dis/satisfaction attributes for the physical restaurant, nine attributes were perceived as giving little information on the web by the respondents while they browsed on TGI Friday's website, the other 5 attributes (flavor, price, marketing campaign, restaurant location, and menu variety) were perceived only between general and much information level. In Table 3, an interesting phenomenon can also be found in the dis/satisfaction column. The higher mean score of dis/satisfaction regarding the 14 attributes were restaurant location (3.6010), flavor (3.4904), menu variety (3.4183), price (3.3029), and marketing campaign (3.1538). These five attributes are exactly the same as the attributes where more information was perceived by the respondents on TGI Friday's website. Besides, with respect to the correlation between these two variables (information perceived and dis/satisfaction level), higher correlation can also be found in four (flavor/0.71, marketing campaign/0.69, restaurant location/0.69, and menu variety/0.73) out of the above five attributes.

Apparently, it seems that a gap exists between the TGI Friday's offerings and its website's offerings. Nine out of the 14 attributes were perceived insufficient on the web and the dis/satisfaction level of these nine attributes were very close to the general level, some even between the general and dissatisfied level (service speed/2.9567, period of waiting time/2.8462, and appearance of employee/2.8942). The other five attributes, namely, the flavor, price, marketing campaign, restaurant location, and menu variety, though they are a little bit higher than the above nine attributes on the dis/satisfaction measure, they are still a little bit away from the satisfied level or very satisfied level.

As an overview, this study finds that the 14 dis/satisfaction attributes emerged from the TGI Friday's that did not fully reflect its website's content design. It also implies that a potential problem might exist if any potential customers browse on TGI Friday's website and attempt to find some important information about the physical restaurant before actually going there for dining. The potential customers would probably find some important attribute information regarding the physical restaurant that are apparently insufficient or even do not exist, as a result, the potential customers' expectation regarding the physical restaurant would be affected. However, according to Yi's (1993) arguments that consumer expectations have direct effects on consumer satisfaction, the above situation may possibly affect the customers' satisfaction directly while they are actually dining in TGI Friday's.

CONCLUSIONS AND IMPLICATIONS

Potential customers surfing the Internet to gain information from the restaurant website should expect more than experienced customers. However, it seems that marketing practitioners remain unsure about the marketing strategies most appropriate to the Internet (Maignan & Lukas, 1997). But from this study a more tangible direction may have evolved.

This research demonstrated that the amount of information provided on the websites could affect customer satisfaction towards the services. As in Yi's theory (1993), it could further affect customer's dining experience as well. The implication for a restaurant's website is that web designers should strategically highlight the information concerning the best offerings dear to their customers.

In addition, several findings are worth noting most. First, in TGI Friday's, the most important attribute affecting customer satisfaction on dining experience was service attitude. However, with the constraints demonstrated on the TGI Friday's website, the information of service attitude perceived by the respondents was very low (2.6779). This variation might be due to the attribute being less tangible compared to other attributes such as: price or restaurant location.

However, as indicated by Murphy et al. (1996), the Web has an unlimited storage space coupled with multi-media capabilities. Also the presentation possibilities of a website are limited by the restaurateur's imagination and financial considerations. With development and popularization of wideband networks and Asymmetric

Digital Subscriber Line (ADSL), nowadays enterprises could definitely offer faster and more diversified services on websites. Virtual reality, talking web pages, online movies, multimedia or other means are able to surpass the constraints of current technology regarding the current problems on restaurant's website.

Advances in technology have definitely made room for creative website designs. But more importantly, restaurateurs should make their sites in a way that allows potential customers to perceive the important attributes before they actually go there. For example, a few pictures with waiters/waitresses smiling as they serve the customers might be a good way to reflect the restaurants service attitude.

In this present study 14 emergent dis/satisfaction attributes were obtained via qualitative approach. The study suggests that practitioners should consider using some website techniques and technologies such as: the on-line survey, polls, guest books, data-warehousing, and data-mining (Olsen & Connolly, 2000; Ziperovich, 2002) to replace the qualitative method. The methods entail several advantages such as cost saving and efficiency. Additionally, the website administrator could update the content more promptly.

Since TGI Friday's was selected as the only study restaurant, this shortcoming limits the general application of the study. Nevertheless, as Wang et al. (2000) and Wang et al. (2002) stated that Taiwan and China are similar in race, culture, and language, the result of this study could be generalized to the huge Chinese market (presently TGI Friday's has 11 branches in Taiwan, 3 branches in Beijing, 1 branch in Shanghai, and 1 branch in Tianjin).

This study merely used Yi's (1993) research concept with regard to the customer satisfaction relationship between the website design and the actual dining experience. If consumers obtain higher satisfaction when dining in the restaurant as a consequence of higher perceived satisfaction on the restaurant's website is still unclear. This seems to be a fruitful area for further research. In addition, future research might use the experimental method to investigate the customer's clicking behaviors on the 14 dis/satisfaction attributes and other content elements. If a positive relationship exists between the clicking behaviors within the 14 dis/satisfaction attributes, the result might further support and reinforce the idea this study has proposed, that is, to integrate the possible satisfaction attributes pertaining to dining experiences into restaurant websites as much as possible.

In conclusion, as indicated by Murphy et al. (1996), future marketing success will be found in giving the customer the easiest, most rewarding access to relevant information before, during, and after the dining experience. Besides, Vandermerwe (1993) also noted that those companies that are and will be most successful have started to look at the customer's entire experience, from the pre- to the post-purchase stage. Our study only focused on "before and during." Obviously, more research is still needed to understand the relationship between the before, during, and after concepts so as to increase the knowledge on customers' dining in relation to website design.

REFERENCES

Bitner, M. J., Booms, B. H., & Mohr, L. A. (1994). Critical service encounters: The employee's viewpoint. *Journal of Marketing, 58*(4), 95–106.

Bitner, M. J., Booms, B. H., & Tetreault, M. S. (1990). The service encounter: Diagnosing favorable and unfavorable incidents. *Journal of Marketing, 54*(1), 71–84.

Davis, D., & Cosenza, R. M. (1993). *Business research for decision making*. California: Wadsworth.

Keaveney, S. M. (1995). Customer switching behavior in service industries: An exploratory study. *Journal of Marketing, 59*(2), 71–82.

Latham, G., & Saari, L. M. (1984). Do people do what they say? Further studies on the situational interview. *Journal of Applied Psychology, 69*(4), 422–427.

Maignan, I., & Lukas, B. A. (1997). The nature and social uses of the internet: A qualitative investigation. *The Journal of Consumer Affairs, 31*(2), 346–371.

Murphy, J. (1999). Surfers and searchers: An examination of web-site visitors' clicking behavior. *Cornell Hotel and Restaurant Administration Quarterly, 40*(2), 84–95.

Murphy, J., Forrest, E. J., & Wotring, C. E. (1996). Restaurant marketing on the worldwide web. *Cornell Hotel and Restaurant Administration Quarterly, 37*(1), 61–71.

Oliver, R. L. (1980). A cognitive model of the antecedents and consequences of satisfaction decision. *Journal of Marketing Research, 17*(November), 460–469.

Olsen, M. D., & Connolly, D. J. (2000). Experience-based travel: How technology is changing the hospitality industry. *Cornell Hotel and Restaurant Administration Quarterly, 41*(1), 30–40.

Vandermerwe, S. (1993). Jumping into the customer's activity cycle: A new role for customer services in the 1990s. *The Columbia Journal of World Business, 28*(2), 46–65.

Wang, K.-C., Hsieh, A.-T., & Chen, W.-Y. (2002). Is the tour leader an effective endorser for group package tour brochures? *Tourism Management, 23*(5), 489–498.

Wang, K.-C., Hsieh, A.-T., & Huan, T.-C. (2000). Critical service features in group package tour: An exploratory research. *Tourism Management, 21*(2), 177–189.

Yi, Y. (1993). The determinants of consumer satisfaction: The moderating role of ambiguity. In: L. McAlister & M. L. Rothschild (Eds), *Advances in Consumer Research* (Vol. 20, pp. 502–506). Provo, UT: Association for Consumer Research.

Ziperovich, M. (2002). Effective use of internet likely will weave web of opportunities to grow business. *Nation's Restaurant News, 36*(27), 26–28.

EXPLORATION OF THE LINKAGES BETWEEN THE GASTRONOMY AND HERITAGE OF TAINAN CITY, TAIWAN

Li-Jen Jessica Hwang, Jetske van Westering
and Hsin-Hui Chen

ABSTRACT

The aim of this study is to understand the diverse ways in which gastronomy and heritage are related and how this specifically applies to tourism in the city of Tainan, Taiwan and their traditional snack food. Interviews conducted with local food commodity experts in Taiwan generated in-depth insights into distinctive cultural traditions and particular historical circumstances well beyond the immediate producers and consumers. Four issues emerged from these interviews: the concept of what constitutes traditional food, modifications in the method of food production, the role of traditional food within society, and historical inheritance through mass media promotion. The drive toward innovation, when opposed by the force of tradition, can indirectly sustain the configuration of cultural heritage which can be expressed through food as the art of gastronomy.

Advances in Hospitality and Leisure
Advances in Hospitality and Leisure, Volume 1, 223–235
ISSN: 1745-3542/doi:10.1016/S1745-3542(04)01015-X

INTRODUCTION

The concept of gastronomy has had a long and old friendship with heritage, which under the influence of the mass gastronomic media has entered the mainstream consciousness. The serving of traditional snack food is being transformed by new logistics and production methods, as the practice struggles to establish its identity as part of a modern, dynamic configuration in a social and cultural society. This paper is intended to explore the modernisation of tradition snack food in Tainan, which was regarded as distinct from elite culinary practices, and the effect this has had on Tourism and the image the city projects to visitors.

Escapism or Liberation

A common phrase used in describing human beings is "you are what you eat." Eating becomes the integration of the qualities of the food you consume. Food can function as a symbol, a sign of communion, a class marker, or an emblem as part of a physiological and social environment, in addition to the hygienic and nutritional values, and psycho-sensorial and symbolic characteristics (Berrière, 1998). It can be argued that when tasting cuisine from other country, the experience becomes one of participating in another culture and relating to people and places with a strong sense of their own identity (Hergarty & O'Mahony, 2001; Rao, 2003; Van Westering, 1999). This drive can be seen to motivate people to escape into different cultures or have a sense of relief in liberating themselves from the modern highly stressed society.

Demand for Greater Authenticity in Food Experiences

The concept of gastronomy suggests that a thoughtful consumer who is concerned more with the quality of life rather than the quantity of life has prioritised their demand for greater authenticity and real experiences when choosing a tourism product (Hall et al., 2003; Hjalager & Corigliano, 2000; Richards, 2002; Van Westering, 1999). The cuisine of another country becomes much more accessible and affordable when providing tourists with the closest of encounters with the authentic and with a sense of having communicated or maybe even merged briefly as part of that culture (Hegarty & O'Mahony, 2001). Coveney and Santich (1997) recognised that by sustaining gastronomy people can benefit through connecting others through food socialisation, which brings a sense of familiarity and authenticity when dealing with food production that is sensitive to the environment, what to prepare and eat in ways that nourish the individual body and collective culture (Corbin, 2002 illustrated the promotion of a heritage village in the North Carolina State Fairgrounds as an example). This fuller cultural experience is enriched more by having local dishes eaten with the local population in a local setting, and cannot replicated elsewhere.

Learning Gastronomy to Continue Heritage

The influences from the mass media through gastronomic magazines and TV programmes have stimulated reflections the relationship between local traditional cuisine and tourism. Compared with ten years ago, three times more gastronomic-related programmes are being broadcast, not only to explore the popularity and curiosity about the heritage of recipes and cooking methods but also to promote the culture as an attraction for tourists to visit destinations (Fattorini, 1996; Ferguson, 1998; Hegarty & O'Mahony, 1999). In the experience economy period, the use of the media machine in its various configurations has portrayed, and to some extent trivialised, the art of living. Because of this, or in spite of it, gastronomy has developed to the point that might be achievable to make it a good degree or even masters dissertation (Pelham, 2002). Snatich (2004) concluded that the study of gastronomy, as the art or science of good eating, provided a gateway towards understanding cultures across the world.

However, Wood (1996) argued that mass journalistic commentary on food have tended to underplay the extent to which this form of public writing perpetuates a culinary hegemony in which popular taste is, if not, effectively denigrated, then dismissed as culturally inferior. Any attempts at understanding how mass markets for food supply and consumption can effectively be ignored or marginalised in everyday discourse in favour of a focus on mere elitist concerns. It can be seen to be a phenomenon, which distorts public perceptions of the nature of food markets, especially in the context of dining out. Like most forms of snobbery, food commentary involves a pernicious and grotesque distortion of reality, in this case the reality of the mass food markets of the developed world and the mass starvation that is to be found in so many parts of the less-developed world. The effect of the consumer targeted food media blurring the boundary between amateur and professional cannot be underestimated (Fattorini, 1996).

Theoretical Identification

Berrière (1998) interpreted heritage as a subjective element, which is recognised as a unifying sign or a collective social memory. Heritage then no longer becomes considered solely as a link between past and present, but also as a reservoir of meaning necessary to understand the work: a resource in order to elaborate a sense of belonging and consequently identity. Food and gastronomy are but one feature of heritage. As an identity maker of a region and/or as a mean of promoting farm products, gastronomy meets the specific needs of consumers, local producers and other actors in rural tourism.

As a reaction to the complexity of the modern world in which social links are either falling apart or weakening, people dream of friendly relationships, true and genuine values – roots. By integrating eating into a new cultural work form both a psychological and physiological standpoint, gastronomy, therefore, offers the possibility for compensating for lost identity and gaining experience of feeling of socialising and finding a community identity as a representation of "the good old days" (Berrière, 1998, p. 22). Gastronomy can be a fundamental component of tourist travelling: eating is an integral part of our holidays and rural tourism can be a part of the re-appropriation of history in terms of eating habits (Berrière, 1998, p. 23).

Processed food can be seen to be devoid of tradition and identity: functionalised, standardised, and recomposed mass foodstuffs, such as a quick sandwich or a Big Mac, merely fulfilling biological needs in the manner that a vitamin supplement might satisfy a deficiency. An increased distrust of agro-industrial products has coincided with the real or imagined side-effects of chemical and processed food, colouring additives and the like. Advertising and marketing professionals are unscrupulous in hoodwinking consumers into believing that they are actually buying grandmother's jam or farm-fresh pâté, which are in fact mass produced. The anonymity of current eating is the result of nutritional industrialisation, fewer structured meals, random snacking, an impoverished culinary legacy and a greater gap between farmer and consumer.

Combining conservation and innovation, stability and dynamism, reproduction and creation, and consequently giving a new social meaning which generates identity and unity. As the daughter or granddaughter no longer inherits secret family recipes, modern home cooking has gone beyond traditional family dishes, creating nostalgia for food eaten in one's childhood and adolescence as if this were a return to the beginning. Heritage elements (Berrière, 1998) can then be produced and reproduced as the result of dynamic interplay between tradition and modernity. Eating farm-fresh products may represent for the urban tourist not only a biological quality but also a short-lived appropriation of a rural identity and integration into a forgotten culture.

Based on Berrière (1998)'s framework, Tainan's culinary heritage has gradually been constructed through the interplay between traditional and modern icons of gastronomy. In the past, gastronomy has played a role in cultural exchange to welcome visitors and provide an authentic experience for tourists. Through time, the dynamism creates ideological conflicts in that adaptation to innovations challenges the conservative ideology that seeks to keep tradition stable and reproducible; in other words, the question lies on what constitutes the shape or form of heritage. This study attempts to explore the questions about the transformation from gastronomic heritage to culinary tourism. What are the constituent elements of this cuisine heritage? What impact has the traditional snack foods had on the local residents in Tainan city? Through the gastronomic media, how far can its rising value be considered part of new drive in developing this culinary heritage and result in attracting tourism?

METHODS

As the literature has demonstrated limited resources in the area of gastronomy and heritage and little direct research has been undertaken in this area, this study has served an exploratory purpose in revealing how the role of gastronomy has been related to the development of heritage. The background information has been gathered from various published resources, particularly from government officials (such as Tourism Bureau of Taiwan and Tainan country council), non-profit organisations (the Foundation of Chinese Dietary Culture, 2003), and organisations related to the Taipei Chinese Food Festival.

According to the Tainan City Government (GIO, 2003) figures in tourism are rapidly rising, with the reasons for tourists to come to Tainan being to visit historic buildings and to taste traditional snacks. Traditional snacks can be found in several cities in Taiwan; however, the most famous amongst these is Tainan City, which is generally regarded as part of the roots and history of Taiwan with regard to traditional snacks. The different ethnic groups that made Tainan their base all brought with them their particular foods; thus each dish or snack reflects a certain period in the development of the city. Tainan itself has trumpeted its local culture and heritage and the important role that food can play. As such, several initiatives have been developed to promote the traditional dishes in conjunction with local heritage: in the Tainan City Tourism guide the five most important historic buildings are combined with the most popular traditional snacks.

Applying a qualitative approach, telephone interviews were carried out during August 2003 with twelve quota-sampled professionals, who are well-known experts in food authorities, journalists, or academics in Hospitality and Tourism in the Tainan area. As Chossat and Gergaud (2003) explained, the reasons why experts' opinions has had respectively large impact in the gastronomic market were simply that the information related to food and cooking was imperfect and very costly to acquire, the quality of messages tended to be subjective, and the most important consumers needed an experts' influence to identify the determinants of these evaluations of product quality. Participants were informed in advance through an introduction letter explaining the purpose of this research and likely areas of investigation, with the stated goal of deriving a maximum theoretical understanding on the development of traditional snack foods in Tainan city.

Four analytic phases (research design, data collection, data analysis and literature comparison of grounded theory building) were followed and evaluated against their reliability and validity to ensure the high quality of the research (Pandit, 1996). Guided by a piloted interview protocol, the priori constructs were built around both traditional and modern perspectives on the topic of recipe selection and the role they play for people, and their implications to local residents and tourists in terms of cultural image and the tourist gastronomic experience. These open-ended questions were defined narrowly enough so that the research was focused and broad enough to allow for flexibility and serendipity. The interview transcripts were verified by the respondents in Chinese, then later translated and then processed in a systematic and rigorous application of the grounded theory method. The synergy in documenting respondents' published articles, research papers, or books was also done to enhance the construct validity and reliability of this study (Yin, 2003).

RESULTS AND DISCUSSION

In the construction of culinary heritage, gastronomy performs a bi-directional function between tradition and modernity as illustrated by the four emerging issues: the concept of what constitutes traditional food, modifications in the method of food production, the role of traditional food within society, and historical inheritance through mass media promotion (Fig. 1).

Meanings of Traditional Snack Food

The concept of traditional snacks has moved on from the locally known delicacies of the past to now become part of the daily meal. From a customer point of view, traditional snack food was small morsels eaten mainly between the three formal meals to show generosity to friends and visitors. This transition may also be indicative of higher disposable incomes and people displaying their increased status, as the majority of families tended to cook for themselves in the past.

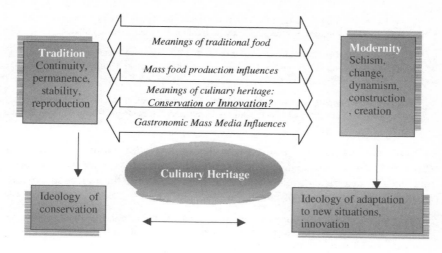

(Adopted from Berrière, 1998, p. 27)

Fig. 1.   The Inter-Relationship of Gastronomy in the Construction of Culinary Heritage.

Traditional snack foods were local dishes that fit the environmental situation in the past.

People would eat traditional snack food before or after dinner when they have earned more money in the past.

The so-called traditional snacks are other kinds of food apart from our daily meals. They have become something more than just snacks after daily meals.

From a business point of view, providers have largely remained Small and Medium Enterprises, mostly involving family members as staff. It was viewed as a low skilled job requiring little risk and investment but with the potential to earn a living.

My father opened a traditional snack shop in order to survive, so that all of our family needed to help my father to run the business. Although there was not so much, it was the way for us to survive.

Deeply rooted in a particular place as well as in a particular space and time, the cooking traditions of Tainan city revealed the character of the society and mentality of its local residents. These traditions were an obvious legacy of their ancestors, and they bear witness to previous eating habits. The distinctive taste of food recalls memories, brings up nostalgic feelings, and infuses heritage with a certain sense of realism. The culinary heritage is strongly linked to a peasant identity and brought a style of eating which is full of imaginary symbols.

My parents would bring me to taste the Wan Ko (a special local dish) when I got a good grade at school. I was encouraged and felt satisfied with traditional snacks in my childhood.

When you sit on that small wooden stool to taste the Tan Tzu noodle (a Tainan speciality food), the memory will jump out, that is the feeling you had when you were a child! It could be the taste or the place that recalls the memory.

When I ate the shrimp meat ball in the square in front of the temple, I would remember when I was a child that I always used to play with my friends there. It made me feel so warm in my heart.

Traditional snacks were found to be intertwined with cultural heritage and attraction tourism. Certain dishes are regarded as cultural symbols and have been influenced by historical developments as Taiwan has moved through as succession of rulers, both foreign and of late, domestic.

The traditional snack food no longer serves just the purpose of filling the hungry, but represents special local delicacies. People visit the local night market with the purpose of tasting that uniqueness of flavour of particular dishes.

Now, when talking about the traditional snacks, people feel it is not just about food but also represents local customs in each city in Taiwan.

Mass Food Production Influences

The majority of respondents agreed that five particular dishes can be linked to the image of Tainan city. The most popular items are Tan Tzu noodles, Coffin Cake (seafood chowder in a pastry), Woa-ko (a steamed rice cake), Shrimp rolls and Fried Eel noodles. The basic ingredients for each dish have not changed, but the production methods and selling tactics have been modified to deal with the larger volumes. The old way to sell the snacks was to peddle them on the street without any regulation or food hygiene policies in place. Little shops may be set up on any corner in any place that attracts attention and foot traffic. Another method was to drive a self-contained kitchen van around the streets during certain hours of the day and announcing their presence via loud speakers. The snacks would only be made to order, cooked to order, or prepared in small batches using a small kitchen, cookers, ovens, or hot plates.

The modern way is to apply mass production methods with assembly at the point of sale in either their own chain of retail shops or outsourcing to other convenience stores. Food factories meet food hygiene regulations and gain quality accreditation from the local council. A successful example is the way the Woa-Ko dish has raised its profile by harmonising the food with traditional tableware and decorations in the shop.

The shop owner now can earn more profit than ever. Some may reach one hundred thousand [NT yuan] per month.

However, the worry was that the true experience of local dishes might become lost as most snack foods were based on the quality and simplicity of fresh ingredients, combined quickly and freshly in front of you, which most of the time did not require sophistication in preparation. Although modern processes have solved the technical production problems inherent in supplying large quantities, the original atmosphere can hardly be duplicated or replaced with new metal or plastic containers in a modern architectural environment.

The reason why a shrimp roll was so delicious was because its ingredients were made fresh and served immediately, but now the dish is brought in either partially cooked and frozen, or pre-cooked before the orders to meet the large quantities of tourist demand. It is dangerous that our next generation cannot understand the taste of the past.

Purpose of Preserving Tainan Culinary Heritage: Conservation or Innovation?

The results found that unlike other heritage, culinary heritage has not been treated as a method of cultural preservation. The general impression from these respondents was that there was no obvious conservation work being undertaken to maintain the traditional snacks. Most night markets have suffered under dirty, unhygienic conditions or with poor infrastructure compared with world standards. The locations were not normally regulated or supported by official policy. The hide and seek situation with the shop owners still occurs when police come to inspect the street for local council regulation. Most importantly, the original recipes, the chef's technical skills and unique cooking styles are often kept as a business secret, which are not usually documented and the children might not be willing to continue the family business. One of reasons suggested for this lack of preservation was that the value and contribution of gastronomy to culture and history was largely underestimated, which has resulted in inadequate funding to promote culinary heritage.

It is a good thing to use traditional snacks to promote tourism in Tainan city. Nonetheless, it is a pity that the sanitation of tradition snack shops is not good enough for the tourist, and it should be improved if they want it to develop further.

Although the culture affairs bureau under the new governor party in Taiwan has created several initiatives to revitalise the traditional snack food as a marketing tool for promoting local heritage and attracting tourism, the promotion was not fully supported with the necessary resources and manpower. Having a clean and open night market could become a rare experience that might give an authentic option for the modern western traveller.

If Tainan wants to use traditional snacks as a tourism attraction, there should first be an improvement in sanitation. We should focus on developing the international market in the future, and let more foreign tourists know about the traditional snacks in Tainan.

Traditional snacks were just normal foods for Tainan residents in the past. We did not think they could be attractive for tourists. However, after tourism became a main point of development, then we started to think that traditional snacks could be a good tool for promoting Tainan city.

Gastronomic Mass Media Influences

The gastronomic media has provided a driving force to sustain traditional recipes and advocate the tourist experiences. In the past, gastronomic TV programmes were neither popular nor associated with tourism activities. The purpose of the food programme was purely to teach housewives how to cook authentic cuisine for their husband or to impress family or friends. The language was strictly technical in terms of food ingredients and demonstrating the complexity of the recipes in a practical way. Under the influence of Japanese culture during their 50 years of occupation of Taiwan, the food programmes have gradually embraced the concept of tourism and begun to view cuisine as a tourist experience which relates to the local culture. The number of gastronomic related TV programmes has recently increased dramatically from only eight in 1993 to 20+ now.

If they had not been introduced to snacks in the gastronomic magazines or TV programmes, tourists would not come to experience the taste. Interestingly, tourism increased dramatically once the shops were introduced by the gastronomic magazines or TV programmes.

However, the concern is that the commercialisation of the food experience may cause a loss of understanding of the history, development and mystery of a dish and the meaning of local food identity. A misinterpretation of these particular dishes in luxurious ways when broadcasting the programmes can have worrisome effects with regard to the cultural aspects of the food.

People that travel to Tainan to visit the historic sites and taste the traditional snacks, do not understand the cultural meaning of the dish or the story behind the ingredients.

CONCLUSION

As the four issues emerging from this study into the changing status of Tainan snack food has been supported by previous research (Bessiere, 1998; Fields, 2002; Hegarty & O'Mahony, 2001), the gastronomic aspects of tradition food should also be pursued not merely for consumption, but also for culture expression, heritage status, and the promotion of food tourism.

Unclear Branding of Traditional Food for Market Positioning

The promotion of traditional snacks is increasing as their image is diversified into providing spiritual memories and nostalgia for tourists. The acquisition of gastronomic experiences can enhance tourists' understanding and appreciation of the cultural and heritage sites. As this study also found, the connotation of tradition food would depend on the levels of transformation from the old production methods with a new modernising touch. Further study should examine the implications of branding the tradition food for its position in the market and the promotional strategies of both food providers and heritage attractions.

Subsequent investigations can examine what elements make up traditional food in terms of its recipes, production methods, or service style. New food production methods, such as cook-chill or batch production, may alter the unique recipes during processing of the quantities required to match the tourist demand. This study discovered that to local food has modified the product to at least some extent in their cooking methods, delivery channels, or product presentation. Further study could investigate food regulation policies and their effect upon traditional food or local dishes and perceptions of unhygienic or unhealthy foodservice.

As the sample utilised in this study only involved one reputable Taiwanese city – Tainan, the relationships surrounding other local cuisine can be explored, as such Devon Cream Teas, Spanish Tapas (bar foods), Vietnamese Phô (noodle soup). Further research could compare the role of gastronomy through cross-cultural research that could redefine the role of culinary heritage among distinctive culture differences, such as European, Oriental, Asia, Mediterranean, or Latin American. As this study was limited by the data, collected at one heritage site in one country, future studies could investigate in multiple sites and/or countries and promote the benefits of a formal culinary heritage designation.

Mass Media Influences on Consumer Behaviour

Preserving the values and uniqueness of the traditional snack may become more difficult under the influences of gastronomic programmes with divergent purposes. Food programmes target different audiences through new styles and techniques as compared to the old-style culinary teaching. This study revealed that the pursuit of popularity might override an understanding of the origin of the snack foods and their heritage development. Further study into the cognitive influences of gastronomic mass media on consumer perception and patronage patterns could contribute relevant information for tourism development.

Sustainable Culinary Heritage Development for Traditional Food

Often traditional recipes are kept secret in the family without documentation and the new generation may not be willing to inherit the family business, this study in Taiwanese culture found that dishes may become lost or gradually forgotten over time. The increased stature of gastronomy in heritage can have a significant role in both cultural exchange and tourism development. Further research into promoting the contributions of culinary heritage can establish the reliability and validity of this newly proposed model (shown in Fig. 1).

As this study explored the concept of "traditional food" as a first small step in looking at the role of gastronomy, the intention is to contribute further direction in the areas of the effects of branding in multiple sites or its cross-cultural aspects, understanding consumer behaviour toward the meaning of traditional food, synthesising modern operations management for traditional food, and the sustainability of culinary heritage. The implications and contribution of gastronomy on heritage and tourism requires is currently only superficially understood and requires more in-depth research.

ACKNOWLEDGMENTS

The authors would like to acknowledge twelve professions in Taiwan for sharing their experiences and giving their time to allow us to complete our work.

REFERENCES

Bessiere, J. (1998). Local development and heritage: Traditional food and cuisine as tourist attractions in rural areas. *European Society for Rural Sociology, 38*(1), 21–34.
Chossat, V., & Gergaud, O. (2003). Expert opinion and gastronomy: The recipe for success. *Journal of Cultural Economics, 27*(2), 127–141.
Coveney, J., & Santich, B. (1997). A question of balance: Nutrition, health, and gastronomy. *Appetite, 28*(3), 267–277.
Fattorini, J. (1996). Food Journalism: A medium for conflict? *British Food Journal, 96*(10), 24–28.
Fields, K. (2002). Demand for the gastronomy tourism product: Motivational factors. In: A. M. Hjalager & G. Richards (Eds), *Tourism and Gastronomy* (pp. 36–50). London: Routledge.

Foundation of Chinese Dietary Culture (2003). Current Chinese food and drink culture catalog, [online] 26/03/2004 from http://www.fcdc.org.tw/html/1-00.htm.

Hall, C. M., Sharples, L., Michell, R., Macionis, N., & Cambourne, B. (2003). *Food tourism around the World – Development, management and markets*. London: Butterworth-Heinemann.

Hegarty, J. A., & O'Mahony, G. B. (1999). Gastronomy: A phenomenon of culture expressionism and aesthetic for living. *Journal of Hospitality and Tourism Education, 11*(4), 25–29.

Pandit, N. R. (1996). The Creation of theory: A recent application of the grounded theory method. *The Qualitative Report, 2*(4), [Online]. 25/03/04 from http://www.nova.edu/ssss/QR/QR2-4/pandit.html/.

Pelham, P. (2002). Book review on European gastronomy into 21st century. *Food Service Technology, 2*(2), 107.

Richards, G. (2002). Gastronomy: An essential ingredient in tourism production and consumption. In: A. M. Hjalager & G. Richards (Eds), *Tourism and Gastronomy* (pp. 3–20). London: Routledge.

Snatich, B. (2004). The study of gastronomy and its relevance to hospitality and tourism education and training. *International Journal of Hospitality Management, 23*(1), 15–24.

Van Westering, J. (1999). Heritage and gastronomy: The pursuits of the new tourists. *International Journal of Heritage Studies, 5*(2), 75–81.

Yin, R. K. (2003). *Case study research: Design and methods*. Thousand Oaks, CA: Sage.

ESTIMATING THE IMMEDIATE EFFECTS OF AN UNPRECEDENTED EVENT OF TERRORISM

Tadayuki Hara

ABSTRACT

The negative impact of unexpected events, such as terrorism and natural disaster, on national and regional economies has been widely recognized, but seldom quantified immediately after the shock. The objective of this paper is to present an alternative quantitative method to forecast immediate short term impacts given an unprecedented negative shock to a regional economy, including tourism related sectors. The result of application to the September 11 attack over New York City shows promising validity of using a deterministic model of an input-output/social accounting matrix, which depicts the annual flow of and interdependency of industrial sectors in the economy. This implies applicability of the method to forecast immediate impacts of negative events, while further required refinements are suggested.

INTRODUCTION

The negative impacts of terrorism on a regional economy and tourism-related sectors have been tacitly assumed, but seldom quantified despite the fact that many national and regional governments have substantial dependence on tourism revenues, which often are one of the largest exporting industries in

Advances in Hospitality and Leisure
Advances in Hospitality and Leisure, Volume 1, 237–254
Copyright © 2004 by Elsevier Ltd.
All rights of reproduction in any form reserved
ISSN: 1745-3542/doi:10.1016/S1745-3542(04)01016-1

developing economies. Negative economic impacts of an unexpected event might be estimated through inductive analysis after all the data become available, but during, or immediately after an unexpected event, the lack of data may hinder forecasting detailed impact using multivariate econometrics or time-series intervention analysis. Regression-based models assume homoskedastic data, i.e. equal variance, thereby making it challenging to predict/estimate sudden unexpected surges/plunges in the value of relevant variables. The negative impacts of unexpected events on tourism have been widely recognized, but seldom quantified not only due to its difficulty in ex-post analysis but also to uncertain definition of "tourism industry" for regional economists. While researchers are faced with those constraints, the World Trade Center attack in 2001 happened in a region that has solid I-O/SAM components and detailed monthly employment data, that became available quicker than any other published ones to have reflected the initial shock.

The purpose of the study is to find an alternative model to capture the immediate negative shock to the economy and forecast with limited amount of available data on what would happen to the regional economy and hospitality-related sectors in the short term before the negative impact goes back to the trend line that the regression/time-series based model would indicate in the long-run. Literature on quantifying unexpected/unprecedented shocks to regional economy and to tourism industry will be reviewed. Estimating shock of natural disasters, of man-made disaster and of terrorism in particular will be reviewed. I will discuss methodologies for quantifying immediate shocks to demonstrate how the shock of the World Trade Center attack over New York economy can be quantified before various data become available, and compare it with other works on the same topic, followed by a conclusion.

LITERATURE REVIEW: MEASUREMENT OF UNEXPECTED/UNPRECEDENTED SHOCK

Among researches on verifying the nature of unexpected impact, this study classifies them into natural disaster, man-made disaster (such as war, oil-spill) and terrorism.

Quantifying the Negative Impact of Natural Disasters

Prominent among studies of natural disasters outside of the Unites States is a study by Horwich, who discussed the economic impact of the Kobe earthquake in 1995

(Horwich, 2000). The paper quoted an estimate made by a Japanese scholar that the damage to capital stock was U.S.$114 billion, by far the most costly disaster on record. Because the earthquake struck a heavily populated modern urban area, 6500 people were killed, and 100,000 buildings were totally destroyed as well. Horwich, based on the swift recovery of the City of Kobe, asserted that natural disasters in major advanced economies tended not to significantly reduce current aggregate output or induce an associated rise in the general price level. Horwich's notion was that evaluating change in capital stock was better than evaluating change in total output. Okuyama et al. (1997) also studied the Kobe earthquake, but in greater depth with intertemporal processes analysis.

From the viewpoint of real estate finance, Brunette (1995) conducted a study on the impact of natural disasters on commercial real estate returns as measured by the Russell-NCREIF Property Index (RNPI). In the history of the index, there had been only three major natural disasters near Metropolitan Statistical Areas (MSAs) represented in the Index – the San Francisco Bay Area Earthquake in October 1989, Hurricane Andrew in South Florida in August 1992, and the Los Angeles Area Earthquake in January 1994. Time-series analyses of each market detected no apparent changes in property prices or in returns on an annual basis, even though each disaster was estimated to have inflicted billions of dollars worth of damages. Murdoch et al. (1993) conducted a thorough econometric study on the effect of the San Francisco Earthquake on housing prices in the Bay Area, with a sample of 9000 home sales data. The study controlled for housing characteristics (structural, neighborhood, community, location) that might be correlated with the occurrence of the earthquake, and concluded that it caused an approximate 2% reduction in housing values.

Quantifying Negative Economic Impacts of a Man-Made
Disaster – Oil Spill, War

Although it was not exactly classified as a natural disaster, Cohen (1995) employed an ex-post forecasting methodology to measure the total costs of the 1988 Exxon Valdez oil spill on south central Alaskan fisheries activities. Based on eleven structural equations, one for each species of Pacific Salmon, Cohen forecasted that the costs were U.S.$108 million in the first year and U.S.$47 million in the second year. Cohen conceded the fair share of difficulties associated with ex-post analysis.

Grobar and Gnanaselvam (1993) used a multivariate regression model to estimate the economic effects of a man-made disaster – the Sri Lankan Civil War. They found a strong inverse relationship between national investment and military spending (namely, if the military spending increased by U.S.$1 million, the national investment decreased by U.S.$1.44 million, with a *t*-ratio of 4.13, which indicated strong significance of this inverse relationship) in their analysis.

Quantifying Negative Economic Impact of Terrorism

Besides Fiscal Policy Institute (2001a, b, 2002a, b), Hara and Saltzman (2003), Hara (2004), I did not find research on quantifying negative economic impact of terrorism events over multiple industrial sectors in the regional economy, while there was good research on the negative impact of terrorism specifically over a certain single dependent variable, such as number of tourists visiting the region in question. Mihalic (1996) analyzed the number of tourist nights to Slovenia with simple linear model to verify the negative effect of war over the tourism demand, with mixed significance over different outgoing markets. Mansfeld (1999) documented comparative analysis of tourist inflow to the Middle East, using international tourist arrivals as a dependent variable. Coshall (2003) also used a single dependent variable, U.K. air travel, to find out whether the threats of terrorism were an periodical intervention on international travel flows. His time-series data were quarterly number of passengers since 1976–1999, and he used a time-series framework (Auto Regressive Integrated Moving Average: ARIMA) to find whether selected three shocks, U.S. bombing of Libya in 1986, the Lockerbie Pan-Am bombing in 1988, and the first Gulf War 1991, had any long-term impact on the time-series trends. Coshall stated that "(the ARIMA framework) can measure the significance of impacts on passenger flows, but it can also assess the form of decay of the (terrorism) impact, be it temporary, gradual, or permanent." These studies did not mention the shortfall and limitations of using regression and time-series models to assess the immediate impact of current terrorism, which the author elaborates below.

REVIEW OF OTHER METHODOLOGY TO QUANTIFY NEGATIVE IMPACTS

Using Multivariate Econometric Models and Time-Series Models

Multivariate econometric based models could be accurate and useful once all the data, especially the independent variables, are on the researcher's table. But immediately after an act of terrorism, all the relevant data are not necessarily available at time = 0, or the event is still fresh or recent past. One could extrapolate what could happen in a similar case in the future, but it may present less guidance when faced with "unprecedented" current events such as is often the case with an act of terrorism.

Unprecedented magnitude of shock itself[1] poses a severe challenge to a series of assumptions on which the regression/econometric based models hold their validity.[2] It is the sudden plunge at time 0 that changes the slope of the trend line more than a similar shock in the middle of a time-series observation, which tends to shift the trend line downward but does not the change of slope. Hendry and Katarina (2000) point out that the problem of classical econometric theory that observed data come from a stationary process, where means and variances are assumed constant over times. A time-series model could be a useful tool to estimate what could have happened without a terrorism event, similar to the method the Federal Reserve Bank of New York adapted to estimate the state's economy without the shock of 9/11 (Bram & Rapaport, 2002). Simple time-series framework has been used to answer the research question of whether the shocks of terrorism caused permanent shift of the trend line (difference stationary) or the impact of the shock is transient (trend stationary).[3] But a major obstacle of time-series model is to digest the sudden change of variance due to an unexpected/unprecedented event, or making a model that incorporates heteroskadastisity of its sudden variance as endogenous.[4] While the multivariate & time-series model are highly versatile for analyzing past data, immediately after or during the shock, when policy-makers, managers and the public endeavor to figure out how deep the shock will plunge the whole economy, the model might at best indicate a comfort that economy would regress back to the trend line as time passes. Also the multivariate & time-series frame are not meant for forecasting detailed analyses on changes in series of multiple variables that are being affected concurrently by the shock of terrorism.

Brief Review of Input Output/Social Accounting Matrix Models

An Input-Output model is basically an accounting framework that depicts how the total output of each industry depends on its inter-industry demands and final demands, by showing all inter-industry transactions in a matrix format. A SAM model is an extension of an I-O model and shows additional monetary flows among the production, factors and institutional sectors in an economy. The model can be expressed in matrix notation:

$$X = (I - A)^{-1} Y \qquad (1)$$

where X = total output (an $n \times 1$ vector), I = identity matrix (an $n \times n$ matrix), A = normalized inter-industry coefficient matrix in cents per dollar (an $n \times n$ matrix), Y = final demand (an $n \times 1$ vector), where n is the number of sectors included in the model.

The merit of using the I-O/SAM model is that it is structurally made to capture the initial shock, usually in the form of change in final demands for selected industrial sectors to predict total shock over each and every sector of economy in question. As a model, the I-O/SAM model has a fair share of limitations including, constant returns to scale, and has no assumptions for supply constraints and for price changes. I-O/SAM model is not a stochastic but a deterministic model, thus without confidence intervals or t-ratios, which may make some researchers feel uncomfortable. Temporal stability of technical coefficients or accuracy of I-O/SAM after passage of time can be questioned. I did not assume significant changes in economic structures because of the World Trade Center attack, as Vaccara (1970) indicated the large developed economy tend to change its structure "slowly and orderly."[5]

I-O/SAM models are often used by governments and economic researchers for estimating impacts of certain actions and policy choices, and they also are used for estimating positive impacts of large development projects in a region, for example, the economic impacts of a housing development, a large industrial development, a tourism development, and changes in income and other tax revenues in a region. The model does not appear to be frequently used for micro-level hospitality projects, such as the impact of a single hotel development on a regional economy, due in part to its apparent relative complexity, and to the fact that the hospitality managers are rather unfamiliar with the model.

I use the I-O/SAM model to determine whether it could reasonably predict the magnitudes of the total negative impacts caused by an initial negative shock to an economy, given a situation of limited availability of public data, amid uncertainty caused by current unprecedented shock, shortly after a major terrorism incident.

ANALYSIS OF THE 9/11 WORLD TRADE CENTER ATTACK: USING AN I-O/SAM MODEL

Basic Assumptions of the "Initial Shock"

External data required for this study were obtained from relevant government publications of NYC, mainly data that were available on the web page of the New York State Department of Labor. Using IMPLAN,[6] I took the decrease in NYC employment from September as a proxy for the initial shock from the attack, and simulated what would happen to the NYC economy in terms of total changes in economic activity including, for example, employment, income, and tax on an annual basis. I also looked into the hotel & lodging sector NYC in order to better understand the specific economic impacts of the 9/11 attack.

The underlying logic for choosing the job-loss as an initial shock is that this assumed direct initial job-loss will result in an additional job-loss due to the indirect and induced effects associated with the initial job loss. While the employment data appear to be a measurement of "stock" in the economy, they are structured into the framework as a proxy for "flows" of output/compensation/income. The model captures how the reduced income flow caused by an initial shock of job losses would subsequently impact all other flows in the economy.

The assumption about the initial impacts of 9/11 were fairly simple ones – whatever the reductions in the number of people employed between September and October of 2001 would be considered the direct effects and were predominantly attributable to the initial impacts of the 9/11 attack.[7]

The Time Frame of the Estimation of Shocks

One question that should be addressed is how long the economy would reflect the anticipated effects in reply to the initial shock. Unlike dealing with numbers in a balance sheet, which is a snapshot of one point in time on how total assets and liabilities are used to generate activities, economic flows are more like income statements. Income statements, however, generally have a defined time-span of one year, and many economic data also use one-year as a defined time span. If I simulate the shock in an I-O/SAM framework based on general economic data, the results are naturally generated on a one-year flow basis. I estimated total shock on the basis of annual flows, whose decomposition may reveal insights about peak impact.

Allocating the Initial Shock to Industries, Including Tourism

Tourism industry analysis is challenging because we do not have a single industry but a group of industry segments that cater to tourists. In the simulation for 9/11, I choose to give shocks to broad seven industry segments (called the SIC 1-digit), which include tourism-related industries. Thus, we are not allocating shocks to each and every small segment but rather are interested in how the initial broad shock across aggregated segments will affect associated smaller disaggregated segments. The services sector consists of various sectors associated with tourism, but I found that according to the data reported by the NYS Labor Department, the overwhelming increase in educational services from September to October 2001 are the source of the increases for "services" as shown in Table 1. These adjusted values enabled us to estimate the adjusted data set for the assumed direct jobs lost due to the initial shock (see Table 2).

Table 1. Adjustment for "Change in Services" for NYC

Adjustment	NY CITY
Change in services	+12,700
Educational services (to be excluded)	+12,800
Social services (to be excluded)	+1,800
Adjusted change in services excluding changes in education & social services	−1,900

Source: The authors based on data from New York State Department of Labor, 2002.

In theory, what is done here with the input-output/social accounting matrix framework will be shown as follows.

(i) Start from the basic structure.

$$X = (I - A)^{-1}Y \tag{1}$$

(ii) Give a negative shock across the final demand of SIC 1-digit sectors as follows.[8] where

$$f - \text{vector} = \begin{bmatrix} 0 \\ +700 \\ -4,300 \\ -4,300 \\ -9,900 \\ -25,400 \\ -1,900 \end{bmatrix}$$

$$\cdots \begin{bmatrix} f_1 = \Delta\text{employment\_in\_Mining\_sector} \\ f_2 = \Delta\text{employment\_in\_Construction\_sector} \\ f_3 = \Delta\text{employment\_in\_Manufacturing\_sector} \\ f_4 = \Delta\text{employment\_in\_TCPU\_sector} \\ f_5 = \Delta\text{employment\_in\_Trade\_sector} \\ f_6 = \Delta\text{employment\_in\_FIRE\_sector} \\ f_7 = \Delta\text{employment\_in\_Service\_sector} \end{bmatrix} \tag{2}$$

(iii) Assume that coefficients in the Leontief Inverse $(I - A)^{-1}$ to be stable, as the inter-industry transactions matrix A are stable, at least over short time.

Table 2. The Adjusted Initial Shock of 9/11 to Jobs in NYC (Service Adjusted).

Industrial Sector	NY CITY
Mining	0
Construction	+700
Manufacturing	−4,300
TCPU	−4,300
Trade	−9,900
FIRE	−25,400
Services	−1,900
Total	−45,100

(iv) Then, change in final demand in *f*-vector (expressed in vector *Y*) will be reflected in *x*-vector, or *X* (total output matrix) as follows:

$$\Delta X = (I - A)^{-1} \Delta Y \qquad (3)$$

I will observe how the elements of *x*-vector would respond to the initial shock given to the *f*-vector in matrix *Y*. This framework will depict how an initial shock caused by terrorism will affect each sector in the regional economy through interdependence of industrial sectors.

FINDINGS: RESULTS OF THE FORECAST

In Table 3, I present the results of the forecast based on the adjusted initial shock as shown in Table 2. The initial shock of a 45,100 (42,780)[9] job loss due to the 9/11 WTC attack was forecasted to cause an indirect loss of 15,216 jobs and a further loss of 15,430 jobs owing to decreased income and consumption for the unemployed workers. According to the calculation, the initial shock of the 45,100 job-loss was expected to result in approximately a 73,400 total jobs loss in NYC with a decrease in total output of $18 billion on an annual basis.

Table 3. Short Term Terrorism Impact Forecasted for the NYC.

Impact on New York City	Direct Effects	Indirect Effects	Induced Effects	Total Effects
Total value added	−$9,726M	−$1,882M	−$1,398M	−$13,006M
Total output	−$13,283M	−$2,692M	−$1,976M	−$17,952M
Total employment	−42,780 jobs	−15,216 jobs	−15,430 jobs	−73,427 jobs
(Services sector)	−1,747jobs	−7,816 jobs	−5,476 jobs	−15,039 jobs

Source: The author using IMPLAN with 1998 data and deflators. The initial shock (direct effects) to the model were based on actual data from New York State Department of Labor http://www.labor.state.ny.us/.

While the total impact affected the regional economy in general, a further detailed look into some of the resulting effects from the study shows several intriguing findings. The initial negative impact of -1900 jobs in the services sector (see Table 3) was increased by the indirect effects of a 7816 job-loss and an induced effect of a 5476 job-loss, to yield a total effect of a 15,039 job-losses. This is due to the service sectors' strong interrelationship with other sectors in the economy, such as "FIRE" (finance, insurance and real estate), which suffered a huge negative initial shock due to the 9/11 WTC attack. The top three sectors that showed the largest resulting negative impacts on employee compensation are: (1) Eating & Drinking: $-\$45.0$ million; (2) Miscellaneous Retail: $-\$26.7$ million; and (3) Hotel & Lodging Places: $-\$15.5$ million. Our simulation by I-O/SAM data of the NYC underlines the assumed vulnerability of the "hospitality industry" to huge negative economic impacts compared to other industrial segments in a society due to the interdependence among sectors. While the FIRE sector in NYC accounts for only 50% of the resulting job loss, it accounts for 66% of the total output loss. The result reveals that the hospitality industry cannot exist in a vacuum when the other sectors are hit severely by an act of terrorism.

REVIEW OF OTHER STUDIES AND COMPARISON WITH ACTUAL DATA

Other Studies in Perspective

To make the analysis in perspective, various other media reports and articles about the possible economic impacts of the 9/11 attack were reviewed. Based on the reviews, most of the relevant media coverage that discussed the economic impact issue appeared either to quote or to base their discussions on one of the research studies conducted by economic and/or policy analyses-oriented institutions. Table in Appendix shows the entity that commissioned each report, which group made the study, as well as the estimated economic impacts on NYC. Impacts on a balance sheet (B/S) or "stock" basis are distinguished from those on an income statement (I/S) or "flow" basis, as some media coverage failed to separate those effects. Note that there is a wide range of estimates of the economic impacts of the 9/11 attack and that our estimates fall within their range (see Appendix).

Historical Patterns of Monthly Change in Employment

In order to find the existence of certain monthly trends, I first collected monthly employment data from 1976 to 2002 to depict specific patterns of employment

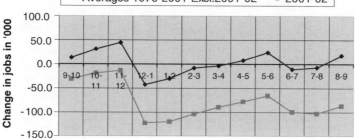

Fig. 1. New York City's Historical Monthly Employment Changes (1976–2001) vs. 2001–2002.

changes in NYC from each preceding September level. Then I plotted the changes for the historical averages and for 2001–2002 in perspective in Fig. 1. The observation is, while the monthly change patterns are similar, the plunge in September/October of 2001 was unusual (an average of +13,800 vs. −30,500 for 2001), the magnitude of the seasonal plunge in December~January was amplified in 2001, and in the remaining months of 2001 it continued to be suppressed for the rest of the 12 month period. Interestingly enough, the observed patterns fits with how the I-O/SAM model is perceived to explain the way such a shock behaves in general. It is noteworthy that of the last 26 years of monthly data for NYS, the other two years in which employment decreased from September to October (1979–1980, 1990–1991) seem to be years in which the economy also slowed.

Comparison of This Alternative Forecasts with Actual Data

To put the simulation further in perspective, I show a graph of the monthly changes in the employed since September 2001. An absolute employment level in September 2001 was set as zero and followed by monthly changes from that point, until September 2002 (see Fig. 2).

Since an I-O/SAM model is deterministic and not stochastic, I cannot infer any confidence limits on these estimates as in a multivariate econometric model.[10] The annual employment loss of 73,400, the forecast that was presented immediately after the 9/11 shock, happen to be close to the actual average employment loss for the subsequent 12 months since the 9/11 incident. The forecast for the New York State as a whole (loss of 113,200) became close to the actual average employment

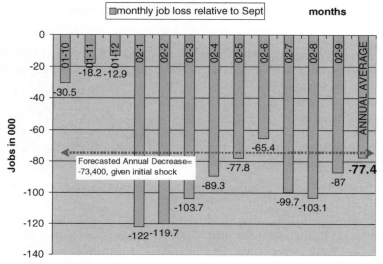

Fig. 2.   New York City Monthly Changes in Employment (from Sept).

loss for the subsequent 12 months since the 9/11 incident (115,900) as well. As previously mentioned, the forecasted figures are not stochastic in nature, therefore there's no confidence interval, or a measure to check its relative significance. However, the forecasted figures turned out to be two of the closest to the actual data respectively, which may provide some external validity of this alternative framework to measure the unprecedented shock to the regional economy.

CONCLUSION

Versatility of the I-O/SAM Model Application in Negative Economic Impact Analysis

An I-O/SAM model in general has its fair share of criticism. One of the widely pointed limitations of an I-O based model is that there are no capacity constraints; that is, supply will increase as necessary to satisfy increased demand and prices will remain unchanged. This underlying assumption might lead to overestimates of economic growth given a positive shock to the economy. Fortunately, this assumption does not hold when the economy receives a negative shock as in the case of 9/11. Indeed, if the criticism of overestimation of total positive impact to initial impact is respected, the diminishing returns to scale notion might then lead to underestimation of the total negative impact of unexpected/unprecedented events.

This study is not the first time I-O/SAM models have been used to estimate the broader economic impacts of negative shocks to an economy nor will they be the last. Because these models are designed to estimate, in addition to the direct effects, the indirect and induced effects of shocks to an economy in question, they could be extremely valuable as tools to measure the total economic impacts of other sudden unexpected, unprecedented events that cause significant negative impacts on a national/regional economy. For analysis of tourism industry, this framework will provide meaningful comprehensiveness of capturing unprecedented shocks than the econometric/time-series framework for short term prediction of total impacts. This approach would provide more accurate and comprehensive estimates of economic impacts than a more traditional one that considers only the direct impacts. This method may help researchers to find alternative ways to model negative impacts when the data behaves outside of the realm of prior events' behavior, or when the data are not yet fully available to use other types of models, which are suited to analyze long-term trends of a variable in question. Unexpected negative events such as terrorism, even if it does not even directly impact a hospitality facility *per se*, can cause severe impacts on other economic activities such as tourism due partly to the interdependence among industrial sectors. Restaurant industry, for example, is revealed to be an important intermediate commodity for the service production of the financial industry.

Quantification of the negative economic impacts of terrorism would help us justify the costs of immediate relief and future prevention measures, if any, and therefore should be further explored for the benefit of practitioners and educators of the hospitality industry and for the optimal allocation of taxpayers' funds by policy-makers.

This study is not an attempt to question the long-term versatility of the regression/time-series based models. This is an attempt to contribute to show how an alternative method could estimate short-term total impacts on the regional economy and tourism industry of an unprecedented negative event. An unprecedented terrorism not only destroys tangible assets but also challenges regression/time-series based models to make meaningful short-term forecasting by blowing away their important assumptions.

NOTES

1. Unprecedented shock of terrorism poses serious challenges to the assumptions of error terms. First assumption is that the error term has constant Variance, or $E(\varepsilon_i^2) = \sigma^2$.

This assumes that the data set is homoskedastic, and thus the use of Ordinary Least Square is appropriate. On the other hand, if this is not the case and the variance changes with i, such that $E(\varepsilon_i^2) = \sigma_i^2$ then the data set is said to be heteroskedastic, and other estimating procedures will be necessary. Suppose we fit a multivariate regression model with household tourism expenditure as dependent variable, and household disposable income as independent variable, we may expect larger variance as the income increases. In the case of terrorism shock analysis, we have to face with sudden increase of variance. Impact of terrorism not only destroys tangible assets, but also blows away the important assumptions of regression-based modelers. Second, the assumption that the error term is statistically independent is thrown into question by the unprecedented shock of terrorism. $Cov(\varepsilon_i, \varepsilon_j) = 0$ for $i \neq j$. Serial correlation, or autocorrelation occurs when the error terms, ε_i in a regression model are correlated with each other. This violates the OLS assumption that the $Cov(\varepsilon_i, \varepsilon_j) = 0$ for $i \neq j$. Serial correlation can occur in time series models, and also in spatial econometric models where cross-sectional data may indicate serial correlation between adjacent regions. While most economic data, such as unemployment rate, or interest rate, would generate positive serial correlation even in normal times, the unprecedented negative shock of terrorism, depending on the interval of data, might cause serious autocorrelation. This topic poses a research question of how long the negative shock of terrorism ringers, or how long it will take to tail off the shock in question.

2. A Bayesian analysis of regressions, which try to incorporate posterior information, and the Kalman Filter, which is a computer algorithm for sequentially updating a liner projection for the system, appear to be worth exploring in the field of unexpected event analysis. While the models may be effective in analyzing long term trend of abundant data, I am not sure how much remedy these models can offer to estimate immediate total shock given the initial shock.

3. In comparison with a simple difference stationary model $y_t = y_{t-1} + \varepsilon_t$ (ε_t has a zero mean), $y_t = \alpha y_{t-1} + \varepsilon_t(|\alpha| < 1)$ is a model in which the sudden shock would fade away as the time passes to revert back to the trend line. If there has been a permanent shock of terrorism, then at the time $= 0$, the shock caused sudden plunge of some constant C, then $\alpha = 1$ for $t > 1$.

4. Engle et al. (1990) found evidence that negative surprise tend to increase volatility than positive surprise, showing asymmetry in stock price movements. The topic of asymmetry of volatility with tourism-demand related variables would be a subject for future research, as it violates an assumption of equal variance used in many modeling.

5. When there are solid evidences that an open, small economy changed its economic structure drastically in a relative short time, violation of the assumed temporal stability of technical coefficients has to be rectified by researcher using available data (Hara, 2004).

6. IMPLAN (Impact Analysis for Planning) is an estimated I-O/SAM database and software available for states and counties in the U.S. Because New York City's 1998 data were available at the time of analysis in November 2001, the deflator was used to estimate shocks in 2001. For the sake of analysis, I did not attempt to change any multipliers or other setting, using default database. (For details of the IMPLAN product, see *www.implan.com*.)

7. This definition of the initial shock is simple and rather ad hoc, and it requires future refinement of how we define the initial shock in terms of time frame. In this applied case, initial monthly change is considered as an initial shock. As shown in Fig. 1, effect of the plunge appears to widen in the following months, the observation in conformity with the notion of spreading effects of the initial shock.

8. In theory, it is easier for us to give contracted final demands $(-\Delta Y)$ in each sector as negative shock. Since the total outputs and the number of employments are in linear relationship in the I-O data, we give the change in employment as a proxy for contracted final demands.

9. Note that we see a slight difference between the impact that we gave to the model and the sum of the direct impacts (in the parenthesis). This could be attributable to our use of deflators to adjust the base data (1998) to the target year of 2001.

10. Ray (1998) suggested several strategies for combining econometric with input-output framework for regional analysis of Southern California, and claimed that integrated models can result in better forecasting accuracy. This is another field that a tourism-related study may explore for the future.

REFERENCES

Brunette, D. (1995). Natural disasters and commercial real estate returns. *Real Estate Finance, 11*(4), 67.

Cohen, M. J. (1995). Technological disasters and natural resource damage assessment. *Land Economics, 71*(1), 65.

Coshall, J. T. (2003). The threat of terrorism as an intervention on international travel flows. *Journal of Travel Research, 42*(1), 4–12.

DRI WEFA (2002a). *Financial impact of the World Trade Center attack* (Vol. January 2002). Albany, NY: Committee?

DRI-WEFA (2002b). *New York State economic and revenue review*, from http://204.168. 97.3/Docs/sfc0102.pdf (March).

Engle, R., Ng, V., & Rothschild, M. (1990). Asset pricing with a FACTOR-ARCH covariance structure: Empirical estimates for treasury bills. *Journal of Econometrics, 45*, 213–237.

Federal Reserve Bank New York (2002). *Impact of the WTC attack on the New York City economy: An update*, http://www.house.gov/maloney/FederalReserve.pdf (April 24, Retrieved July 4, 2002).

Fiscal Policy Institute (2001a). *Economic impact of the September 11 World Trade Center attack*. New York: New York City Central Labor Council and the Consortium for Worker Education.

Fiscal Policy Institute (2001b). *World Trade Center job impacts take a heavy toll on low-wage workers: Occupational and wage implications of job losses related to September 11 World Trade Center attack*, http://www.fiscalpolicy.org/Nov5WTCreport.PDF (November 5).

Fiscal Policy Institute (2002a). *The employment impact of the September 11 World Trade Center attacks: Updated estimates based on the benchmarked employment data.*

Fiscal Policy Institute (2002b). *Joint public hearing on economic development/taxes.*

Grobar, L. M., & Gnanaselvam, S. (1993). The economic effects of Sri Lankan civil war. *Economic Development and Cultural Change, 41*(2), 395.

Hara, T. (2004). *Estimating the economic impacts of the tourism industrial complex on the West Bank and Gaza: An analysis of the crossroads of tourism and terrorism along the road map for peace.* Ph.D. Dissertation, Cornell University, Ithaca.

Hara, T., & Saltzman, S. (2003). The economic impacts of terrorism: An alternative method to quantify the effects on the New York City economy of the 9/11 attack on the World Trade Center. Paper presented at the Eighth Annual Graduate Education and Graduate Students Research Conference in Hospitality and Tourism, Las Vegas, January 5–7.

Hendry, D., & Katarina, J. (2000). Explaining cointegration analysis: Part 1. *Energy Journal, 21*(1), 1–42.

Horwich, G. (2000). Economic lessons of the Kobe earthquake. *Economic Development and Cultural Change, 48*(3), 521.

Mansfeld, Y. (1999). Cycles of war, terror, and peace: Determinants and management of crisis and recovery of the Israeli tourism industry. *Journal of Travel Research, 38*(8/1999), 30–36.

Mihalic, T. (1996). Tourism and warfare – the case of Slovenia. In: A. Pizam & Y. Mansfeld (Eds), *Tourism, Crime and International Security Issues* (pp. 231–245) New York: Wiley.

Milken Institute (2002). *Sept. 11 terror attacks to cost U.S. metros more than 1.6 million jobs in 2002*, from http://www.milken-inst.org/presrel/911prel.html (January 11).

Murdoch, J., Singh, H., & Thayer, M. (1993). The impact of natural hazards on housing values: The Loma Prieta earthquake. *Journal of the American Real Estate and Urban Economics Association, 21*(2), 167–184.

New York City Partnership & Chamber of Commerce (2002). Working together to accelerate New York's recovery update of the NYC Partnership's economic impact analysis of the September 11th attack on New York City, from http://www.nycp.org/impactstudy/EconImpactStudy.pdf (February 11).

New York Office of the Comptroller (2001). *The impact of the September 11 WTC attack on NYC's economy and revenues: preliminary estimate*. New York: Office.

New York Office of the State Comptroller (2001). *State, local government fiscal conditions worsening since September 11*, from http://www.osc.state.ny.us/press/releases/oct01/102201.htm (October 22).

New York Office of the State Comptroller (2002, June 7). *NYC Economy beginning a gradual recovery*.

New York State Assembly (2001). Employment and wages in New York City, Manhattan, and Manhattan localities. *Economic News, New York State Assembly*, 2001–10–01.

Okuyama, Y., Hewings, G. J. D., & Sonis, M. (1997). Interregional analysis of an unscheduled event: The dynamics of Economic impacts. Paper presented at the 44th North American Meetings of the Regional Science Association International, Buffalo, NY.

Ray, S. (1998). The performance of alternative integration strategies for combining regional econometric and input-output models. *International Regional Science Review, 21*(1), 1–37.

United States General Accounting Office (2002). *Review of studies of the economic impact of the September 11, 2001, terrorist attacks on the World Trade Center: Results of work for congressional requesters Corp Author(s):*, from http://www.gao.gov/cgi-bin/getrpt?gao/gao-02-700R (May 29).

Vaccara, B. N. (1970). Changes over time in input-output coefficients for the United States. In: *Applications of Input-Output Analysis* (Vol. 2, pp. 238–260): North-Holland.

APPENDIX

Summary of Other Impact Studies of WTC Attack on 9/11.

#	Name of Organization (Sorted by Timing)	Made by	Timing	NY City		Jobs
				B/S(Stock)	I/S (Flow)5	
1	New York City Central Labor Council and the Consortium for worker Education	Fiscal Policy Institute	9/28/2001		$16.9B for lost output, $6.7B for lost "compensation"	−108,500
2	New York State Assembly Ways & Means Committee	Themselves	10/1/2001			WTC vicinity(S of Chambers & W of Broadway) had 99,200 jobs
3	New York City Office of the Comptroller	Themselves	10/4/2001	$45B WTC building & infrastructure	−$45~60B for lost economic activity, NYC Tax −$1.3B, Insurance +$37B	−115,300
4	New York Governor (New York State Comptroller)	Themselves	10/22/2001	total cost $54B	Quoting Governor: −$15B immediate response, $19B redevelopment, $20B economic recovery Total lost Output: −$21.2B	N.A.
5	New York City Central Labor Council and the Consortium for worker Education	Fiscal Policy Institute	11/5/2001			−105,200 (in 2001/4 Q: revised)
6	New York City Partnership & Chamber of Commerce	Group of consultants[a]	Nov-2001	Total Loss = $83 B: −$30B for capital loss, −$14B clean-up	−$39B of economic output, $37~47 B insurance payment & effects	−125,000, Tourism sector −25,000 by 12/2001
	New York State Senate Finance Committee	DRI-WEFA	Jan-2002	Quoting "Governor −$33.8B, Mayor-$32B, Comptroller-$51.8B," Insurance payments +$36~54B	−$1.4B in 2001,−$8.7B in 2002, −$5.0B in 2003	−70,000 in 2001, −70,000 in 2002, −57,000 in 2003: Tourism sector −19,400 in 2001–4 Q

APPENDIX (Continued)

#	Name of Organization (Sorted by Timing)	Made by	Timing	NY City		
				B/S(Stock)	I/S (Flow)5	Jobs
8	Milken Institute	Themselves	1/11/2002			−44,000 in 2001, −150,000 in 2002 in greater NYC area
9	Senate Finance and Assembly Ways and Means Committee	Fiscal Policy Institute	02/26/2002		Quoting Gov. Pataki "Revenue loss for NYC$2B ($3B for 18 months)"	
10	Fiscal Policy Institute	Themselves	03/08/2002			−84,000 in 2001-4Q
11	Senate Finance Committee	DRI-WEFA	Mar-2002			Out of −78,200 of NYS, NYC account for −70,000
12	Federal Reserve Bank of New York & NYC Independent Budget Office	Themselves	4/18/2002	WTC replacement and cleanup −$25~29B, but uninsured portion of loss is ~$10~14B	FIRE $3.0B, Tourism $1.2B, Quoting City Comptroller"−$0.6B City Tax Revenue" −$6B human loss	FIRE-20,000,Tourism −32,000
13	New York Governor and State Divison of the Budget	Themselves	5/14/2002	Total direct costs and loss of tax revenues due to WTC attack reduced from $54B-46B		
14	U.S. General Accounting Office	Themselves	5/29/2002	Quoting NYC Partnership "Total cost −$83B,+$67B from Insurance, leaving −$16B net loss"	Quoting FEB NY "human loss of $6B" much smaller than earlier estimate.	
15	New York State Comptroller	Themselves	6/7/2002			−140,000(−129k in 2001, −11.9k in01-04/2002)
16	Our initial Simulation	Ourselves	Oct-2001	N.A.		(Simulated on NYS only)
17	Our simulation (Data Updated)	Ourselves	Jun-2002	N.A.	Total Impact on Output: −$16B	−55,500
18	Our Simulation (Data Adjusted)	Ourselves	Jun-2002		Total Impact on Output: −$17.9B	−73,400

ᵃ A. T. Kearney, Bain & Company, Booz-Allen & Hamilton Inc, the Boston Consulting Group, KPMGLLP, McKinsey & Company, PwC Consulting. Compiled by T. Hara based on the quoted reports at the reference.

SUBJECT INDEX

255